FACTORS
UNKNOWN

FACTORS UNKNOWN

THE TRAGEDY THAT PUT
A COACH AND FOOTBALL ON TRIAL

RODNEY DAUGHERTY

Acclaim Press
MORLEY, MISSOURI

Acclaim Press
— Your Next Great Book —
P.O. Box 238
Morley, MO 63767
(573) 472-9800
www.acclaimpress.com

Rodney Daugherty, Author
Dr. Janie Gustafson, Editor
Emily Sikes, Cover Designer
M. Frene Melton, Book Designer
Jeff Jennings, Back Cover and inside flap photos
Tracy Martin, Web Designer
Digital Solutions of KY, Inc., Web Developers

Gator™ is a trademark of John Deere.
Adderall®, Adderall XR® are registered trademarks of Shire Pharmaceutical Industries Ltd.
    All rights reserved.
Dexedrine® is a registered trademark of Abbott Laboratories. All rights reserved.
Gatorade® is a registered trademark of Stokley Van-Camp, Inc. All rights reserved.
Muscle Milk® is a registered trademark of CytoSport, Inc. All rights reserved.
Paracetamol® and Tylenol® are registered trademarks of McNeil Pharmaceutical, Inc. All
    rights reserved.

Library of Congress Cataloging-in-Publication Data

Daugherty, Rodney.
    Factors Unknown: the tragedy that put a coach and football on trial / by Rodney
        Daugherty.
    p. cm.
ISBN-13: 978-0-9841716-1-3 (alk. paper)
ISBN-10: 0-9841716-1-4 (alk. paper)
    1. Stinson, David Jason--Trials, litigation, etc. 2. Trials (Homicide)--Kentucky--Louisville.
    3. Football injuries--Kentucky--Louisville. 4. High school football players--Legal status,
    laws, etc.--Kentucky--Louisville. 5. Gilpin, Max--Death and burial.
I. Title.
    KF225.S75D38 2011
    345.769'440252--dc22

                        2011014842

First printing: 2011
Printed in the United States of America
10 9 8 7 6 5 4 3 2 1

Contents

Acknowledgments

Sometimes life takes us down a road we never thought we would travel, but we follow it anyway. This book is about one of those journeys. It has helped define who I am as a person.

I have to first thank my wife, Ann. I know you have long wished that this whole situation could have been over yesterday, but you patiently stood by while Jason and I were playing Holmes and Watson. Thank you for understanding when many mornings you would find me sitting where you left me the night before. Thank you for listening when this was all I had to talk about; furthermore, thank you for supporting me as I took on one of the greatest challenges of my life. But most of all, thank you for being you. I love you!

There were several people who helped with the book in one way or another. A special thank you goes out to Tracy Martin and the Digital Solutions web design team for the fabulous job they did on the *Factors Unknown* website. Also, I would like to thank Stephanie Oglesby for transcribing trial testimony.

Everyone should understand that without Jason Stinson's blessing, this book would never have happened. Jason always thanks me for "all that I do," but I owe Jason a debt of gratitude that can never be repaid. He gave me an opportunity "to ride shotgun" as football and legal history was made. The sacrifices we made will have a profound effect on more than just football. Hopefully, what we learned will eventually save lives. It is important that coaches, players and parents know the truth about what really happened on August 20, 2008, or they could find themselves in the same position.

This book is dedicated to the memory of Michael Coley.

AUTHOR'S NOTE

I feel I have an obligation to the reader to say up front who I am and where I stand. I have known Jason Stinson for over 20 years. We first met in the fall of 1987 when we attended Fairdale High School in Louisville, KY. I had not seen Jason since high school, but I was glad to be reunited with him in early 2005 through the PRPHS football program. I was involved in the criminal process of the legal proceedings from start to finish, and I was an eyewitness to many events described in this book. I do the best that I possibly can to tell a non-biased, fact-based account of the events that took place. The documentation and evidence filed in this case are staggering. There are over 3,500 pages of documents that, in one way or another, relate to the case.

Much like the JCPS's investigation, I am sure I will be accused of pointing out some facts while leaving out other facts. If this should occur, it was not my intention. I do not side with Jason because he is my friend; I side with him because of the facts. These are facts that I have spent over a year documenting and detailing to bring the whole story to the general public. This case was colossal by anyone's description, so please do not expect every single detail to be included in this book. In order to supplement the book, we have set up a website with additional content.

The reader may want to refer to www.factorsunknown.com from time to time for additional information. It contains all the coaches', witnesses' and players' statements, depositions, media coverage, and exclusive content (such as photos, never-before-seen evidence, and letters of support to Coach Stinson). The additional content is included if the book was purchased on the website. If the book was purchased at a retail outlet, the additional content is available at www.factorsunknown.com for an additional charge of $5.99.

FACTORS
UNKNOWN

THE TRAGEDY THAT PUT
A COACH AND FOOTBALL ON TRIAL

CHAPTER 1

A Day Much Like Any Other Day

The Ohio Valley area usually experiences very hot, humid summers, but this particular August was much milder than previous years. In fact, most of the month did not see 90° temperatures at all. August 20, 2008 was a day much like any other day. A high temperature of 95° was recorded at the nearby Louisville International Airport. Students were just beginning to settle into the new school year.

The day could not have been any more average. It was the middle of the week, and everything was moving along normally. Classes for high school students in the Jefferson County Public Schools (JCPS) end daily at 2:20 PM. At this time, Pleasure Ridge Park High School (PRPHS) students involved with the football team do one of two things. All freshmen and any upperclassmen with D's or U's on their previous grade sheet are required to report to study hall from 2:30 until 3:00 PM. Players not required to attend study hall typically go to the locker room to get ready for practice. On this particular day, just prior to practice, player Adrian Vertrees informed Coach Jason Stinson that he did not feel well. Coach Stinson told Vertrees to go home and skip practice for the day. This is standard procedure for any sick player if the coaching staff is aware of the illness.

Each day's itinerary of practice activities is regularly posted in the locker room for players to see. The players can pretty much judge what the practice will entail by glancing at the itinerary. On August 20, the PRPHS players who did not attend study hall were either getting ready to train in the weight room or preparing to go to the film room. At 3:00 PM, the team was divided into two groups: offense and defense. The defense went to the weight room, and the offense went to the film room. The players from study hall were dismissed by Coach Jason Cook at 3:10 PM, either to attend weight training or film study. Somewhere around 3:25 PM, the

11

players switched rooms; the defense went to the film room, and the offense went to the weight room. At approximately 3:45 PM, Coach Stinson sent everybody over to the locker room to get ready to be on the practice field at 4:10 PM.

While the players were walking back to the locker room to get their gear, Coach Stinson crossed the parking lot to the practice field. There, he had a brief conversation with Craig Webb, the high school's Athletic Director. Webb explained to Stinson that he needed help moving some landscaping blocks that were on the soccer field. Even though Stinson knew that having the football players help would put the team behind schedule, he agreed to assist Webb.

Next, Coach Stinson headed to the shed where he kept the temperature readings on a clipboard. He grabbed the clipboard and walked to an area that would best simulate practice conditions to take a heat index reading. He reached in his pocket and removed an instrument used to measure both humidity and temperature. The hygrometer returned a reading of 94 degrees with a relative humidity of 32 percent. He used the chart provided with the hygrometer to determine that the heat index was 94 degrees.

Stinson then headed over to the vacant lot where the players were moving concrete blocks from the soccer field. (These players started arriving at the soccer field around 3:50 PM, and they continued to trickle in until about 4:10 PM.) At this point, Coach Stinson had each varsity player grab a block and carry it over to the vacant lot. Realizing that there was still a large stack of blocks left, he sent each player back over to the soccer field to grab one more.

By 4:15 PM, Stinson recognized the team was indeed behind schedule, so he told the varsity players to gather under the goalpost, as they usually did every day before practice, and he left the freshmen with Craig Webb to finish moving the blocks. The freshmen remained under Webb's supervision for another 15–20 minutes moving blocks, and were observed by coaches and other witnesses to be drinking water during this time.

At 4:20 PM, the varsity and the junior varsity (JV) players broke into teams. This portion of practice is actually called "team stretches," and it consists of light stretching and a brisk jog. The players participated in team stretches until about 4:30 PM, followed by with what is called "team take-offs." During team takeoffs, the players are separated into offensive and defensive groups. The offensive groups usually consist of varsity, JV, and freshman offensive teams, and the defensive groups are broken down the same way.

During such exercises, the players line up on the 10-yard line and go through the motions of a play. Once they finish the play, they usually sprint to the opposite 10-yard line, turn, and go back to the huddle. This drill is usually performed for about 10–15 minutes.

Somewhere between 4:45–4:50 PM, the players were given a scheduled water break. By this time, most of the freshmen had returned from helping Craig Webb. Following the water break, the players were divided into teams. Once the players were grouped into their individual positions, they began about five to seven minutes of ball drills. These drills normally consist of throwing the ball, catching, turning, catching and turning, and finally, catching along with turning and running. During this time, coaches can send the players to get water whenever they choose. It is standard procedure for the coaches to send the players to water after completing a drill, and the players typically receive three to five unscheduled water breaks during the time they are running drills with their position coach. On August 20, Coach Stinson was in charge of the receivers, and he sent them for water after the ball drills.

There were several other coaches assisting that day. Coach Adam Donnelly and Coach Jason Cook were in charge of the offensive line. Coach Jason Hiser was in charge of the defensive backs and linebackers, while Coach Bobby Deacon was in charge of the running backs. His brother, Coach Steve Deacon, was supervising the quarterbacks. Finally, Coach Josh Lightle was in charge of the defensive line, and Chris Webb (the athletic director's brother) was present to help with many tasks, including managing the field equipment and dealing with the players' equipment when it needed repair or replacement.

Individual drills and the second water break ended a little after 5 PM. The team then went into seven-on-seven drills—drills with seven players on each side of the ball. The players' work on both completing and defending routine pass plays. This permits the receivers (offense) to work on their pass routes, and it also allows the defensive backs to work on their pass protection by covering the receivers. Most often, the "skilled" players (those who are faster and more athletic) participate in these drills, while the "heavy" players (offensive and defensive linemen) usually remain with their position coaches.

Somewhere around 5:20 PM, Coach Stinson called for the third scheduled water break of the day. He blew the whistle and gave the coaches five minutes to "water [the players] down." It seems that everyone can agree on this timeline and the series of events leading up to this point, but the accounts of what happened next differ greatly.

At approximately 5:25 PM, Coach Stinson called the players back from their third scheduled water break for "team period," which can best be described as a scrimmage. For this drill, the offensive and defensive teams would have lined up against one another. As usual, the whole 90–100+ member team did not take part in the varsity team's scrimmage. Coach Bobby Deacon, with the assistance of Steve Ellis, gathered the 30 to 40 freshmen to run team drills. (At this point in the 2008 season, 30 percent to 40 percent of the roster was made up of freshmen.) As a rule, coaches want to separate the upperclassmen from the 8th and 9th graders. Putting a freshman up against a senior is not a good idea because the younger, more inexperienced player can easily get hurt.

As Coaches Bobby Deacon and Steve Ellis were gathering the freshmen for their team drills, Coach Stinson told the rest of the defensive team members to change into their skivvies (colored slip-on jerseys used to separate the offensive football players from the defensive players). By this time it was nearing 5:30 PM, at which point a soccer game was scheduled to begin. Stinson had to yell to get his players' attention because he could no longer blow his whistle lest he would interfere with the soccer game. (At PRPHS, the soccer field runs adjacent to the football practice field, and the two are only separated by five to ten yards of vacant space. Given the close proximity of the two fields, it is easy to understand how having whistles blown on an adjacent field could cause problems. With whistles removed from the equation, there is not much left to do to attract the attention of a player 50–60 yards away other than yell.)

Stinson's first set of verbal commands—telling the players to line up for team period—yielded minimal results. Several players, by most accounts, were walking around and "goofing off." At this point Stinson shouted, "Get where you are supposed to be." Realizing that hardly any players were paying attention to his verbal commands, he decided to "condition" instead of "scrimmage." (It is a very dangerous recipe for serious injury to have 22 players scrimmaging when as many as 10–15 of them are not following instructions or paying attention to begin with.) During conditioning, the players have to run a certain number of "gassers." A "gasser" consists of running the width of a football field four times—approximately 213 ⅓ yards total. It is commonly described as running from one sideline to the other, touching it, running back to the starting point, and then repeating the process.

Some witnesses later testified that the conditioning runs the players performed that day were a punishment; however, after reviewing the evidence, that simply does not appear to be the case. If any punishment was issued on August 20, it would have been not allowing the players to participate in the team drills. The players were going to "condition" regardless, and they would normally run six-to-eight timed gassers.

The significance of timed gassers is this: If the prescribed time is not met, it does not count. Rarely does each group make the prescribed time every day, and that frequently means the players have to run extra gassers. According to the coaches' later depositions and police interviews, none of the gassers run on August 20 met the required times. (If the coaching staff had been enforcing the times, the players probably would only have completed three or four gassers, because so many would not have counted.)

After verbally calling out to the players at least three times, only to have three out of the 22 players show up where they were supposed to be, Stinson then yelled out, "Get on the line." When the players hear that, they know it is conditioning time, "...and they know they're gonna run," stated Stinson during his interview with Louisville Metropolitan Police Department (LMPD). "Get on the line," meant it was time to run gassers. Coach Ellis testified to gathering the freshmen at the south end of the practice field for conditioning once Stinson called the players to the line. The other coaches took up their usual positions on the field as the gassers began.

There were over 100 people on that practice field August 20, 2008, so where they were located can sometimes be confusing. The map on the next page is a dimensional and directional representation of PRPHS' football practice field. Coaches' and players' positions on the field will be described throughout this book. Please use the graphic as a reference when needed.

Coaches Bobby Deacon and Steve Ellis were standing between the SW end zone and the SW 20-yard line with the freshmen. Coach Josh Lightle was around the SW 30-yard line standing with Jim Nichols, a volunteer who has dedicated over three decades to PRPHS athletics. Coach Jason Stinson was standing in the middle of the field on the 50-yard line. Coach Adam Donnelly was on the east side of the field at the 50-yard line. Coach Jason

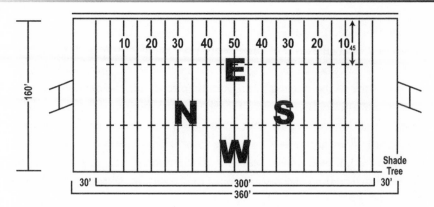

Cook was also on the east side of the field. Earlier, Coach Steve Deacon took three players (Taylor Banks, Sam Ellis, and Demetrius Moore) to the locker room for treatment, and he returned to the practice field sometime during conditioning. Coach Jason Hiser had left for an appointment.

In addition to the three players being treated, two other players were allowed to leave and one was allowed to sit out. Players D. J. Horn and Kyle Frames approached Coach Stinson somewhere around 5:25 PM to inform him of their prior commitments (a doctor's appointment and work, respectively), and he excused them both from the remainder of practice. Player Daniel Farris, who had a previous history of heat exhaustion/stroke, complained of being light-headed prior to the run, so he was instructed by Chris Webb to put an ice bag on his neck and rest in the shade while the others ran.

The first few gassers were completed with nothing substantial to note other than several players were not putting forth maximum effort. The fact that many players were not sprinting (as was customary) should come as no surprise, since many players were not fully following instructions that day. However, some players, including Charlie Mullennex, Logan Vardeman and Antonio Calloway, were running at top speed. Around gasser No. 6, Stinson began excusing players based on their effort, and this continued through gasser No. 8.

By the beginning of gasser No. 8, at least half a dozen players had been excused. A normal day of conditioning would consist of six-to-eight gassers, so the players who ran theirs as they should were excused to go sit under the nearby shade tree. Those who were moving anywhere from a half-sprint to walking were told to remove their helmets and to continue. By this point it was about 5:50 PM. Each group had run about 5,120 feet (just under 1 mile), and the players had been running for about 10 minutes each. It is estimated by both Coach Ellis and Coach Stinson that it was taking at least two and one-half minutes for both groups to complete a full gasser. It had taken about twenty minutes to run the first eight gassers, after which Coach Stinson told the players to remove their helmets.

The first event that would cause great confusion later occurred immediately after Antonio Calloway was dismissed around the eighth gasser. As soon as he finished the run, Calloway began exhibiting signs of breathing difficulty, described by many as a loud wheezing sound. Another player, Dave West, (who had also been excused from further runs), helped Calloway to the bleachers under the shade tree. Coach Deacon was instructing two freshmen on the need to stand up after running, so Coach Ellis grabbed an ice bag and placed it on Calloway's neck as he worked with him to control his breathing. Coach Ellis walked Calloway about 50 yards over to the water supply, and had him put his head under the water to help cool him while they worked on his breathing.

Meanwhile, the gassers continued after the helmets were removed. The pace of the players was progressively getting slower and slower. At this point, players DeAndre Cole and Christian Vincent began to show signs of fatigue. Within moments, both players experienced asthma problems, and Coach Stinson separately asked each player: "Do you have your inhaler?" They both answered "no," at which point they were told to stop running and stand still.

Shortly after Coach Stinson stopped Cole and Vincent from running, he realized he had a group of about eight players who were "dogging it," laughing and joking around. They were described by many witnesses (coaches and players alike) as walking the final gassers while they made jokes and laughed about them. Coach Stinson described these eight players as "my athletes, they're my guys, they can go all day." But Stinson had seen enough and called those players together into a circle. "I told those guys, 'stop where you're at,' and the other guys, I told them to continue running."

Coach Donnelly at this point supervised the gassers, while Stinson told the eight players, "Get your feet moving. We're going to do up/downs, because you all can't do what you're asked to do."

Up/downs are best described as having players chop their feet (run in place quickly) until they are instructed to "hit the ground." Once they hit the ground (dive to the ground, landing flat on their stomachs), they are to jump back up and continue to chop their feet. This technique is commonly used by coaches when they are not getting the desired results from their players. They will have the players perform up/downs as a deterrent for whatever unacceptable behavior the players were exhibiting.

In fact, Coach Deacon had two freshmen doing up/downs at the south end of the field earlier because they were not displaying good posture. (Players are taught to stand up because it helps them to breathe better, and it also allows the coaches to see their eyes.) The two freshmen kept bending over after running, so Stinson told Deacon, "If they are not going to stand up, they can do up/downs." While they were doing the up/downs, Antonio Calloway was excused and began to have breathing problems. Since Deacon was supervising the freshmen up/downs, Coach Ellis went to help Calloway, and shortly thereafter Stinson gathered the eight "problem" players down around the NW 40-yard line. Stinson had them start doing up/downs, while Deacon released most of the freshmen from the run to go to the water and then to wait under the shade tree for the rest of the team to finish.

After the 8 players had completed about 14–18 up/downs, Stinson had 1 of the freshmen in the group say something to the nature of, "We're not gonna quit, we're not gonna quit." Stinson told them, "We are going to do these up/downs until you all get it right and until you guys start doing what you are supposed to be doing."

After the tenth gasser, Coach Stinson told all remaining runners to remove their jerseys and shoulder pads, which took one to two minutes to complete. At the beginning of the 12th gasser, Coach Stinson told Donnelly, "This is the last one." Then he turned his attention back to the group doing up/downs.

Stinson later recounted to Sgt. Butler "I told the guys, 'If anybody wants to quit, feel free to leave now. Just drop your equipment under the tree and walk out the gate.' We tell our guys this from day one. I said, 'If you've got ambitions to quit, just quit now and leave and go off the field.'"

If Stinson wanted to know who would quit, he didn't have to wait long to find out. As the runners were finishing the last quarter of their 12th gasser around 6:05 PM, he found his quitter. Player David Englert said he got tired of listening to Coach Stinson, so he just walked off. He was soon followed by player Chris Bryant. Stinson later told Sgt. Butler, "He never said 'I quit'; he never said 'I'm done.' We were just getting to the point where we were finished, and he walked off."

That was to be the last gasser for the day whether David Englert and Chris Bryant had quit or not, because it was already after 6:00 PM, and some players had to be ready to catch a bus home no later than 6:30 PM. As Englert and Bryant walked away, Coach Stinson uttered a phrase that his players had heard many times before: "Ding, ding, ding…we have a winner."

Coach Stinson was placed under a great deal of scrutiny because of his ding, ding, ding... and we are going to run until someone quits comments. Football can be a rough sport and "tough talk" is nothing new to the practice field. Coaches say sarcastic and demanding things regularly to see how their players will react.

In the game of football, knowing who the quitters are is important, because coaches don't want them in the game when the going gets tough (and it does). They could not only cost the team a game, but they could get one of their teammates hurt. There was actually a blueprint developed by a strength and conditioning coach explaining the benefits of running a drill attempting to get players to quit. In an April 2007 *Stack* magazine article, author Chad Zimmerman quotes Rob Oviatt, head strength and conditioning coach at Washington State University. According to Oviatt, "If you quit during a workout, the odds are you'll quit during a play in practice or a game. So, we create situations within our football training program where our players are forced to think about quitting."

For the most part, the running of gassers could be considered normal and not unusual. Everything about that August 20th practice was perfectly ordinary. It was a day much like any other day…until Max Gilpin, one of the team members, collapsed.

CHAPTER 2

A Day Like No Other Day

The gassers ended, and while players David Englert and Chris Bryant were walking away, Coach Stinson told the players to get their equipment and gather under the tree (like they do after every practice) for a team meeting. It was about 6:06 PM when Coach Stinson headed south to the tree. On his way to the meeting, he crossed paths with player Max Gilpin, who was walking east to west to retrieve his equipment from the west sideline. At that time Coach Stinson didn't notice anything wrong with Max. Later he explained to Sgt. Butler what he witnessed: "So I walk past Max, and this is probably 6:05 to 6:10, somewhere in that nature. At this point, Max is finished running. He finished what we asked him to do. He's walkin', breathin', and sweatin', but he never says, 'Coach I don't feel good.' He's walkin' with the rest of 'em."

Moments after Coach Stinson passed Max, Max began having trouble walking. He experienced what is known as "rubber legs." "Rubber legs" is a term used to describe a player who has overextended himself and is having trouble walking because his legs are shaky. Players Justin Agrue and David Thompson were walking beside Max when he began to have trouble, so they each held under one of his arms to assist him to the shade tree.

When piecing together witness statements, depositions, and trial testimony, the time period of 6:05–6:15 PM appears to have had a substantial amount of activity. Justin Agrue and David Thompson were helping Max. At the same time, Coach Stinson was heading towards the water to retrieve four players who were there instead of being at the team meeting where they are supposed to be. In his later interview with Sgt. Butler, Stinson said, "So I walk around the shade tree, right through where you come in the gate, and those four are in the water drinkin'. I tell 'em, 'You guys need to get to the team meeting; you need to get out of the water and be where you're supposed to be. We always have our team meeting, and then we give you a break to go to water at that point.' None of those guys said, 'Coach, can I go get water?' None of those guys at the water said, 'Coach, I'm not feelin' good; I'm not doin' it.' None of 'em said, 'Can I go over there?' It was the ones who were doin' the up/downs. They were all athletes."

At the same time, Coach Ellis brought Antonio Calloway back over to the bleachers from the water and turned him over to Bobby and Steve Deacon. As Coach Ellis sat Antonio Calloway down on the corner of the bleachers, he noticed "a kid with rubbery legs."

At about 6:07 PM, Justin Agrue and David Thompson started calling for help because Max "went limp." Coach Donnelly told them to lay Gilpin on the ground, and he told the other players who were running up to stay away from him. Coach Adam Donnelly recounted the event to Detective Terry Jones in an interview with LMPD on September 19, 2008. He said, "I was standing over in the end zone side at this point. I saw Max hanging over two players. I told the players to let him walk on his own. They informed me that he couldn't. I then ran out to Max and told them to lay him down. I tried to give Max water. (Somebody had given me a water bottle; I don't know who.) I tried to give water to Max, but realized that he could not take it, and that he was unconscious. I did the "look, listen, and feel" technique to check that he was breathing. I yelled for help at that point. I checked his skin; it was clammy."

Coach Steve Deacon told Detective Jones on September 18, 2008, that he is the *de facto* team trainer and he helps with medical care issues. He stated, "I help kids who need to have ice or any kind of tape treatment or something like that. And then I notify their parents. I let our team physical therapist or team doctor know as well." As Agrue and Thompson were helping Max walk, a couple other players called for Coach Steve Deacon. "At that time, some players yelled out, 'Coach Deacon, Max needs your help.' I turned around and started walking towards them. They were walking towards me, two players. They had Max upright, walking him to me. When I got close to him, he collapsed and fell to the ground on his knees. I then walked around and supported Max underneath his shoulders. I asked him if he needed help, to see if he would respond. He started moaning. It just seemed like he was in 'exhaust' state."

Coach Bobby Deacon also approached the scene to keep the other kids back. In his police interview with Det. Jones, he said, "At that point, all the kids had been dispersed from running. Most were sitting over by the tree for a team meeting. Others were starting to surround the Gator™ to check on Max. So, my focus was breaking them up so we could get the Gator™ out of there." (The Gator™ is a small four-wheel motorized utility cart that is manufactured by John Deere. It is shaped much like a golf cart with a utility dump bed on the back. The entire cart is a little over eight feet long, and it is a little over four feet wide. It has two seats in the front and a dump bed on the back that is just less than four feet long.)

At this time, Coach Stinson was walking up to the team meeting several yards away. He still was not aware that Max had collapsed. He approached the tree where the team members were listening to Coach Steve Ellis address the freshmen players, and he waited for him to finish speaking. Steve Ellis recounted the series of events during his trial testimony. He testified, "It was early on. I wanted to tell these kids basically that we had a rough one, let's have a better day tomorrow. He's (Stinson) kinda looking at me as I'm ready to talk. When I looked at him, I saw Craig Webb, the Athletic Director, come from behind the tree on the Gator™. I wondered where he was going and that's when I looked across the back of Stinson and noticed that somebody had gone down. Whoever had the rubber legs didn't make it, so when I saw that I said to the freshmen, 'You guys listen to Coach.' Stinson had his back to the situation. Then I took off in a dead sprint. When I got to Max, there were already adults there."

Athletic Director Craig Webb, along with Assistant Athletic Director David Bobb, had driven up to where Max was. Tim Keown, a parent, had come over as well as several players. Those who first arrived tried to pick Max up, but they were having trouble getting him off the ground. Steve Ellis later testified, "Max was six-two, 220 pounds, in that range. I couldn't swear to it, but that was about what he was. The first couple of people who reached him couldn't pick him up. This kid had been running, his pants were wet, and he had no shirt on. He was slimy; when you sweat a lot, that's how your skin gets." (According to medical records on August 20th at Norton Kosair Children's Hospital, Max's weight was 100 kg or 220.5 lb.)

As soon as Steve Ellis arrived at the scene, Tim Keown said, "Let's do a fireman's basket." Ellis later testified, "We slid underneath Max, and we put him in the front right seat, which would be the passenger's seat." Max was not able to hold himself upright in the seat so Ellis jumped in the bed of the Gator™ and slid his arms under Max's arms to hold him up by pinning him to the seat.

Craig Webb drove the Gator™ to the water, pulling the front end up by the corner of the watering area where the hose came into it. The watering area is a 6' x 3' rectangular PVC pipe with 14 holes drilled into it. The pipe is fed water from a garden hose run from a separate water source. It allows a large number of players to get a drink of water at one time and cuts down on the spread of germs. It shoots 14 continuous streams of water out away from it.

Steve Ellis told Craig Webb to hold Max while he jumped off the Gator™ to get the garden hose supplying the watering area. He couldn't break loose the first joint he came to, so he moved on to the next one. That one broke loose for him, so he brought it back to where Max was seated in the Gator™ and began hosing him down.

During trial testimony he recounted, "I took Max by the head, and we started to water him down. At that point I was in 'cool down' mode. At that point Max was still making noises. He made a groaning noise. He could not follow commands, but I never felt he was unconscious. I felt he was in there. I had him by the head. I would take the water hose and as I would spray different areas, he would move. We were cooling down the blood. He started to come around. Then he would go quiet on me a little bit. I would move the hose somewhere else. He would kinda' move; he would make a response to the water. Two times while we were doing it, he even had a coughing spell. I was wondering if I was splashing water up his nose."

They continued to cool Max. Craig Webb remained in the driver's seat of the Gator™. Sometimes he was sitting in the seat, and other times he knelt as he administered ice to different areas of Max's body. Max's father, Jeff Gilpin, was at his son's feet, and he removed Max's shoes and socks per Steve Deacon's instructions.

Steve Deacon remained outside the Gator™ on the passenger's side attending to Max. Occasionally he would step a few feet back to check on Antonio Calloway. Deacon recalled that "Max's dad was there at the Gator™ with us. That's when I looked at his dad and said, 'Yeah it's pretty serious. We need to call. Do you want me to call? And he agreed upon that. That was about 6:17 PM, and then I called 911." The following is a transcript of the call:

911: "911 Operator. Where's your emergency?"
S. Deacon: "I'm a coach over at Pleasure Ridge Park High School, and I have a football player who needs an ambulance."

911: "Are you at the school now?"

Deacon: "Yeah, I'm at the school now, back by the baseball field. If they came straight back, they'd have to make a right where the..."

911: "And you're calling from xxx-xxxx?"

Deacon: "Yeah, that's my cell number"

911: "Your name?"

Deacon: "Coach Steve Deacon. D - E - A - C - O - N."

911: "OK, and this is 5901 Greenwood Road?"

Deacon: "Uh huh."

911: "What's the problem? Tell me exactly what happened."

Deacon: "He's just overheated. We've got water on him. He's responsive, and he's got a big rapid pulse, but..."

911: "Are you with him right now?"

Deacon: "Yes. I'm trying to control his breathing. I've got several adults helping me, and then I have his dad here as well."

911: "How old is he, sir?"

Deacon: "Uh, he's 15."

911: "Is he conscious?"

Deacon: "Yes"

911: "Is he breathing?"

Deacon: "Yes, he's breathing, though he's kind of going in and out on us."

911: "Is he completely awake?"

Deacon: "Yeah, he's awake. We're trying to get him to open his eyes right now. He's got a rapid pulse."

911: "Give me one second, sir. I'm updating the paramedics right now." (While he waited for the 911 operator to return, Steve Elllis heard in the background: "Come on, get them eyes open. Keep them eyes open. There you go. Get them eyes all the way up. Get them eyes open. There you go.")

911: "OK, sir, does he have any history of heart problems?"

Deacon: "No."

911: "Does he have any change in his skin color?"

Deacon: "He's a little white."

911: "I'm sorry?"

Deacon: "He's a little white."

24

911: "OK. Now I want you to touch his skin. Tell me what his skin temperature is. Is it hotter than normal, normal, or colder than normal?"

Deacon: "It's probably normal, but we've got water going on him right now."

911: "OK, sir, we're sending the paramedics out right now. I want you to stay on line because I'm going to tell you exactly what you need to do, OK?"

Deacon: "OK"

911: "For heat exposure, you need to remove him from any sources of heat."

Deacon: "OK."

911: "You need to remove his outer clothing."

Deacon: "OK."

911: "Apply cool water to the entire skin surface, while fanning."

Deacon: "OK."

911: "And turn on an air conditioner or fan if you have one."

Deacon: "We're outside. We've got some wind, a little bit."

911: "Reassure him that help is on the way. Please do not let him have anything to eat or drink because it could make him sick or cause problems for the doctor."

Deacon: "OK."

911: "I want you to watch him very closely. Please have someone meet the paramedics. If he should get worse in any way, call me back immediately for further instructions. Now, you said you are back by the baseball field?"

Deacon: "Yes. We need to get some people out there so they can find out where we are."

911: "OK. Have you removed his outer clothing sir?"

Deacon: "Yes, we have."

911: "Socks, shoes, everything?"

Deacon: "Yep, everything."

911: "OK, sir, they've already been dispatched out, and they're coming from Dixie and Gagel."

Deacon: "OK. Thank you."

911: "Thank you."

Deacon: "OK. Bye."

Coach Deacon later described the call to Detective Jones. "She gave me procedures on the phone. I was right there next to Max and that Gator™. I continued to do what she told me to do. I told her that we had done a lot of the things that she'd already requested—like ice on the back of the neck and ice on his lower extremities. She wanted me to feel his skin to see if he was sweating. However, I couldn't determine that because of the water draining down his legs. He was covered in water constantly."

Parent Tim Keown went out to the main road to lead the ambulance back to the practice field. Coach Steve Ellis later described the wait for the ambulance. "I already knew 911 was called. The only thing to do was keep trying to cool this kid. His eyelids came down. His father Jeff was standing there, and he had already taken Max's shoes and socks off. I turned to Jeff and I said, 'Jeff, work his legs.' I was trying to get some circulation, something to pump. So Jeff worked his legs, and we were still watering him down. A couple of times from that point, Max went real quiet on me. I didn't know if we were going to have to do CPR on him."

Ellis continued to describe the agonizing wait. "It seemed like an eternity was going on, just forever. All of sudden things would go quiet, and I would get no reaction. I said, 'We're going to the ground.' I thought we were gonna' jerk him out of this thing (Gator™) and start doing CPR on him. I knew EMS was on the way, if he quit breathing or whatever. He never struggled in his breathing. If anything, his breathing was just light."

Max's mother, Michele Crockett, arrived a few minutes before the ambulance. She was made aware of the situation when she received a phone call from Christina Spiva, a parent present at the time Max collapsed. In later trial testimony, Mrs. Crockett recalled her arrival. "When I pulled in the parking lot, I could see Max. He was sort of being propped up and held in a Gator™ type thing they use. People had to hold him in. People were asking him to open his eyes. His eyes were about half open, and they were really bloodshot."

When the ambulance arrived at 6:27 PM, the day much like any other day had turned into a day like no other day.

CHAPTER 3

A Tragedy Ensues

At 6:30 PM, Louisville Metro Emergency Medical Services (EMS) technicians Joseph Bratcher and Christopher Harris brought the stretcher over to where the first responders had Max located. Steve Ellis relinquished his support of Max's head to the EMS technicians and stepped back to let them take over. They picked Max up from the Gator™ and put him on the gurney. Christopher Harris started supplying Max with oxygen and placed a mask (also known as bagging) over his mouth and nose to assist him with breathing. The technicians wheeled Max out to the ambulance and put him in the back. Max's mother, Michele, got into the front passenger's seat of the ambulance to accompany Max to Norton Kosair Children's Hospital.

Joseph Bratcher got into the back of the ambulance to begin treatment, while Christopher Harris went back to the Gator™ to check on Antonio Calloway. There was a fair amount of discussion as to whether Antonio was going to go to the hospital or not. In fact, in the beginning, one of the EMTs had said that another ambulance was going to have to be called. A phone call was placed to Antonio's grandmother to see if she wanted him to go to the hospital or not.

Antonio was definitely an afterthought when it came to EMS being called. He probably would not have gone to the hospital that day if an ambulance had not already been there. After discussing the situation with Antonio's grandmother, it was decided it would be better to be safe than sorry, so they should send him too. Max's condition was deteriorating quickly and he needed to leave immediately, so the coaching staff was told if Antonio was going, he needed to go now. Hearing this, Steve Ellis stepped in and put Antonio's arm around his neck and helped him with a fast walk to the ambulance. Steve Ellis stepped into the ambulance behind the driver's side door, placed Antonio in the jump seat behind the driver, and closed the door.

Joseph Bratcher requested Mrs. Crockett's permission to intubate Max (put a tube down his nose or throat) to assist him with his breathing. She agreed, and he attempted the procedure three times with no success. He started an intravenous (IV) line and began treating Max with 250ml (8.5 oz) of fluids. Bratcher also administered ice packs under Max's arms and to the back of his neck.

At 6:40 PM, the ambulance left PRPHS traveling Code 3 (lights and siren on). It took 18 minutes to travel the fifteen miles from PRPHS to downtown Louisville, where the Norton Kosair Children's Hospital is located. The ambulance arrived at 6:58 PM, and emergency room medical personnel began working on Max right away. A battery of medical exams and tests was performed as soon as his care was transferred from EMS to the hospital. Max's temperature when he came into the emergency room was 107.4 degrees.

I received a phone call that night at a little after 11 PM. It was Coach Stinson calling to talk to my stepson Christopher "Cookie" Cook. Coach Stinson asked me if Cookie was awake, and I told him no, that he had gone to sleep a little after 10 PM. I informed Coach Stinson that Christopher had told me at dinner about Max collapsing. Christopher didn't mention anything being different about this practice other than Max collapsing. He did briefly mention that a group of guys were "screwing off," but his attention repeatedly returned to Max. He was very concerned about Max, and he had made Coach Stinson promise he would call and update him on Max's condition. Coach Stinson confirmed what Christopher had told me, and went on to say that "Cookie seemed really shook up, and I promised him I would call when I knew something."

Coach Stinson informed me that it was "touch-and-go" at that time. Max was in a critical, but stable condition, and the hospital was moving him to the Intensive Care Unit (ICU). I offered to put my stepson on the phone, but Coach Stinson just wanted to make sure I told Christopher that he called, and that I updated him on Max's condition. I assured Coach Stinson that I would do that as soon as I hung up the phone. I asked the coach how he was doing, because I could hear the pain in his voice. He never spoke of how he was doing; he only wanted to speak about Max.

Christopher seemed to share the same care and regard for Max. He had told me of a story where once he had given Max a nickname to make his name sound somewhat more extravagant. "We will call you Maximus,"

Christopher told Max. It will make you sound cooler. Christopher was a couple of years ahead of Max, but he got to know him because they played the same position. Cookie really took a liking to the young man just has many others, and there was a reason for that. Max seemed to be one of those kids who got along with everyone. He didn't have an enemy, or at least, not one I ever came across. Everyone who spoke about him, held him in high regards, and more than one person claimed to be his best friend.

I hardly knew Max Gilpin before his collapse, and if I was asked to identify him I would have had difficulty. Christopher on the other hand, would not. He shared several stories with me that related to Max, and all of them had the same central theme. The theme was Max was a nice guy, and the way he interacted with others shined though when they spoke about him.

Max's stepmother, Lois Gilpin, shared her high regard for him as she told me many stories about Max. Many times she would have to pause because she loved him so much and to reflect only bought about pain. "He was such a good boy," she would say. Max was described by others as "a one of a kind, and all around good person" and "one of those people who everybody wishes they could be like." Those words say a lot because these words come from his closest friends. One of Max's closest friends had a tattoo put on his rib cage to remind him of Max, he said "this way he will forever be by my side."

I understood why Jason only wanted to speak of Max, he could be an overwhelming presence even though he demanded no attention. Max was content to blend into the background, but his warm and inviting personality would not allow it. It was this personality that surely made Coach Stinson speak of Max during our call, but it was also something more. I guess I could say you would have to know Jason Stinson to understand him, but even then it might not fully explain the guy. He is one of a few "selfless" people I have ever met in my life. He would think of someone else long before he would think of himself.

I remember a man attacking Jason's character after hearing Jason had stated he only coached to give back and to make a difference. The man stated "If he wants to give back and make a difference, why don't he go work with the homeless?" I replied, "He does, every Monday night. He goes downtown and works with Valley View Church and the Salvation Army. He gives out food, clothing and whatever else the homeless might need." "He also….," I continued, but the guy didn't need to hear anymore as he realized Jason was the real deal.

The sarcastic gentlemen realized, Jason didn't help others for any other reason than it was the right thing to do. I had to come know this about Jason twenty years earlier, but for some it was a surprise. Shortly after Max's collapse Jason was vilified in the media and it left many who didn't know him with an inaccurate picture. There could not be a guy that I would trust my children with more than Jason Stinson. He loves his players and students like they are his own kids. I can think of a kid I would have gave up on long ago, but Jason didn't. Jason stayed on him, mentored him and guided the young man. I still believe today that the young man has succeeded and prospered because Jason didn't toss him aside.

Jason learned these values early from his parents, Don and Regina Stinson. Mrs. Stinson worked very hard to see that Jason and his brother Daniel were exposed to as much positive stimuli as possible, and it paid great dividends. Mr. Stinson would not allow a moment of sassy or disrespectful behavior and those lessons led Jason to be caring and respectful regardless of who it was. It was a combination of these role models as well as a strong foundation in the Christian religion that led Jason on a path to help others. Jason always seemed to be worried about everyone else long before he thought of himself, and his call to Christopher only proved that.

I let Coach Stinson know how earlier in the evening I had told Christopher not to worry, that Max would be fine. I recounted to Christopher the numerous times I had seen players moaning and lethargic only to recover after a little ice and water was poured over them. Once the blood starts cooling down, the person always comes back around. I also told Coach Stinson if there was anything I could do for him or for the Crockett/Gilpin families to let me know, and I would do what I could to assist in any way.

I walked downstairs and woke up Christopher. I told him that Coach Stinson had called, and I gave him the latest information on Max. I assured him again that everything was going to be OK and that he should not worry. I told him I loved him, not something I did regularly, and I told him to go back to sleep. As I walked out of his room and shut the door, I wondered to myself if Max would be OK. I had my doubts, because from what I was hearing it did not sound very good. I hoped I wasn't promising Christopher something I could not deliver.

Practice on Thursday, August 21, was cancelled. Also cancelled was the scrimmage scheduled with Bullitt East High School for Friday, August 22.

Any decisions on cancellations for the following week would be reserved until the weekend to see how things went with Max.

A few years earlier at a game played at PRPHS, a soccer player from Western High School (a neighboring high school a few miles away) died after being kicked in the throat while diving for a ball that was being kicked at the same time, so PRPHS had some prior experience with a tragedy surrounding an athletic event. It was surreal having that player later die, but most people at PRPHS forgot about it quickly, since the student did not attend PRPHS.

After Max's hospitalization, everything practically stood still. I am talking about the lives of 2,000 students, as well as many members of the community. By Friday, August 22, things had not changed and the outcome appeared bleak. Students, parents and community members were overwhelmed with worry and grief. Traffic on the football team's website spiked tremendously; people were looking for any information they could get about what was going on. By Friday morning, anyone with ties to the high school or football team knew about this. No real information was being released out of respect for the privacy of the Crockett and Gilpin families.

A blood transfusion was performed on Max on Thursday, but that did not seem to help much. As a last resort, a highly evasive procedure called Extracorporeal Membrane Oxygenation (ECMO) was performed. This technique provides both cardiac and respiratory support oxygen to patients whose heart and lungs are so rigorously damaged that they can no longer serve their function.

Max was pronounced dead on Saturday, August 23, at 10:23 PM. After a consultation with Deputy Coroner Sam Weakley at 11:35 PM, Max's parents chose to decline permission for an autopsy. (Deputy Coroner Weakley incorrectly advised Max's parents that an autopsy was not necessary, because it would not show anything that they didn't already know from Max's extensive medical records that were compiled over his three-day stay.)

The Commonwealth of Kentucky has a very clear list of circumstances that by law require an autopsy. Max's death fell under at least two of these circumstances, yet Max's body was released to Owen Funeral Home (located in southwest Louisville on Dixie Hwy) to be prepared for burial.

It seemed that the bad news spread quickly, although not everyone heard about it Saturday night. It did not take long for the majority of the PRPHS student body to notify each other of Max's death. The kids were in

31

full-blown text mode as they sent text messages to one another. A spur-of-the-moment gathering of several players at Charlie Mullennex's home began shortly following Max's death. Coach Bobby Deacon had coached many of these boys since youth league, so he felt a personal connection to them. He went over to the Mullennex's to sit with the boys and chat about life, death or whatever anyone wanted to talk about. Needless to say, most of these young men were in shock.

Shortly after Max's death, I was speaking with Shawn and Celeste Mullennex about the unusual series of events that had taken place since Max's death. Celeste wanted to emphasize how important it was to her son Charlie that Bobby Deacon had come over that night. She said his presence made a big difference. (Celeste was suffering from ALS—Lou Gehrig's disease—so it was difficult to understand her at times.) Celeste was concerned that I didn't understand her, but I understood her just fine. Not only could I understand what she was saying, I could also see the admiration that she held for Bobby Deacon. (Sadly, Celeste Mullennex lost her battle with ALS on April 15, 2009.)

Those in the PRPHS community who did not hear about Max's death Saturday night awoke to the news on Sunday morning. It was one of the *Courier-Journal*'s front-page stories. I awoke fairly early that morning and went to the end of the driveway to collect the Sunday paper for my wife and me to share, as we regularly do on Sundays. I was only expecting to see a little blurb about Max's death, since it occurred so late the night before. I underestimated that one. It looked like it was a full-blown feature story, but once I skimmed it, I realized that it only contained a few new paragraphs. It appeared to be the same article from Saturday, with some new content added about Max once his name and information were released late Saturday night.

As I walked up the driveway and flipped the paper over, Max's football picture was the other thing besides the headline that caught my eye. It made me wonder. Where did they get this picture? As I stood in my kitchen reading the article, it occurred to me that probably only four or five people had that picture of Max. The picture of Max in his #61 football jersey was taken a couple of weeks before his death. Team and individual pictures had been snapped by Assistant Principal Jeff Jennings and his wife Amy. As I understood it, the only people who had a copy of that picture were the Jennings, Coach Jason Stinson, maybe Max's parents, and me as webmaster of the team's website. I knew no one from the newspaper had contacted me for permission to use the picture, and I found it highly unlikely that Coach Stinson or Max's parents would have been available to give consent, so it had to be Jeff Jennings who gave it to the newspaper. If Jeff Jennings didn't give the newspaper permission, that meant the picture was more than likely taken without permission from www.prpfootball.com. I was not sure, but I intended to find out whether the *Courier-Journal* or any other news agency had permission to use the picture they were all splashing around.

Craig Webb called me shortly after I finished reading the article to inform me that a vigil was going to be held Sunday evening at the PRPHS/Greenwood Elementary complex. (PRPHS and Greenwood sit side by side, and you can walk from the front door of one school to the front door of the other within two minutes.) Max's mother, Michele Crockett, was employed as a counselor at Greenwood, so it looked like the vigil might be centered at Greenwood. Craig asked me if I could contact as many parents as possible to let them know, and I told him that Ann and I would do our best.

Six hours and 60 phone calls later, I arrived at the high school to help out wherever I was needed. There were not many people there yet, but most of the high school's administrators were present, as well as the local print and television media. As I approached Principal Dave Johnson, Craig Webb, and Jeff Jennings, Assistant Principal Jerry Mays was showing the media where they could set up. I asked Jeff if he had given Max's picture to the newspaper, but he didn't know anything about it. I stood on the campus lawn looking back across the street at the media that was gathering, and somehow I knew this would only be the beginning.

Mike Frames, one of the PRPHS football parents, walked around the gathering crowd of several hundred. He handed out candles that were pushed through the bottom of a wax-paper cup to prevent hot wax from falling on your hand. Once Max's parents arrived, Pastor Joel Carwile of Valley View Church took the role of spokesperson for the family. He climbed up on a platform in front of Greenwood Elementary and delivered a semi-impromptu speech to the crowd. As he spoke of Jesus, pain, sorrow, life, death and even football through a handheld megaphone, I could feel positive energy and relief flowing across the crowd.

But then I looked over to see the media again. While most people focused on Pastor Joel, I stared at the news van with the satellite dish on top, video cameras and a photographer across the street. Something told me that some people might not like the fact that there was a pastor preaching on school property. Separation of church and state had been a point of emphasis for some local groups over the past couple decades, and a preacher praying on school property could definitely strike a nerve in some. It probably would not matter that Max's mother was employed at that school and the young man who had just passed away less than 24 hours earlier attended school next door.

There had already been a minor controversy in the past regarding coaches leading players in prayer, so I felt this prayer vigil would really draw some negative attention. However, when this event was planned, I don't think anyone was considering religion and school property. Death and religion go hand in hand. After all, isn't death a cornerstone of any religion? Religion says there is an afterlife, and if you follow your particular religion's disciplines, you will be rewarded upon your death. It should almost be expected that a religious leader would be in attendance and furthermore address the crowd directly following such a tragic event. Many of the people in that crowd were members of Valley View, the third largest church in Jefferson County.

Once Pastor Carwile spoke to the crowd, he crossed Greenwood Road to give a statement to the local media outlets that had gathered. My concerns about the perception of the evening's events seemed to be correct. Later that evening, when I read the comments section on the *Courier-Journal*'s website, the mood and atmosphere were already beginning to change. The tone had already gone from sympathy and sadness to an anti-Christian slant. All people have a right to their opinions, and the message boards of the *Courier-Journal*'s website seemed to be the place for people in Louisville to share theirs. A vocal minority started to speak out against the prayer vigil, and they quickly seemed to stray away from Max Gilpin.

Visitation for Max began on Monday, August 25, at the Owen Funeral Home. The mood was very somber. Classmates, family, friends and the surrounding community members came to pay their condolences to Max's family. Jeff Gilpin, Max's father, estimated that over 3,000 people came to the funeral home during the visitation period.

Max's parents had divorced when he was four, and both had remarried. Michele married Aaron Crockett, with whom she has two children, and Jeff Gilpin married a woman named Lois. Jeff and Lois did not have any children together, but Lois has a 16-year-old daughter from a previous marriage, who was also a part of Max's life.

There were several hundred people at the Owen Funeral Home on Tuesday, August 26. Once I found what seemed like the last available parking spot, I was only present a short time on Tuesday evening. Even though my stay was brief, I saw a wide variety of people come in to pay their respects. Max's parents had stepped away briefly when a very surreal moment occurred. A neighboring high school's entire football team showed up wearing matching team apparel to offer their condolences. As Butler High School's football team members approached Max's casket, they were welcomed by some of the PRPHS football players, who shook their hands and thanked them for coming.

As they filed by—one-by-one—peering into Max's open casket, I wondered what they were thinking. I can't remember any of their faces, but I sure can remember their shirts. I stood there watching as each young man approached. Some would stop longer than others, but none of them looked at Max very long. Did they think that same thing could happen to them, or did they think this could never happen to them? Only one thing seemed clear to me. Before the tragedy ensued on August 20, every one of these boys who walked by the casket was just like Max Gilpin.

CHAPTER 4

DID THAT REALLY HAPPEN?

Max Gilpin's funeral service was held on Wednesday, August 27, 2008 at 1:00 PM at Valley View Church. There were hundreds of, if not a little over a thousand, people in attendance. PRPHS's Principal Dave Johnson said that over 300 students had permission slips signed by a parent/guardian allowing them to attend the funeral. Valley View has a lower level and a spacious upper balcony. Both sections were filled with groups of families and close friends. All the team members, wearing dress shirts and ties like they were required to do on game days, walked by Max's casket. Each one of the players paused briefly to hug Max's immediate family as he went by.

Pastor Joel Carwile gave a sermon that seemed to build on the speech he gave Sunday evening at Greenwood Elementary. One of Max's close friends, Josh Healey, stood up and gave a brief eulogy. Due to the *Courier-Journal* having representatives perched in the church's balcony during the funeral, we were able to have a detailed description later. In an article entitled, "Man of honor is laid to rest," published in the August 28 *Courier-Journal*, writer Antoinette Konz described the somber occasion.

> Yesterday, dozens of flowers in black, red and white—the school's colors—surrounded Max's casket at the front of Valley View Church, where his funeral was held. The service consisted of several songs, a poem written by family members, and words of encouragement from the Rev. Joel Carwile, pastor of the church and the team's minister.
>
> "Our hearts are saddened, yet there is joy within us because we know where Max is. ... He is now on God's starting team," Carwile said.
>
> Before the service, hundreds of people stood in line to offer

condolences to Max's parents, Jeff and Lois Gilpin and Michele and Aaron Crockett. They included members of the football team, all dressed in shirts and ties. As they stood at their teammate's casket, hugging Max's mother and shaking his father's hand, many had tears running down their faces.

The same newspaper had a couple of reporters follow the funeral precession to the gravesite, a little over a mile from the funeral home. At the gravesite, Coach Jason Stinson asked *Courier-Journal* reporters Antoinette "Toni" Konz and Jason Frakes if they were there to pay their respects for a fine young man or to write a story. They shook Coach Stinson's hand and told him they were there to pay their respects. (Now whether that is true or not is subject to interpretation. It seems unlikely, considering Toni Konz wrote dozens of articles about the case over the next year. Every detail of this situation appeared to be of interest to many members of the local media, and this was starting to spread to a national story.)

On the day Max was buried, the *Courier-Journal* ran this headline: "5 who saw practice say coach denied players water." The article quoted Mary Frazier, Brian Bale, Robyn Kirchner (Bale's ex-wife), Rhonda Barnett (Frazier's daughter), and Jo Ann Gayle (Bale's girlfriend). The information and quotes below were obtained from the article written by Andrew Wolfson on August 27.

"A couple of them asked for water and he went off on them," said Mary Frazier, whose granddaughter was playing soccer. "He said, 'Don't you ask for a water break; I'll tell you when you can have a water break.'"

Brian Bale, who was at PRPHS on August 20 to watch his daughter play soccer, told the newspaper yesterday that he heard a football coach ridicule the players' requests for water, noting that they had had the previous day off, yet couldn't finish their practice. Bale, who said he once played football at Waggener, said he understands the need to push athletes, but thought the coach's behavior was excessive.

Bale's former wife, Robyn Kirchner, who estimated she was one of about 30 soccer fans, said she saw three or four football players walking off the field to get water when a coach yelled that he hadn't given permission yet and to "get your butts back over here."

Rhonda Barnett, whose daughter attends PRPHS, said she had been watching the soccer game for about 10 minutes when she heard one of the football players ask if he could stop to get a drink of water. The coach's response was to yell, "Did I tell you that you need a drink of water? You don't tell me when you need something, you got that? We are the professionals here; we'll tell you when you need a drink or a break or anything else."

All four people who said water was denied players at the August 20 practice at PRPHS also said they heard a football coach yell at the players that they wouldn't be allowed to stop running until one of them quit the team.

Another witness, Bale's girlfriend, Jo Ann Gayle, said: "Kids were bent over and puking and gasping for breath, but he kept running the drills. He kept screaming, 'If you stop, you're off the team.'"

Barnett, a registered nurse, said she walked onto the football field after seeing Max collapse. She said he appeared to be unconscious, but his coaches assured her that he was awake, and one of them said he had "just overheated and would be fine." She said she didn't identify herself as a nurse once she was told Max was OK.

This was sure a lot to digest as we got ready for Max's funeral Wednesday morning. My first question was, "Did that really happen?" I had a hard time believing that players were denied water. I have seen numerous practices; the water runs constantly, and the players are at the water quite frequently. My stepson Christopher didn't mention being denied water, and he didn't mention Stinson saying the players would have to run until someone quit the team.

As far as I knew, there were water breaks in the schedule. These breaks are to be taken whether it is 54° or 94° because hydration is necessary, regardless of the temperature outside. It seemed like players were at the water almost constantly. When they were not over as an entire team, they were coming over in groups of 6–12. It was something the kids were doing during the whole practice. I wasn't there that day, but I was having a hard time believing what I was reading. Denial of water? That didn't sound like any practice I have ever attended.

Where were all the football parents when this was going on? I know several parents who regularly attend practice, and I cannot imagine any of them standing by while something like this was going on. The witnesses said, "Coach denied players water." This sounds horrible, and it really doesn't sound like anything Jason Stinson would say. Which coach? What did this coach look like? I had all kinds of questions after reading that article. As I was making the short drive to Max's funeral, my thoughts were dominated by what I had read. I should have been thinking about Max's family and what they were going through, but my mind kept going back to the newspaper article. I read it, and I re-read it. Did that really happen?

These people would not just make up this stuff. This wasn't the first time I read about that practice being different. There were a handful of people posting on the newspaper's message board online implying that Max hadn't been cared for and that the practice was abusive. I wondered if the people who had been posting on the message boards were the same people quoted in the newspaper. You have to take things you read on message boards with a pound of salt (not a grain), because some people post negative things just to get a reaction. I have heard these people referred to as "trolls." They troll the message boards posting comments, looking for a reaction.

The information I was reading on the message boards about that practice was not what my stepson Christopher had described to me. He said that "a bunch of players were screwing off, so we ran gassers instead of practicing." He said it was a hard practice, but he had been through much worse several times in the three years prior under the former head coach, Chris Wolfe. (Chris Wolfe resigned a few days after the 2007 season ended with a first round playoff loss, and he was replaced by Jason Stinson.)

I knew Christopher would speak up if something had been wrong. I had spoken with at least five other people who had been there, and they didn't describe anything like what I was reading on the message boards, and now in the paper. I had so many questions. I had two different pictures of what happened that day. I heard rumors of all kinds of things.

One fact was clear: Max's father, Jeff Gilpin, was there that day. I thought about it, and I concluded that there is no way that Jeff Gilpin would have stood by while these things were being done to his kid. I didn't know Jeff personally, but I remembered him and Michele from a friendship they shared with my sister and brother-in-law. (My brother-in-law and Jeff had worked together as mechanics at a Ford Dealership in the mid 90s, and they would meet outside the workplace in social circles.) I always had the opinion that Jeff was a "hothead." I never witnessed anything to prove that; it was just my "read" on the guy. In any event, I couldn't imagine this guy standing by while his kid was being mistreated.

I kept thinking, maybe these people heard some things that others didn't. I pictured they would have been near the middle of the field while most of the football parents would have been at the southwest end sitting on the bleachers under the tree. Coach Stinson usually stands somewhere around the middle of the field, so they could possibly hear him when the football parents could not.

I knew Christopher had been running somewhere near Max, so I asked him about what Stinson was saying out there that day. Christopher informed me that he was actually much closer to Stinson than he was to Max, and he didn't hear any of the things that were being reported. I didn't even have to ask him if he was one of the gasping and vomiting players, because I already knew the answer. I could think of three players right off the top of my head who vomit almost every day (they have been doing that regularly since youth league), and Christopher was at the top of the list. I used to describe his vomiting as "his very natural reaction (vomiting) to what he considers a very unnatural action (running)."

I asked him if the practice was as bad as it sounded after reading the accounts in the newspaper, and he told me it wasn't. He went on to say that there wasn't anything that was abnormal. I remember laughing when he said, "Of course we were gasping for air; we were running gassers. What did they expect?" I also asked him directly about the water denial allegations, and he said that he didn't witness anyone being denied water. He even said, "We can get water about anytime we want it. I don't know what they are talking about." I would have to believe Christopher, because he would spend as much time as anyone at the water.

This whole catastrophe seemed to be spiraling out of control. I felt like I was right at the center of some concoction being dreamed up in the mind of a mystery crime writer, only this was really happening. There were completely opposite stories from witnesses, allegations made about the practice and rumors that Max was sick that day. I had so many questions. However, the rumors I was hearing had me asking a couple of new questions. Why Max? What made Max so different from any other player practicing that day?

When I came home from Max's funeral, I turned on the noon news and saw Commonwealth Attorney R. David Stengel announce that he had asked the LMPD to open an investigation into Max Gilpin's death. In an interview with the *Courier-Journal*, LMPD spokesperson Lt. Col. Troy Riggs was questioned about the investigation. An article titled, "Police will investigate PRP player's death," written by Antoinette Konz and Andrew Wolfson, reported the following:

> Lt. Col. Troy Riggs said the review of Max Gilpin's death was requested by Jefferson County Commonwealth Attorney Dave Stengel. "The review 'doesn't mean there was or wasn't' anything criminal involved," Riggs said.
>
> Stengel said he made the request after reading a story yesterday in the *Courier-Journal* in which four witnesses said a coach denied water to players at the Aug. 20 practice, when the heat index was 94.

Wow, a police investigation? Well, at least we would truly know what happened out there on the field that day. There were so many things swirling around, and I hoped a police investigation would help prove or disprove some of the information that was being reported.

Practice started back up the next day—Thursday, August 28. It was the first time the team had practiced since Max Gilpin's collapse. The season opener, scheduled for August 29 against Valley High School was cancelled, and it was announced that PRPHS would resume its regular game schedule beginning with a JV game at PRPHS against Ballard High School on Monday, September 1.

The first day back at practice was anything but normal. Parents were huddled up recounting what they recalled from that day, while the players seemed to be emotionally numb. There are certain points in practice when coaches will see "fire" come out of the players, but the first day back was void of any excited behavior. That was understandable considering the players had just attended their teammate's funeral the day before. The topic of discussion between the parents was about the media coverage and what many saw as slanted reporting.

The story that was printed in the *Courier-Journal* on the first day back to practice was about the police investigation and a sixth witness who had come forward to tell what he saw. The article reported the following:

> An additional witness, Phil Compton of Valley Station, who took his 11-year-old daughter to watch the soccer game, told the newspaper yesterday that when players began walking toward a water fountain at the far corner of the soccer field, the coach "pretty much called them out. They turned around and went back on the field."

Most of the parents discussed the remarkable turn this situation was taking. They all said they didn't know what the witnesses were talking about, because it was just a normal practice. Most parents in attendance recounted that conditioning started early, but understood why—with the way the players were behaving that day. Most of us were listing the allegations one-by-one, asking each other if they really happened. There were at least five different allegations of water denial, and many of them were reporting that the coach said the players would run until someone quit the team.

Did that really happen? Well, the answer to this is "yes" and "no." Some of it happened; almost all of it occurred, but most of it was taken out of context. Most of the situations, statements, and actions reported in the newspaper occurred away from Max Gilpin and had absolutely nothing to do with his collapse. Only some of what was being reported was related to Max, so by this time I had a good idea of what was really said that day and by whom it was said.

It turns out that water denial allegations and comments from Mary Frazier, Brian Bale, and Rhonda Barnett came from one interaction with a player at the SW end of the field, which was the opposite end from where Max Gilpin was running. The exchange took place around 5:40 between Coach Bobby Deacon and a freshman player who is known for asking for water repeatedly during drills. (In attempts to avoid conditioning, this player, in the past, has actually asked for a water break after the first gasser.) Bobby, being Bobby, replied with one of his sarcastic comments, knowing that the request for water was a ploy by the player to get out of running. Joking with the player, Bobby told him he didn't need a break because he was not even sweating yet. The player responded, "Yeah I am, Coach. Look at me." Coach Bobby Deacon then replied, "Well, if you are sweating you are hydrated. I read that in my paraprofessional book." Then Coach Deacon turned to some of the other coaches and said, "Since I read a paraprofessional book, does that make me a professional?" One of the other coaches replied jokingly that they were all professionals and told the player, "We'll let you know when you need water."

This was the first strenuous exercise that the player requesting water had participated in all day. Prior to this he had only stood on the sidelines throwing pass routes to receivers, so Coach Bobby Deacon told him that they were almost done and asked if he could wait. The player replied, "I'm fine Coach." The statement about having a couple of days off was said to a player, but it also was said in joking manner. Somehow along the way, a couple of statements that were intended to be funny got turned into an insensitive, fire-breathing denial of water by a tyrannical football coach.

Denial of water allegations mentioned by Robyn Kirchner and Phil Compton both happened. It was when Coach Stinson went after the four players who went to the water instead of going to the team meeting where they had been instructed to be. Coach Stinson telling the players, "Get your butts back over here," is about as harsh as the language got.

The allegation made by Jo Ann Gayle about the players gasping for breath and puking appears to be true also, but it happens every other day of the week too. At one point, one group of kids was told that they were going to keep doing up/downs until one of them quit the team or they started doing what they are supposed to be doing. However, the statement, "If you stop, you're off the team" isn't recalled by anyone else. These words simply did not happen. That might be what Jo Ann Gayle remembers, but as we discovered later, many of her recollections of the day's events proved to be absolutely unfounded.

Some of witnesses' statements were misquoted by a word or two, and it makes them sound much worse than they truly were. These quotes were also taken out of context, and it was the context of these quotes that was not known to many at this time. Collectively, it was all sounding horrible. Nevertheless, I still believed this would all get straightened out. The truth would come out during the police investigation.

CHAPTER 5

You Might Want to Hire an Attorney

We needed a public relations person to take the lead and straighten out this situation before it completely got out of control. Granted, the newspaper should be given some latitude, since there was "no comment" coming from the coaching staff and players at PRPHS. The allegations could have been easily explained, but it is kind of hard to deny an allegation if you do not make a comment. With a police investigation underway, no comments could be made. It was a real catch-22 situation—a "perfect storm" of events—that helped the situation grow into what it became.

The only way to clear up the confusion was to make a public statement, but any public statement could put you at greater risk of criminal charges whether you had done anything wrong or not. Nobody involved with the situation was experienced with public relations, so no one really knew what to do. The high school relied on the Board of Education to address this publicly before it got out of hand. The Board of Jefferson County Public Schools did not sufficiently do that, so once a police investigation was announced, it was a little too late for a public statement. It is fair to say that, at this point, the situation was out of control. It was definitely too late to resolve the allegations simply. LMPD announced that it would be interviewing every player and coach in attendance that day, and it would also try to interview any witness who may have been at PRPHS on August 20.

At PRPHS's first practice since Max's death, the area was swarming with media trying to get some video. (By that time, the media had been notified that they were not allowed on school property and would have to film all of their video from outside the perimeter of the campus.) The east and north sides of the practice field are bordered by about a dozen houses, and they are only separated in some areas by a six-foot high chain link fence. At one point, Richie Sutton, who is a football parent and the head coach of the

Panther Youth League Seniors, went around the neighborhood to run off one of the TV stations that had set up camp in a nearby backyard. (It turns out that the homeowner was not aware of the intruders, and eventually wrote a letter to the news station to complain about it.) Not being able to find a suitable place to set up on the ground, the media resorted to using a helicopter. I am not sure which station did it, but at least one of them had a helicopter circling practice for a brief period. Everyone just wanted to shield the kids from the media, which was becoming more and more aggressive.

There were not very many comments coming out of PRPHS from players, coaches, or administrators. That was probably the best action to take, because it seemed like everything being said was getting twisted. This had gone so far that I felt like a JCPS spokesperson should be the only one commenting at this time, but JCPS had been limited in its public comments. It seemed that every time someone from the Board made a statement, the worse it got. It was perceived that they were either being insensitive, or that they were glossing over the situation. It appeared like whatever direction anyone from JCPS or PRPHS took, it was dissected and scrutinized until an angle was found to make that person look bad. We did not want our kids being pawns in the media's pursuit of a story, so we tried to keep the media away from them.

I had already gotten an early indication of what the media's behavior might be like when I realized no one had granted permission to the media to use Max's football picture in the newspaper. (The picture was taken without permission off a website that clearly states the photo was copyrighted.) I called three television stations and the newspaper to complain. For the most part, they were all apologetic. The representative from the *Courier-Journal* was somewhat combative in the beginning, but eventually apologized when he realized he had no one's permission to use the picture. He said the picture had been given to the *Courier-Journal* by someone at WHAS 11-TV. By the time I spoke to WHAS 11-TV, I was pretty angry, and I took it out on reporter Renee Murphy and her producer. She was trying to be professional about it and immediately apologized, but I ranted and raged at her anyway. (Actually, she was the first person who admitted knowledge that the photo was off the website, and she was probably the only honest person that day.) Up to this point, people were apologizing, but they were also blaming others. They reminded me of a bunch of vultures; PRPHS was the dead meat. The media was swarming to get anybody on camera who had anything to say.

Witnesses were talking to the media so much that they had difficulty keeping their details straight. There was one witness whose story was already being conflicted by one of her relatives. On Wednesday, August 27, Mary Frazier appeared on WLKY 32-TV's news, and WLKY's website ran a transcript of the story. Part of it read, "Frazier said she arrived at the soccer match at 5:45 when her attention shifted to the football practice, and she said her daughter, who's a nurse, offered to help Gilpin but was turned down."

That's strange. When I reviewed Rhonda Barnett's statement in the *Courier-Journal*, nowhere did it say she offered to help, but was turned down. She asked Bobby Deacon if Max was going to be all right, but she never offered to help, nor did she identify herself as a nurse.

The next scheduled event was the JV game at PRPHS against Ballard on September 1. At the game, Mary Frazier and Rhonda Barnett were main topics of discussion. I stood at the corner of the concession stand with Steve Ellis, discussing the entire event from the time Steve started helping Antonio to the time EMS took over with Max. I mentioned Frazier and Barnett along with the media stories they had been a part of, and I asked Steve if he remembered anybody offering help. He was fully aware of what Barnett had said, and I will never forget what he said to me. "I fix bulldozers for a living. If that lady had told me she was a nurse, I would have put Max in her hands. She did not say anything about being a nurse."

I told Steve about discussing the nurse with Bobby Deacon several times over the last few days. Bobby clearly remembered the woman walking up to him. She approached him as he was clearing players out of the area and securing the scene. One of the worst scenarios possible is a bunch of observers getting in the way while coaches were trying to load Max in the Gator™ to take to the water. Bobby Deacon was the first person the woman reached.

Barnett asked Bobby Deacon, "Is he going to be all right?" and Bobby replied, "Yeah, Mom, he'll be OK. He's just overheated." Bobby called her "Mom" because he thought she was Max's Mom. (Michele Crockett and Rhonda Barnett do not look anything alike, but Bobby would not have known that since he could not recall meeting Crockett prior to Max's collapse. He just figured, since this woman was walking up to the situation, she was more than likely the player's mother.) She never offered to help, nor did she identify herself as a nurse. Barnett would not have been turned away if she had identified herself. Her experience and expertise may have quickly determined that Max was suffering from heatstroke and not heat exhaustion, but whether her help would have made a difference will never be known, since she didn't offer to assist.

Heat exhaustion can present itself just like heatstroke, and the differences can be extremely subtle. Having no experience with heatstrokes, the coaches probably thought they were dealing with heat exhaustion and that, with some water and ice, Max would come back around. No one delayed in caring for Max. Once the coaches got him to the water, they were applying treatment that was appropriate for heat exhaustion or heatstroke. They put ice bags in his groin and under his arm, as well as rubbing a bag of ice across his chest, neck, and back. In another attempt of cooling him, they hosed him down with water. However, he didn't seem to be cooling down. Something was different about this kid versus the others. Once you place ice where the arterial blood flows, it doesn't take long for the blood to start cooling down. Once the body temperature starts coming back down, the player will come around. It won't be long before he will want the ice pack out of his underwear. (To test this theory, all you need to do is walk around with an ice pack in your underwear for a little while. You will want to remove it before long, just as most people being treated for heat-related illness do as their body temperature starts to drop.)

It was a real mystery to us. What made Max different? Why wouldn't he cool down? It didn't appear that Antonio Calloway's hospital stay was heat related, because his body temp when he arrived at the hospital was 98.7 degrees. The practice appeared to be tough since the players were running gassers for 15–20 minutes each, but never was it excessive. Contrary to what many of the players said, if they were a 10th grader or higher, they had run more gassers than 12 before. However, the whole situation just kept gaining momentum, and there was no stopping it.

There was no autopsy, so all kinds of speculations were being made. I was starting to hear rumors about steroids and bodybuilding enhancers. Bobby Deacon told me that his nephew, who is one of Max's close friends, saw Max take Creatine just a couple of weeks before his collapse. Creatine is an over-the-counter muscle enhancer that is considered a supplement. It is used to help pack on muscle mass by removing water from the vascular system and storing it in the muscles. Users are advised to discontinue Creatine 30 days prior to training in the heat, because of water issues created by using this supplement. Someone else told me Max was on Adderall®. Adderall® is an amphetamine, so I wondered if that played a role. There were so many factors unknown. What was rumor, and what was the truth?

I ran into Coach Jason Stinson at the JV game. I walked with him to the press box and sat with him for a few minutes. I needed to discuss some fundraising issues, and I wanted to ask him how he was doing. It was ironic, because I had a concern over a sponsor that was advertising with us for the 2008 season. The company was a law firm specializing in personal injury litigation. I wondered if I should return the firm's money, given the situation that had just occurred. Jason told me not to worry about it, and to go ahead and hang the firm's banner with the other advertisers. (Nevertheless, I had it in the back of my mind that there would be a lawsuit filed. I felt hanging the banner would be extremely ironic, especially if that law firm ended up being the one who grabbed the case.)

Three days later on September 4, Christopher brought home the following letter from Craig Webb.

> Dear Parent/Guardian:
>
> Next week, members of the football team will be interviewed by Louisville Metro Police. If you feel it necessary for you to be with your child during the interview process, please call Sergeant Denny Butler @ _____ by Friday, 3 PM. Leave your name and contact number, and he will call you back. The department will then set up a situation for your child to be interviewed. If Sgt. Butler does not hear from you, then he will assume you approve. The police will conduct interviews here at school starting next week.
>
> Thanks for your time and cooperation.
>
> Craig Webb, Athletic Director

Most of the parents I spoke with wished to be present when the police department interviewed their son. My wife Ann left a voicemail for Sgt. Butler to inform him that we would like to be present during Christopher's interview. We were contacted back by Detective Terry Jones, and we agreed to meet at the high school on Tuesday, September 9, at 5:30 PM.

When PRPHS's varsity team took the field for the first time since Max's death on September 5, it was a media feeding frenzy at Ballard High School. The football team had to travel with a police officer to maintain order on the sidelines. Ballard High had set up "media zones" at each end of the football field from which the media was to film, but for some that was not enough. A reporter from a local TV station continued to remain on the sidelines after being asked to move. When PRPHS's Assistant Principal Jeff Jennings said something to her about it, she called him an asshole. (I guess her behavior could have been overlooked since she went to the designated area right after that incident, but she went back to the station and told her boss that Jeff had called her an asshole. The only problem with her claim is that all the people standing there heard her say those words, not him. Ultimately, she ended up having to write Jeff a letter of apology, and management at the TV station informed Jeff that she was suspended for one week.)

PRPHS led a defensive battle 6–0 until late in the fourth quarter. Then Ballard scored a touchdown in final seconds of the game to win 7–6. It was heartbreaking for the boys who had really wanted to win this game for Max. It was this stated goal that had caught the attention of some media members. Generally, players will say some word or phrase in unison as they leave their huddle before each play. Many times you will hear the huddle leader say something like "defense on three" or "win on three," and then the team will break with that word. The media wanted something like that to run on the 11 o'clock news. There were actually a couple of reporters moving up and down the line of players shaking hands after the game. They were seeking comment about anything but the football game in which the players had just played their hearts out. I hoped this was not the way the rest of the season was going to go.

Ann, Christopher, and I met with Detective Terry Jones at 5:30 PM on September 9, as agreed. He first wanted to get into his car to conduct the interview, but he decided against that since Christopher is 6' 3" and was wearing his equipment. He had a sheet of paper with a list of questions on it, and he pretty much followed it question by question. Below are the questions the detectives were instructed to ask the players:

- This statement is being tape recorded, does this meet with your approval?
- I am taking this statement in reference to the events on 08/20/08 that occurred during the PRP football practice. Please describe the events of 08/20/08 from the beginning to the end of practice.

- How were water breaks given—individually or as a team?
- On 08/20/08, how many water breaks did you take?
- After the last water break, what did practice consist of?
- Why was the team running sprints?
- How many sprints did your group run?
- What group were you in?
- How many sprints did you run before taking off gear?
- After taking off gear?
- How long do you think the team was running sprints?
- Did you or any of your teammates ask for water breaks or try to get water during the running of sprints?
- If they were denied, who denied them?
- Did you or any of your teammates become ill during the running of sprints?
- Who?_____ When?_____
- Who?_____ When?_____
- Who?_____ When?_____
- Who?_____ When?_____
- During any practices this year, have you personally seen or heard of any teammates being injured or quitting the team?
- Has anyone influenced you in any way to withhold information or change any of the facts that actually occurred during the practice?
- Is this statement truthful?
- Do you have anything else to add?

I was alarmed by what I had just witnessed. It appeared to me that the Commonwealth Attorney and LMPD had an angle they were pursuing. I was troubled that they did not seem to be concerned about how Max was cared for, but instead they were looking at the events leading up to his collapse. They were focusing heavily on water breaks, the amount of gassers run, and if anyone got sick during the run.

Once Detective Jones completed his interview, Christopher went back to practice, while Ann and I got into our car and went back home. I told her as we were pulling out of the parking lot that LMPD was going for wanton endangerment and reckless homicide, and that Christopher just made their case. They had no concerns about how Max was treated after his collapse, so it was clear to me the path that they were on.

As soon as practice ended, I returned to the high school to warn the coaches of what I feared. I remember that Steve Deacon, Jason Cook, and Bobby Deacon were there, as well as at least one more coach. I really can't recall if the meeting occurred on the practice field or in the locker room, but my statement could not have been more prophetic. I was mainly talking to Bobby because I knew he would understand what I was talking about, but since everyone else standing there was in the same jeopardy, I shared my theory.

I said, "Where is your KRS book? I know where they're going with this, and it's not good." (The KRS book is a handbook of Kentucky Revised Statutes that contains all laws on the books in the Commonwealth.) Bobby told me he had one in his car and asked me why I thought that. I looked at the coaches standing there, and I said, "You all had better shut your mouths and hire an attorney." I went on to explain that it was my opinion that the police were looking for about five or six counts of wanton endangerment for the vomiting players and Antonio Calloway, and reckless homicide for Max.

It was clear that someone somewhere had an agenda, and everyone coaching that day could be at risk.

CHAPTER 6

A SEASON CLOUDED IN CONTROVERSY

Although it was not reality, it felt like almost every day had some big breaking news story about the investigation. No sooner than Max was buried WHAS-11 TV obtained an interview with Max's father, Jeff Gilpin, on August 28. Jeff did not want to go on camera, but he was willing to talk to Renee Murphy. What he told her sounded much different than the story the *Courier-Journal* ran the day before.

WHAS-11 TV posted the story on its website. It stated:

> Max Gilpin's father says he doesn't blame the coaches, and that his son actually died of a heatstroke. WHAS-11's Renee Murphy had the chance to talk to Jeff Gilpin. He says the teachers and coaches always looked after his son at PRP. He says he is not angry at the school. At PRP High School, players are back on the field for their first practice since Max Gilpin died.... "Max's father tells me he was at practice last week when his son collapsed, and he says his son died of heatstroke. He says his son looked okay just before he collapsed and says he is not angry with the school. He says he didn't see the coaches do anything wrong that day at practice."

Please remember these statements, because you may want to refer back to them later. The August 28 interview with Renee Murphy would be the first of several statements Jeff Gilpin gave regarding the day Max collapsed. (Unfortunately, as he gave multiple statements, he ended up with multiple stories. The only time any consistency was found was when the statements first began. For the first couple of months, his story didn't waiver much at all.)

On August 31, which was the Sunday following Max's funeral, the *Courier-Journal* ran a big front page spread with the headline, "Max's Mom: 'I just want the truth.'" In addition to that story, an editorial by Bennie L. Ivory was published in response to criticism coming from the PRPHS community. (The editorial written by Ivory was published August 31 in the *Courier-Journal* and was titled, "Tragedy requires tough questions.") Ivory stated:

> There are stories and there are stories, and every now and then, there are stories like that of 15-year-old Max Gilpin. It's the kind of story that—contrary to what some believe—most journalists would prefer not to have to cover—the death of someone so young, so full of hope, so full of potential. It is also the kind of the story that demands tough questions, deliberation and honest answers.

If most reporters did not want to cover this story, someone forgot to give them the memo. Furthermore, no news organization was more aggressive than the *Courier-Journal.* The television stations usually had a maximum of one reporter working this story at a time, but the newspaper was throwing multiple reporters at this. I remember thinking it was a good thing that they preferred not to cover this story, because if this was their preference we might find a *C-J* reporter hiding in the bushes or in the back seat of one of our cars.

We did not find any reporters in our back seats, but a *C-J* reporter did ambush some parents and a player after a game. The reporter was literally hiding behind a bush and presented himself once they walked by. The parents recounted that the reporter was a large, heavyset man, and he initially frightened them when he appeared from nowhere in the dark to say, "Excuse me, I am a reporter with the *Courier-Journal.* Can I ask you a few questions about…." Before he was able to complete his request or even say what he wanted to ask, he was told "no." (He and others at the newspaper would frequently be told "no" when asking for comment from people at PRP.)

It seemed to me that the more parents, players, and coaches of PRP refused to talk to the media, the more aggressive the media became. The reporting on this story was becoming slanted to present one side, and that side in many ways was not even based on facts. (Several people had already begun to say that this story was going to sell newspapers "as long as it lasts.")

Ivory went on to say in his editorial:

This case is a classic example of the delicate balancing act that news organizations across the country face every day in weighing the rights of the people we cover and the public's right to know.

It seemed at this juncture of this ever-changing story, Ivory could taste a Pulitzer Prize, and this editorial was intended to lay the groundwork for an application. (Bennie Ivory is the vice president and executive editor of the *Courier-Journal*, and it seems he wanted the public and perhaps the Pulitzer Prize board to know that this story would not exist without the newspaper's "watchdog journalism.") Ivory also stated:

> While our stories may have been difficult for some to read, they have raised serious questions about Max's death. Had we not published the eyewitness accounts, would the Jefferson County Public Schools be taking a deeper look? Would the police department be involved? Probably not.

JCPS publicly stated that it opened an investigation prior to the story about water denial allegations being published. There had been an e-mail sent by Brian Bale two days after the practice, and JCPS received phones calls on Monday after Max's death. It may have appeared that JCPS was glossing over the situation, but behind the scenes a full-fledged investigation was forming. It is highly unlikely JCPS considered calling the media to inform them of this investigation. It was publicly declared by Lauren Roberts (the JCPS spokesperson) that it is JCPS's policy not to disclose details of ongoing investigations to the media until they are complete. The statement that caught me off guard as I read the editorial was when Ivory wrote:

> You also should know that Max's mother, Michele Crockett, fully supported that story and others we have done. And, as for covering the funeral, she approved our request to cover it.

I didn't want to judge, but it seemed to me that a newspaper photo/videographer would be the last thing I would want at my son's funeral. I am not saying that what the newspaper did was wrong, because I may not fully understand the reasons behind that decision; however, I am saying that it appears the newspaper operated on the fringe of several boundaries in this situation.

Michele Crockett told the *Courier-Journal* that she "just wanted the truth," and the article listed several questions she wanted answers to. (It would probably be Christmas before she got those answers, since the police department was now involved. Anyone involved that day sought legal counsel, so their only answer will be coming from that pending investigation.) There were over 90 players, six coaches, and one or two dozen witnesses to be interviewed, so it wasn't going to be any time soon before all of that information could be compiled.

The article quoted Crockett as saying, "I want to know what the coaches were saying. I want to know how many sprints the boys were running. I want to know if they were denied water, and I want to know what they did to help my son after he went down." Actually, those were all good questions. In the same article, Crockett said one of her friends had frantically called, telling her to get over to the practice field. The friend said, "Your boy has been down on the ground for (several) minutes, and I don't think they are moving fast enough to help him. You may want to get over here."

Stories were circulating that told of the coaches leaving Max on the field for nearly fifteen minutes before anyone offered to help him. There was even a story that Coach Stinson had witnessed Max go down, stepped over him, and continued to have the team run gassers. When I first heard these things, coupled with what Michele Crockett was saying in the paper, I really began to ponder some of these allegations. I knew most of these coaches, and it did not sound like anything they were capable of doing. I just was not buying the denial of water allegations, but the rumors and allegations about some of the coaches' behavior had me asking questions. Fortunately for me, people were answering my questions, so I would not have to wait for the LMPD to tell me.

We never knew what new allegation the next day might bring, and this whole process was taking a toll on some of the boys. The news stories just kept coming, so many of the players were finding it difficult to gain closure. If it was not a new allegation being released, it was an editorial or columnist's point of view stirring the pot.

On September 6, the morning after the Ballard game, Rick Bozich—one of the newspaper's senior sports columnists—added his opinion. In an article titled "Finding the truth is the best way to honor Gilpin," Bozich described the Ballard game—all while mixing in emotional tidbits about Max Gilpin and his death's influence on the game. Then with his closing,

Bozich expressed his frustration that none of the players or coaches at PRP had any interest in talking with him. After only being able to get a comment by speaking with a player who was not traveling with the team, he wrote:

> Nobody else from the PRP football team—players or coaches—talked to the media last night. That's certainly their right. They can wave off sportswriters and TV people. But they should not wave off the Louisville Metro Police, who are investigating the circumstances surrounding Gilpin's death at the request of Jefferson Commonwealth Attorney Dave Stengel. T-shirts, wristbands and moments of silence are a wonderful way to honor Max Gilpin. Getting the answers to everything that happened on the practice field would be the best way.

Wow, Bozich seemed really peeved at the PRP players and coaches declining to comment. The PRPHS football team was forced to travel with a uniformed LMPD officer for security. Reporters simply refused to accept "no comment" or leave the sidelines when asked. Many times, the only way to back up the reporters was to have a police officer make an ultimatum. The media was a huge distraction for the team at best, but the players did their best to put it out of their minds.

After the initial storm of media reports, there seemed to be a minor calm. PRPHS hosted its second opponent of the year, Doss High School, on September 12. (Doss is located just a few miles from PRP, and the team wanted to show its condolences. Prior to the game, Jeff Gilpin was presented with a wreath from Doss High School's head coach, LaKunta Farmer. A red flag with an emblem of a football and the number 61 was prepped to fly below the U.S. flag that flies over the scoreboard. (The flag honoring Max is to fly there every football game until the end of the 2010 season, and then it will be hung in the locker room.)

Both of Max's parents were invited to the ceremony, but only his father, Jeff, and his stepmother, Lois Gilpin, attended. The student pep club, "the Black Hole," had raised over two thousand dollars by selling t-shirts. (The shirts had "For Max" printed on the front and "Gilpin #61" on the back.) The student pep club presented half of the money it raised to Jeff Gilpin, along with the shadow-box frame of Max's jersey. (The other half of the money, along with another one of Max's jerseys, was given to Michele Crockett at a later time.) Compared to the Ballard game, the media presence wasn't as thick, but they were definitely there to film and report on the memorial.

On the Sunday following the Doss game, hurricane force winds ripped through Louisville. At the same time, Coach Jason Stinson was in the office of his attorney, Alex Dathorne, submitting to an in-depth interview with LMPD Sgt. Denny Butler. Upon exiting the building, the three men were greeted with downed tree limbs and power lines all over the city. It took nearly a week before Louisville Gas & Electric (LG&E) was able to restore power to all the homes and businesses that had experienced power outages.

Due to the widespread outages, JCPS was forced to cancel school for the entire week of September 15–19. All games scheduled for that week were also cancelled. The windstorm took the attention off PRP for a short while. This was a much-needed break from relentless coverage of this tragedy.

After LMPD wrapped up its interviews with most of the players and coaches, everyone hoped that the boys could start grabbing some sense of normalcy. PRPHS's next scheduled game was against district opponent Butler Traditional High School on September 26. Butler High was another school located only a short distance from PRPHS, and PRP's real rival is undoubtedly Butler. (In a knock-off of the slogan, "friends don't let friends drive drunk," several PRP students wore t-shirts that read, "friends don't let friends go to Butler.")

Ever since the storm, all had been calm on the media front. But that came to a screeching halt when the inevitable occurred. On September 26, the morning of the Butler game, the *Courier-Journal* ran the article "Parents sue 6 PRP coaches" written by Andrew Wolfson. The article said:

> The parents of a 15-year-old Pleasure Ridge Park High School football player who died after collapsing at practice have filed a wrongful-death lawsuit against head coach Jason Stinson and five other coaches on the team. The lawsuit, filed yesterday in Jefferson Circuit Court, accuses the coaches of negligence and "reckless disregard" in the death of Max Gilpin, who died three days after collapsing Aug. 20 of apparent heatstroke. Glenna Michele Crockett and Jeffrey Dean Gilpin, who watched part of his son's practice, sued the coaches individually, saying the men had a "duty to exercise ordinary and reasonable care for the safety" of Max.

Jeff Gilpin was suing the coaches? That was fast. It had only been 30 days since Max was buried. This turn of events was not one bit surprising, and actually I had expected and predicted it. But I didn't think it was going to happen that quickly. This article, of course, overshadowed the game and was the topic of most conversations. Jeff acknowledged his name was on the lawsuit, but he said he was only in it so he could get information. He claimed if he was not listed on the lawsuit, he would not be privy to any information into Max's death. In the beginning, many at PRPHS skeptically accepted there had to be something to that statement, since Jeff continued to come around. On the day this article appeared in the paper, he attended the football game, and he continued to come to football games for the remainder of the season.

Regardless of all of the distractions around this game, the players once again seemed to be focused. They defeated the Butler Bears 18–0 and moved their season record to 2 wins and 1 loss. PRPHS's next opponent would be Seneca High School seven days later on October 2. Once again, things would hopefully settle, now that a whole new dust cloud had been rustled up.

PRPHS hosted Seneca High School for the fourth game of the season. It was a very close game, but PRP prevailed in the end, 27–14, and moved its season record to 3 wins and 1 loss. The media attention was drastically reduced, and it seemed that things might be calming down again. (It had only been a week since the last bombshell had been dropped, so it was a little premature to tell.)

On October 9, PRPHS played DuPont Manual High School at Kentucky's oldest football stadium, DuPont Manual Memorial Stadium. (This venue is nestled right in the middle of the historic Germantown area of Louisville.) PRPHS played district opponent Manual, losing its second game of the year, 15–23. That loss moved the 2008 season record to 3 wins and 2 losses. PRP had really hoped to pull off a victory against Manual to build momentum for the next game. (The boys would need all the momentum they could get because the following week they would be facing Trinity High School, the defending state champion in Class 6A football.)

The media had really pulled back recently, so most people were starting to relax. Then, on Monday, October 13, the *Courier-Journal* printed an article titled "Fallen PRP player's mother still wonders 'why?'" The article was written by Andrew Wolfson, and it quoted Michele Crockett on several questions she had. She wanted to know why she had not been interviewed by JCPS. JCPS said it had to contact her through her attorneys, but her attorneys said no one had contacted them to speak to their client. The article went on to state:

> And most of all, Crockett said she questions why PRP head coach Jason Stinson and his assistants are still on the job, given that teachers suspected of improper conduct with students, such as inappropriate touching, are immediately suspended and reassigned... Roberts [JCPS's spokesperson] said the PRP coaches are still on the job because the school district must have "reasonable suspicion that a violation of rules has occurred, in order to take action against an individual employee."

Jeff Gilpin appeared on WHAS-11 TV several days later on October 15. He stated several things that were contrary to what was being reported elsewhere. He spoke of Max not feeling well the day before he collapsed, and he went on to elaborate that Max had visited Greenwood Elementary School (GES) to lie down for a while that Tuesday. He said that this was "odd." He said Max didn't eat as much as usual at dinner, and he went to bed early complaining of a headache. There was also talk that Max had gone to GES to lie down on Wednesday, too, but this was never confirmed.

Douglas Higdon, a custodian at GES, told LMPD during an interview that he saw Max in the building on either Tuesday or Wednesday, but he was not sure which day. GES became "the iron wall to the east" when attempting to find out what truly happened there on August 19 and 20. (It seems everyone other than Douglas Higdon was looking another way.)

PRP was next scheduled to play on October 17 at Trinity High School in the St. Matthew's neighborhood of Louisville. Trinity is an all boys' Catholic high school that had won six out of the last seven state championships in football, so it would be a tough game. (Trinity is regularly favored to win the state title, and 2008 was no different.) PRP was defeated 27–56 by the eventual champion of the 2008 season. This loss took PRP's record to 3 wins and 3 losses. The media seemed to be present more for Trinity than to chronicle the ever-changing PRP soap opera, and for the people from PRP, that was OK.

PRP's next foe was another all boys' Catholic high school. St. Xavier's (St. X) football pedigree is not quite as strong as Trinity's, but the school has won state championships and its team regularly competes for the championship. St. X's visit to Joe Young Stadium on October 24 yielded them a 57–6 victory over PRP. Much like the Trinity game, the media in attendance seemed to focus their reports on St. X. There were no questions being asked of PRP about the police investigation. It was almost like old times. The media could care less about PRP football, and we just took our annual spanking from St. X.

PRP took its record of 3 wins and 4 losses on the road to Radcliff, KY, on Halloween night. North Hardin High School is located just a few miles south of Ft. Knox. PRP played very well against North Hardin and earned a 36–10 win for the final regular season game of 2008. PRP concluded the 2008 regular season with 4 wins and 4 losses. Typically, high schools in this area would play 10 games during the regular season, but due to Max Gilpin's death and the windstorm, one game was cancelled and two open weeks in the schedule were not filled.

After the North Hardin game, PRP had an open week, but the school did not stay out of the news. The 911 tape from Steve Deacon's call to Emergency Services was released on November 7, and that seemed to be the hot topic. You could catch excerpts of the call on any local new broadcast, or you could listen to it in its entirety at the *Courier-Journal* website.

If you did not know Steve Deacon, you could easily misconstrue his tone during the 911 call. His calm demeanor was portrayed as unhurried and lacking concern. Some people were implying that there was no sense of urgency on the coach's part. When I listened to the tape, I thought his actions sounded correct to me. He was supposed to be calm. If he was panicking and screaming, the 911 operator would first have to settle him down in order to get information. That was not the case at all. Steve had assessed the situation, and the coaches had begun to apply treatment. Moments later, when Max was not responding, Steve called 911. The civil suit claims that he did not dial 911 fast enough.

On November 14, PRP traveled to Meade Co. for its first playoff win in seven years, winning 27–7. The team earned another match with St. X for the second round on November 21. Much like the regular season game, PRP lost 6–48. PRP finished the 2008 season 5–5. The team was only nine points away from finishing 7–3 with those three losses coming against Trinity (defending state champs) and St. X twice. Even still, 5–5 is not too bad, considering it was a season clouded in controversy.

CHAPTER 7

COMMONWEALTH VS. FOOTBALL

The police investigation ended on November 13. LMPD passed its investigative file on to the Commonwealth Attorney's Office for its review. Once the investigation was handed off to Stengel's office, there was not much else to report. Before we knew it, Christmas came and went, and it was a whole new year. We normally have the football banquet sometime before Christmas, but we had kept postponing the date. The reason was mostly because the person who normally took care of setting everything up was dealing with more than he could handle.

Coach Stinson's wife, Monica, recounted what a rough period Christmas 2008 was for her entire family and, more specifically, for Jason. She remembered that the longer the investigation went on, the more depressed Jason seemed to become. The onslaught of media coverage would have drug down the strongest man, so it should have been no surprise that Jason was being affected. Monica recounted that "not knowing what the outcome of the investigation would be" was hard on Jason, and he would be relieved once it was announced whether he would face charges or not. Either way, at least he would know.

In 2007, my wife and I made a PowerPoint presentation for the senior players at the suggestion of another parent. This presentation included a recorded message from each player's family. It would play in the background while pictures of the player were shown on the screen. The pictures of the boys usually began with them in the first or second grade and would go up to their senior football picture. Most parents would recount how quickly their son grew up or how proud they were of him. Everyone seemed to enjoy the video, so we put one together again for this year's senior class.

Most parents preferred to stop by my office and make their recording. We had a system going where Ann would scan the pictures while I recorded the parents' message to their child. The recordings were usually completed before the pictures were scanned, so casual conversation would begin. The topic was always Max Gilpin's death and the criminal investigation surrounding it. At least 15 players' parents stopped by in December–January to complete their recordings. Their opinion was unanimous. This was a terrible tragedy, and the police investigation was unnecessary.

I spoke with Sheila West after her recording, and some of the things she said really left an impression on me. Sheila's son, David West, Jr., was the starting quarterback for the 2008 varsity team, so she was no stranger to athletics. In fact, she currently coaches the JV softball and JV girls' basketball teams at PRPHS. She is also a physical education teacher in the JCPS system, so she has multiple points of view. Her son was at the practice on August 20, and she felt his account of the day's events didn't sound that uncommon for a football practice.

She asked, "How far is too far? Can you go to jail for coaching?" She said that the investigation had opened many coaches' eyes, but not necessarily in a good way. She said that if Jason Stinson was to be charged and convicted for what happened, she would surely resign from any and all coaching duties. Perhaps she would do that as a symbol of protest, but mostly out of self-preservation. It is bad enough to live with a tragedy like this on your mind, but then to end up facing criminal charges is just too much to take. There are so many things coaches do not know about their players, and the coaches cannot be expected to know everything.

Something that was working one day at practice could have an entirely different affect on a player the next day. Medication, supplements, illness and many other factors could entirely change things. "How far do we push kids?" Sheila asked. "What if something happens that we could not have possibly known?" The prospect of what risks modern day coaching might bring were unsettling to her, to say the least.

Shelia brought up some good points that most certainly will be debated for some time to come. "How far is too far?" Contrary to what was being reported, this was not the most running the players had ever experienced. Perhaps some players with little or no experience would have definitely seen this as their most grueling practice, but that was not the case for most of the players. Jeff Gilpin even told LMPD investigators on September 4 that he had seen Max run harder in hotter weather, and he did not know what happened. He then went on to tell WHAS-11 TV on October 15 that Max had "run further in hotter weather for longer."

Sheila wondered if coaches could be held accountable for circumstances beyond their control. She asked me, "Do you really think they are going to charge him?" We looked at a calendar to speculate when the case might be presented to a grand jury, and we figured that by the end of January we all would know. I told her that it looked like the police were chasing five counts of wanton endangerment for the kids who vomited, and one count of reckless homicide for Max's death. If and how they presented it to a grand jury would determine the final outcome. It appeared that LMPD had lined up its investigation to focus on some things, while choosing to ignore others, and it concerned several people that this was becoming a witch-hunt.

Early in the new year, I took a cell phone call from Bobby Deacon that will be forever etched in my memory. My mind was racing as he told me what he had just learned. I had a gut feeling that Coach Stinson would probably get indicted, but until it really happened it was only speculation.

> "Hello."
> "Rodney, this is Bobby Deacon."
> "Hey, what's up? What are you doing?"
> "Nothing. I just heard they indicted Stinson."
> "What? You have got to be kidding me."
> "No man, I wish I was."
> "Is he the only one they indicted?"
> "As far as I know."
> "I don't know if it is possible to be stunned and not surprised all at the same time, but that is what I feel right now. What the hell is he going to do? He can't afford to pay attorneys to defend this."

I talked to Bobby many more times over the weekend, and I told him I was going to go to Jason's arraignment the following Monday. He said that he planned on attending too, and he would meet me down there a little before Jason's hearing was scheduled.

It was now clear that both football history and legal history were going to be made in Louisville, KY. I had reporters coming from various outlets to my home and office seeking my comment. When I walked off the elevator, there were at least a dozen cameras set up in a semicircle fashion. They were all fixed on the courtroom door to guarantee a shot of Jason Stinson as he entered the courtroom. Commonwealth vs. Football had begun, and the whole country was watching.

After a "not guilty" plea was entered and the next hearing date was set for March 20, attorney Alex Dathorne escorted Jason to Metro Corrections to be booked for the charge on which he had just been arraigned. One reporter ran up from behind to be present during the procedure. The reporter demanded that he receive a copy of Jason's mug shot, and he led the early news with it.

Once Jason was fingerprinted and had his picture taken, he was immediately released on his own recognizance and ordered to appear at his next scheduled hearing. Stinson's co-counsel, Brian Butler, stayed behind to address the media that was hungry for comment. Butler explained the situation to the drove of reporters waiting outside the courtroom. He said, "The courthouse is filled with people who have committed murder, robbery or rape; this man is a football coach. A tragedy happened, and unfortunately in life, tragedies do happen sometimes, and there's not always someone who is at fault. That is our position."

Those comments from Brian Butler were run coast to coast as the media geared up to follow a gripping story. There were legal implications from a case that was a first: social judgment had to be passed, and maybe there would even be a change in how coaches train athletes across America. ESPN, CNN, FOX-NEWS, CBS, ABC, and several more networks ran the story. It was a hot topic. A coach allegedly denied players water during practice, and later a player died from heatstroke as a result. The topic was widely debated and even more widely misreported. There were on-air television personalities going on the air spreading information that just wasn't true. Nationally, many people were under the impression that this was the second practice of the day and that PRP coach Jason Stinson had denied Max Gilpin water.

There was only one practice August 20, 2008, and it was shorter than normal. It appeared it would be difficult for Jason Stinson to escape the damage this situation would cause his reputation, regardless of the outcome. Many people believed he was running a grueling two-a-day practice schedule and that allowing no water had something to do with the player's death. Neither of those things could have been further from the truth, but that didn't stop people from saying it.

2008 Pleasure Ridge Park Panthers
COURTESY OF AMY JENNINGS

2008 PRPHS coaching staff
Front row (left to right): Bobby Deacon, Steve Deacon, Jason Hiser. Back row: Chris
Webb, Adam Donnelly, Jason Stinson, Jason Cook, Josh Lightle.
COURTESY OF JEFF JENNINGS

Pleasure Ridge Park High School, Louisville, Kentucky.
COURTESY OF JEFF JENNINGS

PRPHS Head Coach Jason Stinson speaking to the team after a game.
COURTESY OF JEFF JENNINGS

2008 PRPHS Panthers praying after a playoff win at Meade County.
COURTESY OF JEFF JENNINGS

2008 PRPHS Panthers listening to Coach Jason Stinson after a playoff win at Meade County.
COURTESY OF JEFF JENNINGS

Greenwood Elementary School's announcement board shortly after Max Gilpin's death.
COURTESY OF JEFF JENNINGS

Pleasure Ridge Park High School's announcement board shortly after Max Gilpin's death.
COURTESY OF JEFF JENNNINGS

Above and below: Memorial service for students held at PRPHS shortly after Max Gilpin's death.
COURTESY OF JEFF JENNINGS

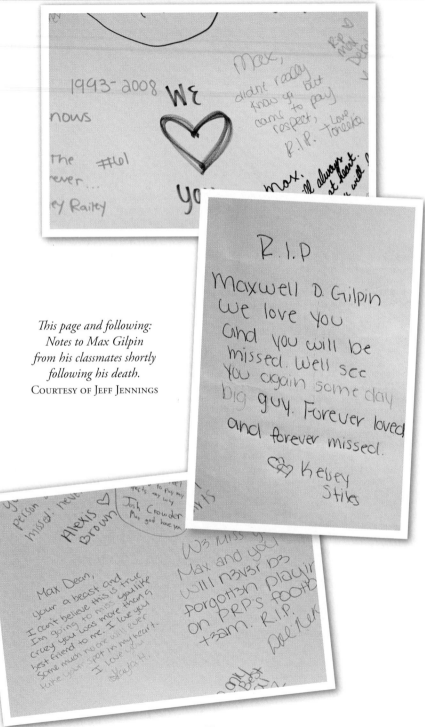

*This page and following:
Notes to Max Gilpin
from his classmates shortly
following his death.*
COURTESY OF JEFF JENNINGS

MAX -
a panther forever.
you will always be
loved and missed.
Love,
Morgan Fife

I'm gonna miss
you, you were
always that strong
and nice guy everyone
loved. I'll always
remember that time
you were on the
D-Line with me.
You did ur best even
though you didn't
know the plays. But
It doesn't matter,
I'd love to have you
on D-Line with me
as line backes anyday.
Love from your

Maxey,
I love you so much and more
im gonna miss you so much more
Chemistry and lunch wont be the
Some without you and I just want
you to know that you will never be
forgoten im glad we became as close
as we were but I want you to know
I will never forget about you and I'll
think about you everyday im gonna
miss rommin and junnin on you everytime
I see you. I love you
- amanda matte Kilby
R.I.P

i'll remember you

i love you!

Doss High School Head Coach LaKunta Farmer and players walking to present a wreath to Jeff Gilpin.
COURTESY OF JEFF JENNINGS

Doss High School Head Coach LaKunta Farmer hugging Jeff Gilpin after presentation of the wreath.
COURTESY OF JEFF JENNNINGS

2008 PRPHS Cheerleaders hugging the Gilpin family.
COURTESY OF JEFF JENNINGS

2008 PRPHS players watching a ceremony for the Gilpin family.
COURTESY OF JEFF JENNINGS

Gilpin family during a ceremony for Max Gilpin.
COURTESY OF JEFF JENNINGS

Black Hole members presented Jeff Gilpin with a t-shirt in Max's honor as well as half of the money raised from selling the shirts.
COURTESY OF JEFF JENNINGS

PRPHS Principal Dave Johnson and Tyler Williams
COURTESY OF JEFF JENNINGS

Black Hole member Tyler Williams presented Jeff Gilpin with Max's jersey.
Pictured: Pam Larimore-Skinner, Tyler Williams, Jeff Gilpin, Lois Gilpin
COURTESY OF JEFF JENNINGS

Jeff Gilpin holding up Max's jersey after it was presented to him.
COURTESY OF JEFF JENNINGS

*Jeff Gilpin and PRPHS Athletic Director Craig Webb leaving the field after a
ceremony for Max Gilpin. Jason Stinson is pictured in the background.*
COURTESY OF JEFF JENNINGS

Memorial Flag raised in Max Gilpin's honor. It was flown for the 2008-2010 seasons.
COURTESY OF JEFF JENNINGS

Max Gilpin, 2008
COURTESY OF JEFF JENNINGS

Lois Gilpin family photo
Left to right: Max Gilpin, Lois Gilpin, Amber Green
COURTESY OF LOIS GILPIN

Courtesy of Jeff and Amy Jennings

I left the courthouse genuinely concerned about Jason. I was waiting for Ashton Kutcher from MTV's Punk'd to jump out of the bushes screaming, "Haaaaaaa, you've been punked." Unfortunately that never happened, so the next question was how this was going to be paid for. It was no secret that a JCPS and KY State employee—especially someone in Jason's position— makes about $45,000 a year. As soon as I arrived home from Jason's arraignment, I wrote the following e-mail.

Jason,

I am dropping you an email for many reasons, but please don't feel obligated to reply. I understand you have a lot on your plate, but I wanted to reach out and let you know that Ann, Christopher, and I care about you. Ty Scroggins was at the arraignment today, and I promised him I would let you know that he had showed up to support you. I told Ty to send you an e-mail, or even to drop by your house to pay you a visit. Deacon and I told him how to get there, so don't be surprised if he drops by.

I have a business associate who runs a prayer group on the west coast, and I asked him to pray for you. Here is his response to me.

Rodney,

I am so sorry for your friend. I cannot imagine what this is doing to his family.

Yes, we will pray and have already prayed. This is definitely a situation where faith in Jesus Christ as Lord and Savior is vital. Rodney, have you ever committed your life to Jesus? If not, let's chat about it. Without knowing Jesus as your savior, you miss out on the opportunity to help your friend the most. And that help is by going to your heavenly father in prayer.

In the Bible there is a very important promise from God:

Are any among you suffering? They should keep on praying about it. And those who have reason to be thankful should continually sing praises to the Lord. Are any among you sick? They should call for the elders of the church and have them pray over them, anointing them with oil in the name of the Lord. And their prayer

81

offered in faith will heal the sick, and the Lord will make them well. And anyone who has committed sins will be forgiven.

Confess your sins to each other and pray for each other so that you may be healed. The earnest prayer of a righteous person has great power and wonderful results. Elijah was as human as we are, and yet when he prayed earnestly that no rain would fall, none fell for the next three and a half years! Then he prayed for rain, and down it poured. The grass turned green, and the crops began to grow again. (James 5:13–18)

Rodney, I pray for you because you and your family are important to me. My earnest prayer is that you would know Jesus as your personal Lord and Savior as your friend and I do.

Phil Crocker

Phil is a wonderful man, and he had already begun prayer for you without me ever having to ask. I know Phil has prayed for me on many occasions without me ever requesting it; however, today I asked him (among others coast to coast) to pray for you because I believe that an indictment on scholastic sports has been laid on your shoulders.

Jason, I don't know how I can possibly help you outside of prayer, requesting others to pray, and just being there for you. If there is anything I can do to help your legal team, tell them to call me and I will provide any IT support needed, free of charge. Whatever they need technology wise, I will be glad to help. I suspect that a lot of people (mostly attorneys) will be stepping forward to help you, and all of this may create some IT needs. If this does happen, I can set up whatever they need. I am willing to provide the computers, the networking devices, VPNs, and the labor it will take to set up any of the aforementioned. Beyond these things, I don't know what else I can do. You and Monica are in my thoughts. I don't know if I have ever had so many internal feelings than I feel right now and felt once I knew they were going to go through with this madness. There are bad people in this world, but you are not like that, and you have never been. This is a fact that all will know in the end.

I have one question for you if you do get time to respond to me. How are you going to pay for all of this? I can't imagine that this is being done *pro bono* at this time. I am a great fundraiser, and I believe I might to be able to help here. I am not above panhandling in the street for you if it helps raise money to defend you. I don't have any real link to all of this. (I was not at the practice, so I feel free to do what you need me to do.) I really believe, given the high profile nature of this case, we might be able to bring some of the biggest defense attorneys to Louisville (free of charge) to help in your case. I don't know, man; I have so many things running through my head. Anyway... I am here for you.

Your friend,

Rodney

I don't know if the e-mail helped Jason feel better, but it certainly helped me feel less helpless.

CHAPTER 8

THE STINSON LEGAL DEFENSE FUND: PART 1

My e-mail to Jason is essentially how the Jason Stinson Legal Defense Fund was born. Jason contacted me right before Valentine's Day to see if I would help by putting up a Web page. I am the general manager of a company that does web design and hosting, so it was no trouble for me.

So far I had not discussed any facts of the case with Jason, and that was for a reason. I would joke and say things like, "Don't tell me anything; there's a reason your attorneys tell you not to talk." I figured I had heard the story from so many others, there was no need to hear Jason's take on things and have him risk his defense. Besides, at this point, there was no evidence released yet, so I had formed my opinions based on conversations with witnesses. I wanted to see what the police had before Jason and I really talked about it. I thought I knew what happened that day, but I still had my doubts. The Commonwealth Attorney's Office had to be pursuing this for a justified cause. There had to be something I didn't know.

I spent a tremendous amount of time asking questions about Max Gilpin's death as soon as the allegations started to surface. Before Christmas, I had a good idea about the unknown factors in Max's death, and they mostly appeared to be medical. I have a very limited medical background, but it was obvious that there was something different about Max that day. It did not seem the football practice was the cause of these mitigating factors; rather, it was a catalyst that brought them all crashing together with tragic consequences. There have been many terms used in the last year to describe all the things that had to happen collectively for Max to die. I heard the co-incidents called "lightening in a bottle," "one in a million," "a tragic accident," and "a perfect storm." All of those accurately described the situation, but they still didn't explain the indictment. In February 2009, I did not have access to the police department's investigative file, so I surmised there could be a variable litany of legal evidence in there. Who knows? I knew Jason Stinson, the man, and knew Jason Stinson, the football coach, and what was being alleged was not him. Not even close. Until evidence was presented to me to prove otherwise, I was going to stand and fight for him. I felt he was a victim of circumstance. The storms were swirling from all around, and he needed help.

It had been estimated that a competent defense for a high profile case like this could cost $250,000. Where are we going to get a quarter of a million dollars? We tried not to worry about that in the beginning, and we were curious to see if we could even get the first dollar. The Greater Louisville Football Coaches Association (GLFCA) began accepting checks on Jason's behalf from other coaches and coaches' organizations around the country. We wanted to try to build on that movement, so the first page of the website was developed. It was not pretty, but it was functional. The webpage told the visitor where he could mail a check and who the check was for. The first page was mostly meant to be informational and a placeholder as we worked on really putting the defense fund together. It also began to get "indexed," so whenever someone searched Jason Stinson's name with a search engine like Google, www.supportourstinson.com would come up on the first page.

I contacted the fathers of several football players to seek assistance in formally starting the Jason Stinson Legal Defense Fund. Don Fell, who is a construction manager with Padgett Industries, and Steve Healey, who is employed as a narcotics detective with LMPD, both agreed to lend their support. We couldn't be considered a 501c3 non-profit organization because that requires five years of history, so we registered as a for-profit business so we could obtain an Employer Identification Number (EIN). (An EIN is much like a social security number for a business.) Once we had an EIN, we could get a bank account for the defense fund.

There are several corporate banks located in Louisville, KY. The plan was to set up a bank account where people could walk into any branch of that bank and leave a donation. We wanted to use a corporate bank, because such banks almost always have more branches available citywide than a small independent bank. I found a not-so-warm reception when I told each bank what I wanted to do. Some banks gave politically correct reasons for saying "no." A few said they didn't want to upset their customers, and one just flat out said "no," that they didn't want to be involved. We finally were allowed to open an account at Republic Bank, which had several locations.

Once we had a bank account, we could then accept money online through PayPal. (PayPal acts as a middleman, allowing anyone with a checking account to accept credit cards.) We paid a small fee, but PayPal allowed us to collect donations via the Internet by giving potential donors the ability to use their credit/debit cards.

Once the EIN and bank account were established, we began to adjust the website accordingly. Readers were greeted upon entry with a brief explanation that the site was collecting funds for Jason Stinson, and they were given three options to donate. People could mail a check to the GLFCA, donate at the site using PayPal, or walk into any Metro Louisville Republic Bank and tell the cashier they would like to donate to the Jason Stinson Legal Defense Fund. The bank would deposit the funds directly into the defense fund's account.

Donations began to come in from all over the country. We received support coast to coast as states such as Oregon and South Carolina contacted us, pledging their Coaches Associations' public support as well as monetary donations. The donations from these coaches' organizations ranged anywhere from $200–$1500, but we were going to need more. We began meeting every Monday night at Larry Breeding's house, and it was at these meetings that most of the fundraising ideas were conceived and developed.

Larry Breeding is Jason Stinson's father-in-law. Before Jason was thrust into the spotlight, Larry was most commonly known as a deacon at Valley View Church and the proprietor of a local barbershop. Larry's Haircutters is located in the Dixie Manor Shopping Center, which is the largest and perhaps oldest shopping center in the PRP area. Larry has run this shop for over 40 years, so it is easy to imagine he has trimmed thousands of heads in his barbershop. (I first met Larry when I visited his establishment several years prior for a haircut. At the time I was not even aware that he was Jason Stinson's father-in-law.)

Jason asked me to attend a meeting about fundraising for him March 4, 2009, at Larry's house. The inaugural meeting was attended by several dozen people ready to help in any way they could. The people present that first night were almost always at every other meeting we had following the first one—Bonnie Abbott, Terry Abbott, Barbara Blakenship, Jerry Blakenship, Brenda Breeding, Larry Breeding, Bobbie Bryant, Warren Bryant, Phyllis Coffman, Steve Coffman, Jason Cook, Ann Daugherty, Rodney Daugherty, A.B. Deany, Judy Deany, James Frech, George Garrett, Sue Garrett, Cathy

Henn, John Henn, Herman Honaker, Velma Honaker, Kenny Meurer, Pat Meurer, Jim Nichols, Mama Lou Nichols, Debbie Spafford, Richard Spafford, Larry Peercy, Sharlett Peercy, Doug Pope, Melanie Pope, Dwight Reed, Patty Rock, Ray Rock, Darlene Rush, Jeff Rush, Cleve Sheilley, Holly Sheilley, Ken Sheilley, Peggy Sheilley, Sarah Sheilley, Don Stinson, Regina Stinson, Eric Sullivan, Marsha Sullivan, Lisa Watts, Tommy Watts, Jason White, Alan Wolfe, and Kathy Wolfe.

We would usually meet on Monday nights, but we could easily get together just about any night of the week. I met a lot of wonderful people through the fundraising efforts, and I am very grateful for all their help. Had these volunteers not stepped forward to rally around Jason, we probably would not have experienced very much success. We would regularly joke that, if it weren't for all the volunteers, the fundraising effort would have been Jason Stinson, Jason Cook, and I with tin cups panhandling on Dixie Hwy. As profitable (and dangerous) as the panhandling might have been, the alternative was much better.

The Benefit Dinner/Auction was one of the very first ideas that began to take shape at our initial meeting. The plan was to hold a dinner followed by an auction. We wanted to get as much donated as we could, and we needed several things in order to pull it off. In addition to food, we needed people to work, a place to hold the event, and items to auction. This sounded like a tall order, considering we were preparing to hold the event in less than two months.

There was so much positive energy in the air, it was clear whatever challenges we might face would be conquered. There were some very talented and intelligent people, and they were all focused on one mission: to raise money for Jason Stinson's legal defense. At this point, most of the people helping were lending their support on blind faith because we didn't really have any tangible evidence to disprove what the Commonwealth was saying. It made me wonder how many people would attend the dinner/auction given the type of articles that were being written about Jason in the newspaper.

Debbie Spafford helped arrange the use of the old K-Mart building on Dixie Hwy in Valley Station. It was owned by Ed and Benita Alvey, and they offered to let us use it for one night. (Their current tenant at the time was a bingo parlor, and it was not operating again until the next month.) The building was perfect in every way. It already had tables and chairs to accommodate several hundred people. The night before the event, Jason Cook, James Frech, Jason Stinson, and I all spent the night in the building to keep an eye on things and to continue setting up. Work on prepping the areas had began early that morning and went through the night and the next morning until just before the doors opened to the public on the following afternoon.

We used the large open area to seat guests, and we used the space along the right side wall and front wall to serve food and drinks. Sharlett Peercy helped lead a crew that graciously supplied a dinner of salad, baked spaghetti, garlic bread, and assorted deserts. All the food was donated by local grocers such as Pic Pac and Gordon Food Service, thus keeping costs of the event very low.

We turned the back left corner of the building into the auction area. We used a smaller room with two doors to house the silent auction items, and we then used the slightly larger open area to hold the live items. There were over 100 silent and 100 live auction items, so these spaces were packed. This setup proved to work very well, as runners were quickly able to bring an item over to be placed on the auction block. Each item was then shown throughout the building on dozens of television screens visible from just about anywhere inside the structure.

George and Sue Garrett, among others, did a marvelous job preparing the room for the hundreds of potential bidders who were sure to arrive. (We had a good idea there would be at least 500 people, because we had presold over 400 tickets before the event.) Jason's supporters did not disappoint that night, as over 600 people showed up.

We utilized the website to promote the event, and it turned out to be a big success. Several bidders at the auction mentioned that they had been able to look at all the items on the website, and it made selecting what to bid on so much easier. (The silent auction items were to be bid on by writing a bid on a sheet of paper associated with the item. Anyone wishing to bid subsequently would have to bid a higher amount.) We had placed a "buy it now" price on each item, which was usually three times the stated value of each basket. The bidding on the silent auction items began when the doors opened at 3 PM and went right up to the last moment at 7:30 PM.

There was a wide assortment of items available in the baskets. Successful bids went from $11 for a Juice Plus basket to $400 for two suite tickets for a U of L men's basketball Big East game. It seemed there was something

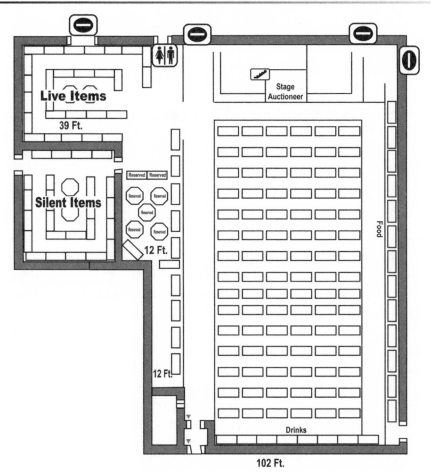

for everyone. Other baskets contained items ranging from blankets to car cleaning materials.

The live auction items were auctioned off by a trio of auctioneers. Some high dollar items available for auction had reserves going from $500 to $2000. There were autographed items from football coaches Howard Schnellenberger, Rich Brooks, and Steve Kragthorpe, as well as from basketball coach Rick Pitino. The bidding climbed up to several hundred dollars on some of the balls, with the FAU football signed by Schnellenberger bringing the most money.

This was by far our largest fundraiser, and it brought in a third of our financial goal in one night. It could not have gone better, and it really set the tone for our future events.

CHAPTER 9

THE STINSON LEGAL DEFENSE FUND: PART 2

Candy for Caring is an organization set up by Sister Margaret Regina and Sister Mary James. Cleve Sheilley worked with the sisters helping them with their candy-making operations. He had mentioned Jason's situation to them, and they wanted to know how they could help. They offered to sell us the candy for cost, but ultimately it was agreed we would pay a little over $1 of the cost per box.

Sister Margaret Regina is also known as "Candy Sister" because of the reputation she has earned making her legendary almond brittle. In 1996 she came up with an idea to make and sell candy. The proceeds were given to those who were hungry, homeless, sick or in need of clothing. After the first year, she had to seek out a larger facility to run the blooming business. A house belonging to St. Mary's was renovated and furnished for the expansion. The new facility allowed her to greatly increase production and to pass necessary inspections by the State.

With the help of Sister Mary James, Candy for Caring has grown tremendously. There are 40 volunteers organized by types of candy. For instance, one group comes on Monday morning to make fudge, and another group makes almond brittle in the afternoon. In a week's time there are 10 different groups—all volunteers making their own specialty.

In 2007, approximately $100,000 was generated by Candy for Caring to fund charitable organizations. (The two agencies that benefit the most from the vision of Sister Margaret Regina are the Healing Place and St. John's Center.) Candy for Caring contributed to the playground project at the Americana Apartments and the Psychiatric Residential Treatment Facilities (PRTFs). Sister Margaret also pledged a $10,000 scholarship at Presentation Academy.

Cleve Sheilley worked with several businesses in the southwest part of the county to set up donation containers for the Jason Stinson Legal Defense Fund. Cleve purchased candy from Candy for Caring, and he would set the boxes out at the counters where the donation buckets were located. If a donation of $10 or higher was given, the donor was offered a box of candy. Cleve reported over $20,000 was raised in donations given for candy. Cleve said, "People liked making the donation and getting the candy because they felt like a part of it, and they knew they were helping out." It was even reported that people sometimes would donate $10 or more, and then they would say, "Keep the candy. I just wanted to donate."

Cleve stated that when the sisters first started, they had no idea they would go through that much candy, and at first it was hard to believe that the demand was so great. He declared that Larry's Haircutters was the largest collector of donations for candy, but he also mentioned that Frontier Diner on Dixie Hwy also handed out a huge amount of candy.

Cleve set up donation containers at two different Phelps Hardware Stores, Hair Dimensions Beauty Salon, a Moneypenny Hardware Store, the OK Tire Company and Shack-n-the-Back BBQ restaurant. Jason was well known at Phelps Hardware from when he was in high school and that seemed to help. "Everyone remembered him from back then, and they knew him and loved him," said Cleve.

Jason is the kind of person who can leave an impression like that on others. The amount of money collected in the PRP and Fairdale areas showed that Jason was cared for by many. It was Jason's interaction with others throughout his life that awarded him the benefit of doubt from many people.

Mark's Feedstore Night was also a very successful fundraiser. The restaurant scheduled six days for the Jason Stinson Legal Defense Fund. Guests would provide their server with a voucher noting the fundraiser, and 15% of the food and beverage bill was donated to Jason's legal defense. The vouchers were valid only on the reserved days, and they could not be used for purchasing gift cards. (The JSLDF received over $2500 from this fundraiser.)

This was definitely a win-win situation for all, considering Jason's supporters spent over $16,000 at the restaurant. The first night was the biggest. The server who waited on my table told me that it was one of the busiest Thursdays ever. There was no reason to dispute her claim, considering there was a wait to be seated that night. The second night was almost as good, but it was a little less crowded because it was the night before the benefit dinner/

auction. These events were scheduled on the third or fourth Thursdays of March through August.

In May we held a golf scramble, organized and run by Doug and Melanie Pope, Ken and Sarah Sheilley, and Alan and Kathy Wolfe. We were able to make money from the entry fees, hole sponsorship, and the "closest to pin" and "hole in one" contests. There were 26 teams in the morning and 14 teams in the afternoon. This event was also very profitable.

Jeff and Darlene Rush organized and ran the SOS Fun Run motorcycle ride held on June 20. It began in the parking lot of Beef O'Bradys in Hillview. It included stops in Boston, Bloomfield, and Mt. Washington, and it ended back in Hillview where it started. There was a fairly decent sized crowd, considering how hot it was and how many other bike runs were being held that day. The first place prize was a Bristol Motor Speedway suite package to the Sharpie 500 that included two suite seats, food and beverage, two garage passes, and one parking pass.

The final Mark's Feedstore fundraiser was held Thursday, July 23, and it was followed up with a pancake breakfast at the Shively Applebee's on July 25. We presold tickets for $5 beginning in mid-July. We sold well over 200 tickets, but we only served a little over 50 breakfasts. For every person served, we were required to pay Applebee's $1. The $1 covered all you-could-eat pancakes, along with your choice of orange juice, coffee, soda, or water.

The volunteers (Brenda Breeding, Bobbie Bryant, Emily Bryant, Warren Bryant, Rodney Daugherty, James Frech, John Henn, Dwight Reed, Clay Stretch and Lisa Stretch) were asked to help with all aspects of the restaurant business except for cooking the pancakes. We mixed the roles of greeters and waiters as each volunteer would greet the guests, seat them, take their drink order and return with pancakes and drinks. We were very well staffed, and no one had to wait to be served. Once the guests were finished, it was our responsibility to bus (clean) the tables, wash the dishes, and restore the restaurant to its original condition. Clay Stretch washed dishes as they were brought to the back, so it was easy to get everything back in order. After wiping down the tables and cleaning the floors, the manager was paid for each guest who attended. Everyone then left to begin prepping for the next event, a picnic and concert held July 26 at Eric and Marsha Sullivan's farm in the southwest part of the county.

There were several hundred people in attendance to enjoy the concert, food, and assorted entertainment. The first musical performance began at

3:30 PM, with the final performance beginning at approximately 8:00 PM. A donation of $10 per adult and $5 per child, with a $30 family maximum was requested for admission. That price included admission, three food tickets per person, inflatables, the concert, and access to all entertainment activities.

John Wade and Dwight Reed smoked several pigs, and the pork sandwiches just melted in your mouth. The volunteers were treated to a special meal prior to the event. Ribs had been prepared and Mama Lou brought six gallons of her homemade cole slaw and four gallons of baked beans. The cole slaw and beans did not last long once the guests began arriving. Multiple games and events were set up around the two-acre area we used to hold the event. There were three inflatable bouncies, a dunking booth, cornhole boards, and basketball, along with several water games.

Doug Slaughter, Robby Wolf, Dave Crowe, and Brent Greco worked very hard to arrange for the bands and musicians—Fishers of Men, Refuge, Blacksmith, Chekane, Jeff Baxter & Joe Frech, Mary Wolf Band, and Kiana—who played free of charge. A flatbed trailer was used as a stage, and then everything else was set up around it.

A cookbook was put together, and Morris Press Cookbooks was used for the printing. Bobbie Bryant, Phyllis Broghton, Cathy Henn, Amanda Ott, Allison Patton, Marsha Sullivan, and countless others worked diligently as they collected and prepared the hundreds of donated recipes. (Some of these recipes were generations old, and a few recipes had received ribbons from the Kentucky State Fair.) The response was incredible, but we were only able to publish 500. From July through December, 2009, we handed out over 1,200 copies of the cookbook to individuals who donated $10 to the defense fund.

There is a high probability that someone who helped a great deal with fundraising was inadvertently left out of these two chapters, and if that is the case, please forgive me. So many wonderful people came forward to help. The support they showed for Jason still overwhelms me to this day. It was awe-inspiring because these people not only reached into their pockets, they also donated countless hours of work necessary to raise over $90,000 in less than six months.

Most of the names listed in these two chapters are members of Valley View Church. Before, during and after the height of the publicity, some posters on the *Courier-Journal* message board said that Valley View had done the fundraising and, even worse, that Valley View had redirected donations for the church to Jason's Defense Fund. That simply is not true. Every event held for Jason was either at a public or privately owned facility, and nothing was held at Valley View Church. The Valley View connection is only through its members who were acting as individuals and not as representatives of the church.

The goal was to raise $100,000 in six months in the most depressed economy in over 25 years. It seemed like an insurmountable hill to climb, but event-by-event, we ascended to our goal. Jason has said "thank you" many times, but he will never be able to say enough to all of those that contributed in one way or another. So allow me to say it again: "THANK YOU!"

CHAPTER 10

COMMONWEALTH VS. FOOTBALL MARCHES ON

The first publically released evidence of Jason Stinson's possible innocence came in early March, 2009. The civil attorneys hired by Jefferson County Public Schools (JCPS) had asked the former chief medical examiner for the Commonwealth of Kentucky, Dr. George Nichols, to independently investigate the case. After reviewing the evidence, Dr. Nichols came to the conclusion that a prescription drug Max was taking for attention-deficit hyperactivity disorder (ADHD) most likely triggered the heatstroke that led to his death, because it contained amphetamine, which can cause overheating.

On March 8, the *Courier-Journal* ran a huge story written by Andrew Wolfson on Dr Nichols' findings titled, "PRP player who died wasn't dehydrated, experts say." For this story, the *Courier-Journal* requested that Dr. Bill Smock independently investigate Max Gilpin's death. The article stated:

> Dr. William Smock, a professor of emergency medicine at the University of Louisville, who has no connection to the case and reviewed Max's medical records at the *Courier-Journal*'s request, agreed with Dr. Nichols that Max's heatstroke was not caused by lack of water.
>
> Smock, who is also director of the clinical forensic medicine program at University Hospital, said he believes Adderall® prompted Max's heatstroke and death.
>
> "There is no indication this kid was dehydrated," Smock said.

Dr. Smock is also a paid consultant for the Commonwealth Attorney's Office. He is paid to offer advice to the CAO on medical matters in criminal cases. Dr. Smock's review of Max Gilpin's medical records exposed the possibility that the prosecution had secured an indictment for homicide without ever consulting a medical expert. If that was the case, this would pose a huge problem for the prosecution because, under Kentucky law, you must show what caused someone's death in order to convict a person of homicide. It was obvious that the prosecutors had not consulted with Dr. Smock, since he had no connection to the case prior to the *Courier-Journal* contacting him. Perhaps the CAO had consulted some other medical expert? That would not make sense, considering Dr. Smock is on retainer to advise the prosecutors. But there had to be some logical explanation. It was hard to believe that the CAO would indict someone for homicide unless they knew, or least thought they could prove, the cause of death.

Two highly respected medical experts publically stated that Max Gilpin's death was a "terrible tragedy," and that dehydration did not cause the heatstroke. Talk began to circulate that the prosecutors might drop the charge against Jason. After all, there was not an autopsy, so proving the cause of death was going to be an insurmountable challenge. Coupled with the fact that Dr. Nichols stated that in his 35 years of examining deaths he had never seen a homicide case without an autopsy, it didn't seem like the CAO had many alternative options. A pre-trial conference hearing date had been set at Jason's arraignment for March 20, 2009. If Dave Stengel was going to drop the charge, March 20 would be as good a time as any.

It would have probably been best for Jason's criminal defense not to have released Dr. Nichols' finding until the trial. Prior to this story being run, there were maybe only one or two positive stories about Jason Stinson, and there was practically no evidence supporting his innocence. Once LMPD's investigation was released, it appeared that Jason was being hammered by the media. (The print media seemed to carry the most responsibility. The *Courier-Journal* even ran a headline that read, "Stinson admits to denying some PRP players water." Several people were not quite sure how the newspaper got that out of Coach Stinson's statement, but the *C-J* ran the headline anyway. In our many conversations about the *Courier-Journal*'s behavior, it would almost always lead me to say, "Whatever sells newspapers." I repeatedly told Jason, "They don't care about you, Max, Michele, Jeff, or anyone else. All they care about is selling newspapers.")

The Dr. Nichols and Dr. Smock press conference dramatically turned things around for Jason. This story was a completely different point of view than what was regularly being fed to the public. It should have been hard for Jason to be pleased with the *Courier-Journal*, regardless of what it was now saying, considering the borderline libelous statements it had previously run. Yet, Jason was thankful the *C-J* had run a fair and balanced story, unlike most others he had read since August 2008.

Considering the new information that was coming to the surface, it seemed plausible that the charge against Jason would be dropped. The Commonwealth's own medical expert said this was a tragic accident and not a criminal act. Dr. Bill Smock has been rendering opinions in court for nearly 25 years, and in the Commonwealth he had never testified for a defendant. In fact, this situation appeared to be the first time that he had ever publically gone against the CAO. Bill Smock did not mince his words, and it was perfectly clear that he did not agree that this particular situation was a crime. Who would know better? After all, he had testified in hundreds of cases rendering medical opinions. It was those opinions and his testimony that helped convict many men sitting in prison today.

The emerging fact that the CAO secured an indictment without consulting a medical expert was a real eye-opener. Dr. Bill Smock is their guy. How did they move forward on a homicide case without talking to him? Additionally, how did they charge someone with another's death if they could not positively say how the person died or how the accused contributed to that cause of death? (That question has never been satisfactorily answered, and it probably never will be.) A cause of death determined without an autopsy is most surely not enough to move forward. The CAO would almost have to drop the charges now.

However, the Commonwealth Attorney's Office did *not* drop the charge against Jason. In fact, at his March 20 pre-trial conference, a trial date of August 31, 2009 was set.

The media attention on this case was unreal, and if there was not a story, the media would make one up. On April 25, 2009, the *Courier-Journal* ran an article titled "PRP Players Allege Retaliation." The article was written by Antoinette Konz, and it made some pretty strong allegations. However, as soon as it fell under scrutiny, the article was exposed to be nothing more than a ploy by the attorney representing Max Gilpin's parents to manufacture negative press against Stinson. There was absolutely no truth to this article, and the *C-J* didn't leave the article on its website very long.

On April 27, 2009, *The Ville Voice* (a small local newspaper) exposed many issues with the *C-J* article in its own article, titled "Shaky reporting on PRP allegations." Writer Rick Redding summed up the situation in pretty clear terms:

> The main story on Saturday's front page *C-J* was that parents in Pleasure Ridge Park have called the paper and complained that kids are being retaliated against for their testimony against Coach Jason Stinson. This story ... provided no details on what the retaliation was or who were the sources of the charges.
>
> It was planted by Todd Thompson, the attorney for the late Max Gilpin's parents, and the *C-J* went along for the ride.
>
> We've got a problem with the reporting, and want to know why the newspaper would protect parents calling in with complaints by hiding their identity. Here's a passage from the piece:
>
> > The *Courier-Journal* has received several calls from PRP parents who said their children were being retaliated against because of the statements they gave police. They asked not to be named.
>
> First of all, there's no journalistic justification for reporting allegations without identifying the accuser. How about at least telling us how many parents are complaining?
>
> Here's why—because there aren't that many.
>
> Does it make you wonder about the paper's source, just a little bit, when you consider that the parent(s) involved apparently didn't call a single TV station and didn't contact Jefferson County Public Schools (JCPS) with these retaliation charges? Is it too weird that the topic came up only when JCPS superintendent Sheldon Berman was being questioned by the attorney for the parents involved in suing Stinson and the school system?
>
> As long as *C-J* is protecting those making charges, we really don't know if *C-J* reporter Toni Konz is actually getting calls from parents. She throws in, at the bottom of the story, additional allegations about fund-raising practices that we know are false. It's interesting that these sources are allowed to vent their frustrations

in print, despite repeated denials from the officials involved—all while hiding behind anonymity granted by the newspaper.

Our investigation into this indicates that there are very few (maybe one) players whose testimony reflects negatively on Coach Stinson and who might be the target of this so-called retaliation. We hear that only six players could have been targeted based on their testimony—a few were seniors and one was suspended from participation in spring drills. The point being that the newspaper could have easily figured out who the players involved were. And if their parents want to influence the coverage of the case, they should have the courage to make their accusations public.

The paper goes further, protecting more parents from identifying themselves while repeating additional charges against the school.

Several other parents who have contacted the newspaper said they are concerned that fundraising is being done during school hours to raise money for Stinson's defense and that their children are being encouraged to wear T-shirts supporting Stinson.

This doesn't have anything to do with whether you think Stinson is guilty of a crime or not. But as a result of *C-J*'s reporting, we don't have any doubt where the *C-J* stands.

It was pretty clear where Rick Redding stood too, and it was refreshing he was willing to say it.

The *C-J* article was a real downer after the successful fundraising event the night before. It also appeared the article was used as an excuse for prosecutors to redo the botched interviews conducted by the LMPD. (These are the same interviews that were conducted without most parents present.)

I had "call Leland Hulbert" at the top of my list of things to do on Monday, April 27. If these allegations printed in the *C-J* were true, the CAO needed to investigate and hold the responsible parties accountable. It was my intention to tell Hulbert that the CAO needed to send a clear message that this type of behavior would not be tolerated. However, before I could call Hulbert, he called me. He mentioned the newspaper article that was published on Saturday, but when I pressed the issue that an investigation needed to be conducted, he quickly moved on to the real reason for his call. He wanted to re-interview my stepson regarding the practice.

I told him that Christopher would be available to discuss any allegations of retaliation, but he was not going to recount the events of practice. I clearly stated that he had given a verbal statement to the police and a written statement to JCPS, and he was not going to talk about it anymore. (It was widely reported by parents who live in Pleasure Ridge Park that they were telling Hulbert the same thing. The CAO decided to wait until June to resume interviews so they would not interfere with the school year.)

If there was an alliance between the *Courier-Journal* and the Commonwealth Attorney's Office, then Jason was going to have a very tough fight ahead of him. It appears that an investigation into these allegations was never conducted, leaving the validity of *C-J*'s story in question.

Commonwealth vs. Football marches on!

CHAPTER 11

THE BERMAN REPORT

The Jefferson County Public Schools' report into Max Gilpin's death was highly anticipated by many. Originally the report was to be released sometime in April of 2009. The day after the evidence was released by LMPD, JCPS spokesperson Lauren Roberts said it would take four to six weeks to digest the police file. She went on to explain that the district needed the police department's case to complete its own investigation.

In the middle of April, JCPS stated it could be another four weeks before its complete report would be ready. Four weeks came and went, and on May 27, JCPS announced another delay in the report's release. On June 3, Stengel's office, which was willing to wait no longer, subpoenaed the school district's investigative file into Max's death. The Commonwealth Attorney said he needed it in order to proceed with the criminal case against Stinson. The attorneys for JCPS disagreed, and on June 9 filed a motion to quash the Commonwealth Attorney's subpoena. They argued that the investigation was incomplete and was protected because it was an attorney work product. The month of June was like watching a tennis match as the Commonwealth and the Board of Education spent countless taxpayer dollars on legal maneuvers back and forth over the school district's investigation.

The Commonwealth Attorney wanted this file very badly, and it appeared he was not going to let the school board's motion to quash stop him. On June 11, the CAO filed a motion to force. This motion asked presiding Jefferson Circuit Court Judge Susan Schultz Gibson to force/compel the district to hand over its findings.

An attorney for JCPS, Byron Leet, argued feverishly to prevent the order, but he was unsuccessful. On June 19, Judge Gibson ruled that JCPS must surrender its interviews with players, coaches, and other witnesses that were a part of its investigation into Max Gilpin's death; however, due to publicity and presumed pressure on witnesses from others, the judge ruled that the interviews were to be sealed from the public.

JCPS released its findings a few days later. The following is the transcript of a statement issued by JCPS Superintendent Sheldon Berman on July 1. It was also published on the *Courier-Journal* website and in the newspaper on July 2.

> Today brings to a close the district's administrative investiga-
> tion of the PRP coaching staff and head coach Jason Stinson and
> whether there was any violation of Kentucky High School Athletic
> Association (KHSAA) or JCPS rules and regulations in the events
> of Aug. 20, 2008, when student athlete Max Gilpin collapsed and
> later died.
>
> Max's death was truly tragic for his family, the PRP commu-
> nity, and for all of us at JCPS. We all want the same thing—to
> see athletics have a positive influence on the lives of our children.
> Max's tragic death has affected high school athletics nationwide.
>
> The investigative report was delivered to me last week. A
> meeting was held as required by our employee practices with Mr.
> Stinson on Monday, June 29, after he returned from out of town.
> And so, today I am able to release the final report.
>
> Some have continued to ask why this investigation has taken
> so long. Let me be very clear—this report and findings represent
> the most extensive investigation ever undertaken by the Jefferson
> County Public Schools.
>
> Our investigation initially began in partnership with Louis-
> ville Metro Police, but we were soon asked to wait until their
> interviews were completed.
>
> In early March, JCPS received more than 2,000 pages of doc-
> uments from the LMPD investigation. It was several weeks after
> that when we received medical records.
>
> The JCPS investigation involved interviews with over 125 wit-
> nesses, players and coaches; a review of the LMPD evidence; a re-
> view of our own athletics program; a review of medical files, and
> consultation with an independent medical expert. Investigators
> then compiled all the evidence into the final report that consists of
> more than 270 pages of findings and supporting evidence.

I want to thank our investigative unit for their diligence in pursuing the evidence in this case and in compiling and analyzing the findings. It has been a long, arduous and, heart-rending task. I am confident that we have considered and addressed this situation with the utmost concern and integrity.

After careful review of the investigators' and the medical expert's findings, I am satisfied with and support the conclusions drawn in this report.

I determined the need for an investigation on Monday, Aug. 25, prior to learning of any allegations against the coaching staff.

We learned later that there were some adults attending a girls' soccer game at an adjacent field, who alleged that the PRP football coaching staff denied players water during the Aug. 20 practice. Based on the evidence, this was not the case.

The evidence shows that on Aug. 20, Coach Stinson and the PRP football coaches complied with the KHSAA rules and regulations for heat play.

Although it was a hot day, the football practice that afternoon was a typical practice with sufficient water breaks and adequate supervision on the part of all the coaching staff.

The football team was well conditioned and had been training for several months prior to Aug. 20.

The Aug. 20 practice was a shorter than usual practice. Water was available on the practice field and the team received 4–5 water breaks during the practice. Some players received additional water breaks during individual drills. Ice packs were available on the field and were in fact used to treat Max Gilpin.

The coaches monitored the players and pulled some players from the conditioning when they showed signs of stress. The last water break on Aug. 20 began around 5:20 PM with practice resuming at around 5:30 PM and 30–35 minutes of conditioning involving running, started soon after.

Because the team was split to run in two groups, each player individually ran for 15–17 minutes resting in between each gasser during that time frame. Each group ran a total of approximately 1.5 to 1.9 miles.

In comparison to the football team's conditioning activities on Aug. 20, it is important to note that because the heat index was below the 95-degree benchmark, the girls' soccer game at the adjacent field played out as a normal game with two 40-minute halves. Soccer officials determined that water breaks at 30-minute intervals were not required.

While the football team was running the gassers, a player experienced breathing problems and shortly thereafter near the end of the conditioning period and between 6:05 and 6:12 p.m., Max collapsed.

Multiple people responded to assist Max. His father also went out to the field. Max was placed on a Gator and transported to the running water. Ice packs also were applied in addition to the running water as per heat-related response protocol.

The evidence shows that 911 was called at 6:17 p.m., approximately 5–12 minutes after Max collapsed.

At the end of practice, Coach Stinson instructed players to go under a shade tree for a brief team meeting as was their normal protocol. A few players began walking to the water fountains and the coach instructed them to go to the meeting first.

Max was not one of those players. The players were then dismissed to get water or leave.

Again, the investigation did not find any violation of KHSAA or JCPS rules.

It is clear from the evidence that the allegations by a few witnesses at the soccer game, were based on their accounts of only a few minutes of the practice that day.

As a result of allegations that the players were denied water, the JCPS investigation included a review of Max Gilpin's medical records.

After reviewing the medical records, an independent physician, Dr. Daniel Rusyniak, a specialist at Indiana University in emergency medicine and medical toxicology, confirmed that the results of tests performed during Max's hospitalization are not consistent with dehydration.

A University of Louisville emergency medicine physician, Dr. William Smock, who has no connection to the case, previously reviewed records for The *Courier-Journal* and also concluded that Max's heat stroke was not caused by lack of water.

The conclusions of the investigators clearly indicate that Max Gilpin did not die as a result of any restriction in water breaks, or denial of water, or any violation of KHSAA or JCPS rules.

Dr. Rusyniak concluded that the evidence suggests that Max was ill prior to football practice on Aug. 20. The key findings are cited in the summary as well as in Dr. Rusyniak's findings in the full report.

According to Dr. Rusyniak, a history and physical form completed at the hospital based on information supplied by Max's parents, indicated that Max was suffering from fever, congestion and difficulty breathing prior to practice that day.

Dr. Rusyniak concluded that the cause of Max's death—sepsis secondary to a bacterial infection—could have resulted from a pre-existing illness and that the absence of an autopsy makes the cause of Max's sepsis more difficult to confirm.

He concluded that a viral or bacterial illness would have made Max more susceptible to the heat. Dr. Rusyniak concluded that a combination of many factors may have made Max more susceptible to the heat on Aug. 20, but again that the results of Max's hospital tests are not consistent with dehydration.

While the evidence did not reveal any violation of KHSAA or JCPS rules, I am extremely troubled—actually I am outraged—by the statement made that day by head coach Jason Stinson—that the running would end when someone quit the team.

While this kind of negative motivation may be used in some amateur and even professional sports, that kind of culture has absolutely no place in JCPS's athletic programs.

Coach Stinson's statement is not an appropriate means to motivate student athletes, but the statement is not a violation of any KHSAA or JCPS rule; therefore, I am unable to initiate disciplinary consequences to Mr. Stinson for his remark.

However, I am taking action to ensure that this kind of culture is not tolerated in JCPS.

I want to deliver an unambiguous message to Mr. Stinson and to all JCPS employees that such motivational techniques are not acceptable.

Sports venues provide opportunities for positive motivation. At the same time we encourage students to stretch their limits and work hard to achieve their athletic goals, we need to teach them that the competitive spirit is compatible with respect for others.

Even as we expand our CARE for Kids initiative, which strives to create caring and respectful communities in our classrooms and schools for both students and adults, we must demand the same approach on our athletic fields.

I have instructed our district Director of Activities/Athletics to immediately develop and present training for all members of our coaching staff on workout strategies that are rigorous, yet incorporate positive motivation and language. These will begin prior to the start of the school year.

Nothing will bring Max back. It deeply saddens all of us that one of our students passed away after collapsing on the practice field. This tragic event has heightened our awareness—as parents, teachers, coaches, athletic directors and administrators—of the need to constantly seek ways to improve safety for our student athletes.

In April 2009, I forwarded a set of recommendations to KHSAA for their consideration in reviewing the state's athletic rules including heat protocol.

Additionally, JCPS committed to implementing some of those recommendations immediately for the coming school year. They include:

- Expediting the new KHSAA rule requiring assistant coaches to join head coaches in attending approved sports safety courses;
- Requiring that each athlete and a parent attend a seminar on healthy habits, nutritional recommendations, injury prevention and treatment, medication and supplement use, and heat-related guidelines; and
- Requiring that every JCPS athlete list all non-prescription medications and supplements he or she is taking; this list is to be reviewed by the physician who conducts the student's physical examination prior to athletic activity.

As a community, we must all continue to work together to keep the safety of our young people in and out of the classroom as a top priority.

A copy of this final report is being delivered to the civil attorneys representing Max Gilpin's parents, to the Commonwealth Attorney's Office, to KHSAA, and to the Kentucky Education Professional Standards Board. Our attorney also will inform the court that the investigation is complete.

The head coaching position at PRP has been advertised and interviews are pending. When the coach is hired, it will be at the coach's discretion as is normal protocol, to recommend the coaching staff. The assistant coaches involved in this investigation may be eligible to be hired for those positions.

Mr. Stinson meanwhile must remain reassigned to a non-instructional position pending the outcome of the criminal trial scheduled in August.

Max Gilpin's family and friends have suffered a great loss. I hope that the findings of our investigation provide a clearer understanding of what actually happened on the practice field on Aug. 20.

It is my hope that the release of this report will bring some measure of solace and healing to all who have been affected by the loss of this fine young man.

Just as when Nichols and Smock released their opinion in March, it seemed a real possibility that the charges against Jason would be dropped. There were multiple doctors, in addition to Nichols and Smock, who opined there were contributing medical factors, and now Jason Stinson's employer, as well as his governing body, had publicly stated that he did not break any rules. When we heard the outcome of the investigation, it was hard not to be positive. I guess we were being naive to believe that this investigation would not be attacked.

It was clear right out of the gate that *C-J* columnist Rick Bozich liked the report about as much as he liked being waved off by PRP players and coaches at the Ballard game the year before. Within a few minutes of the conclusion of the press conference, Bozich posted a blog on *C-J*'s website, dismissing the report. It seemed he had made his decision about the report before he even read it. Within six hours of the press conference, an article by Rick Bozich was posted on *C-J*'s website and it appeared in the newspaper the following day, July 2. The piece, titled "JCPS report blames only Max Gilpin," was a scathing review of the JCPS investigation, and furthermore, a personal attack on Jason Stinson and his coaching staff. Somewhere in all the venom and malice seething from the critique, one of the true underlying motivators of this situation again reared its ugly head. Blame, and/or the need to find someone or something to blame in the event of a tragedy, could no longer be denied.

We currently live in a litigious society where blame or liability is regularly put under a microscope. Someone has to be at fault. There is no such thing as a no-fault accident. Once criminal charges are filed and lawsuits are filed, someone has to be blamed, and many times people do not like where the fingers are pointing when it is all said and done.

JCPS didn't blame Max Gilpin. If anything, the report blamed his parents. At some point parents must accept some responsibility for their children. If Max Gilpin was indeed sick and was in fact using bodybuilding supplements that many outlets require an adult to purchase, his parents must shoulder some responsibility for this tragedy. It clearly bothered Bozich that JCPS was not willing to accept responsibility for Max Gilpin's death, and how dare they lay the blame where it might belong! Blaming the parents just doesn't sell newspapers nearly as well as being able to pin this tragedy on an overbearing, out-of-control football coach. A parent's responsibility for a body-building supplement not sold to minors, a prescribed amphetamine, and an illness that suggested he should not have been at school, let alone at practice, is not nearly as Pulitzer Prize worthy as an abusive, tyrannical, water-denying coach who ran the child to death, all while he was dying of thirst.

The JCPS investigation looked at medical evidence, whereas the LMPD examination did not. In addition to the medical evidence, there were a few glaring differences in JCPS' inquiry versus LMPD's inquest. On July 2, the *Courier-Journal* compared these differences:

Denying Water

JCPS: Stinson did not deny players water. A few players, but not Max, were told to attend a team meeting before getting a drink at the end of practice.

Criminal investigation: Stinson repeatedly denied players water.

Wind Sprints "Gassers"

JCPS: Players ran between 12 and 15 "gassers"—four widths of the football field.

Criminal investigation: Several said they were required to run more than 30.

Nature of Practice

JCPS: Practice was "normal" until the end when Max collapsed.

Criminal investigation: Witnesses including players and assistant coaches, told police that Stinson made players run more than usual because he was mad about players' performance.

Result

JCPS: Neither Stinson nor any other coach violated state or school district rules. The school district's findings in some cases differ from the accounts of witnesses who were interviewed by JCPS and police. The district explains its conclusions by stating in the report that witness statements "vary widely" and the report is based on "the weight of all available information."

Criminal investigation: Indictment of Stinson on charge of reckless homicide.

Water

JCPS: No players were denied water, and all were given four to five scheduled water breaks.

Witness accounts: One player told the district that after the players had run 10 "gassers," one of his teammates asked to get water but was told he could not by an assistant coach. A parent watching a soccer game on an adjacent field told police that a player who took a bottled water for a teammate brought it back saying the teammate wasn't allowed to drink it. Another soccer spectator said that after the players ran sprints, Stinson told 10 to 12 of them who'd gone off for water to come back. Stinson told police that he told four players they couldn't drink until after a team meeting.

Prior Illness

JCPS: An independent doctor says Max was sick before practice and that his illness may have made him more susceptible to heatstroke.

Witnesses: Max's parents have said he was not sick, and Max's friend, Chelsea Scott, who had lunch with him on the day of practice, said he was tired but not sick.

The parent the newspaper is talking about under the "water" section is Susan Fife. Fife was running the soccer concession stand. In her statement, she said the player said, "he couldn't drink it." She did not say he wasn't allowed to drink it. Never did the player (who actually was not a player, but a student manager—Trae McFarland) say he wasn't allowed to drink the water.

When asked for comment concerning the release of the JCPS investigation, Commonwealth Attorney Dave Stengel said the trial would proceed. "We'll do our talking in court," he said.

Who knows what that will entail?

CHAPTER 12

THE ONSIDE KICK

JCPS enacted some new requirements for student athletes and their parents before they could participate in any 2009 fall sport. One of those requirements was that parents and players had to watch a video. When the 2009 PRP football team members showed up for this mandatory health and safety meeting, they were greeted with a surprise.

Asst. Commonwealth Attorney Leland Hulbert took the floor and essentially complained that over 500 calls had been made, and that they were still unable to contact some players and witnesses. He commented about these calls going unreturned, and he explained they would subpoena the ones they could not reach.

He also implied that these individuals might have to sit at the courthouse during the entire trial to be called if the prosecution needed them. WHAS-11 TV's Renee Murphy interviewed a couple of parents about the meeting the next day. On July 14, the TV station ran the story. It stated:

> Some parents of players at Pleasure Ridge Park High School say prosecutors crossed the line. Parents say a prosecutor on the case showed up at one of their organizational meetings and badgered players.
>
> Their former coach will soon be on trial for Reckless Homicide, in the death of 15-year-old football player Max Gilpin.
>
> The meeting was a mandatory health and safety meeting for parents and players at PRP High School.
>
> Some parents say the Commonwealth Attorney's Office used the meeting to threaten people.
>
> The meeting in the cafeteria of PRP High School was sup-

posed to be straightforward and about football. But parents say when they got to the school, the meeting took a dramatic turn.

PRP football father Tim Keown said, "We were...blindsided... I felt threatened."

PRP football parents tell me that Leland Hulbert with the Commonwealth Attorney's Office showed up at their mandatory organization meeting, passed out a letter about the case involving Jason Stinson, and then asked for anyone with information about the case to come forward or they could be subpoenaed.

Tim Keown said, "Our statements have been given. We were truthful in our statements. I don't know if they are fishing for something else."

PRP football parent Gary Vincent said, "I didn't think it was the right place...I didn't think the kids should have to go through it."

The prosecutor was talking about the case of PRP's former coach, Jason Stinson.

Stinson is charged with reckless homicide in the death of 15-year-old Max Gilpin, who collapsed during a hot practice in August 2008, and subsequently died a few days later.

We talked with the Commonwealth Attorney's Office and they said they did not threaten anyone at the meeting. The CAO says they were there to pass along information about Stinson's trial and to ask for information.

The school district says the prosecutor had permission to be at the meeting.

What the story did not tell was the reaction Hulbert received from the mostly stunned crowd. Many sat there with looks of amazement and/or confusion as Hulbert told the crowd what they were going to do. It would be safe to say that the majority of the crowd took exception to how Hulbert delivered his message. Several attendees that evening later stated that he came to a private meeting unannounced, and that they felt ambushed.

One parent stated, "If I wanted to hear what he had to say I would have returned one of his multiple phone calls, but I don't care what he has to say." Collectively, the parents were upset and felt "trapped" because this meeting was mandatory for their child to play football. Had Hulbert's appearance been after the mandatory meeting, he may have found himself talking to a nearly empty room. However, his speech was not at the end; it was at the beginning, and everyone was forced to sit there.

Some parents stated they initially thought the high school was responsible for this, but they quickly learned differently once defense attorney Brian Butler addressed the crowd. Butler was forced to show up on Jason Stinson's behalf since Hulbert would be speaking about his client. In fact, many in attendance felt the opening arguments of the trial began that evening in the cafeteria of PRP.

Once Hulbert finished, Butler took the floor. He was very brief and began by apologizing to everyone for this event even occurring. He told the crowd he was only there because he had to be, because the CAO used its influence to force its way into the meeting. He went on to tell everyone that they didn't have to listen to Hulbert if they didn't desire to, and furthermore, they could throw the paper he was distributing in the trash if they wanted.

Butler stated, "You can listen to him, or don't. The choice is yours. You can keep that piece of paper, or you can throw it in the trash can if you want to." He quickly made his points and then once again apologized for this happening. He thanked the crowd, and what happened next blew me away. Almost everyone in attendance gave Butler a warm round of applause. Something I had known for some time was now clear to those who supported Stinson: Brian Butler was a good attorney, and he was not backing down.

In a matter of less than two minutes, the crowd's mood went from angry and resentful to warm and accepting. As the cheers for Butler rang out, Hulbert and the other representative of the CAO calmly picked up the stack of papers they had come to hand out. They then exited the cafeteria front door shortly after the applause died down.

The CAO probably did not have a worse person for this task than Leland Hulbert. Essentially he forced his way into a private meeting, telling people in attendance what they were going to do. He should have rolled his sleeves up, loosened his tie, and explained to the crowd how he needed their help. But that isn't how he played it. He showed up in a working class neighborhood with a pompous attitude that just did not fly. By the end of the evening, most of the papers he managed to hand out had found their way to the trash can at the front of the cafeteria. It was amazing how quickly things changed when speculation about what prosecutors could or could not do to witnesses was cleared up. If anything, this meeting only hurt the prosecution because many lost their fear of the prosecutors that evening. Until Butler spoke, most of the parents and witnesses had only heard from the LMPD or the CAO on what was required of them. Now they didn't seem so threatening.

Most of the month of July was spent writing letters to anyone I thought might read them. I implored people to publicly call for the dismissal of the criminal case against Jason Stinson. With e-mails sent to politicians, television station general managers, and even national columnists, it was hard to believe that not one of them would take up the cause. Yet as July came to a close, it was clear that this case was going forward.

The message sent out simply stated that this prosecution was unnecessary and that the charge should be dropped. The message also declared that, much like the JCPS report, Stinson's defense would place the responsibility of this tragedy on factors beyond Jason Stinson's control. Furthermore, most of these factors should have been monitored by Max Gilpin's parents. I really didn't think the prosecution could garner a conviction, so all this would do is prolong the torture that most parties involved were going through. Many coaches and players could not gain any closure from this tragedy. Every time they turned around, there was a news story reminding them of the situation.

Shortly after the JCPS report was released, the Commonwealth Attorney's Office filed a motion asking the judge to exclude the report from evidence. In an article titled "Prosecutors: JCPS inquiry into Gilpin 'self-serving'" printed July 21 in the *Courier-Journal*, Jason Riley wrote:

> Jefferson County prosecutors want a school district report on the death last year of Pleasure Ridge Park football player Max Gilpin excluded from ex-coach Jason Stinson's trial because it selectively used information to reach a "self-serving and wholly inaccurate conclusion." Arguing that the Jefferson County Public Schools investigation is "factually and logically unsound," the Commonwealth Attorney's Office is asking a circuit judge to keep the report out of Stinson's Aug. 31 trial.
>
> Superintendent Sheldon Berman released the report earlier this month, concluding that neither Stinson nor his assistants violated state rules or district policy at the practice last Aug. 20 where Max collapsed.

JCPS had been heavily criticized for glossing over its initial investigation of the August 20 practice. It seemed that the school district was being very thorough in its investigation of the practice, especially once conflicting witness accounts began to surface.

There were several differences between the JCPS and LMPD investigations that have already been noted, but something else that stood out was that JCPS had the witnesses give written statements. The important difference between a written statement and a verbal statement is that the investigator is less likely to lead the witnesses one way or another. The witnesses are allowed to tell the series of events in their own words and in their own time. It also gives them the ability to ponder and recall without feeling the pressure of someone waiting on an answer to a question.

The Commonwealth Attorney fought feverishly for months for this information to be released. Then prosecutors didn't want it once the report did not support its version of events that took place. Dave Stengel said that JCPS's investigation and subsequent report were "the biggest cover up since Watergate." Wow! He was comparing this case to Watergate. Perhaps that would make the *Courier-Journal*'s Jason Riley and Antoinette Konz a modern-day version of Woodward and Bernstein. After all, the *C-J* had recently run an ad touting their "watchdog journalism," noting how their stories were responsible for this case not getting swept under a rug.

In addition to attacking the validity of the report, CAO seemed to be questioning whether JCPS's investigators were competent to handle an investigation of this magnitude. The CAO was not the only one attacking the JCPS investigation. As mentioned earlier, the *Courier-Journal* had published articles and opinions attempting to discredit the report. To imply that these investigators and their supervisor were not qualified, or even worse, were involved in a cover up, was absurd.

All but one of the investigators were retired from the Louisville Division of Police (LDP), the Jefferson County Police Department (JCPD) or the LMPD (County and City governments merged in 2003 to form LMPD). These were not just retired "beat cops." With the exception of one, they all held at least a Bachelor's degree, and all held at least the rank of Detective. In fact, Stan Mullen, Barbara Warman, and Stephen Cheatham retired as high-ranking officers from LDP or LMPD.

In addition to Mullen, Warman, and Cheatham, additional investigators were Danny Harrell, Mike Mulhall, Keith Kiper, and Jim Hearn.

When the team's credentials were challenged, JCPS released their resumes.

According to a JCPS press release, Stanford T. Mullen, Jr. is currently the Chief of the Law Enforcement Division of the JCPS with responsibilities for the security and safety of 97,000 students, 14,000 employees and the investigation of criminal activity on JCPS property to include 1,000 buses and 60,000 bus stops. Director Mullen, with 22 years of successful experience, retired in 2003 from the Louisville Division of Police as Lieutenant Colonel, Associate Chief of Police and, with 17 years of experience, he retired from the Kentucky Army National Guard as a Lieutenant Colonel.

Director Mullen began his career with LDP as a Patrol Officer in 1980, and during that time he received both a Bachelors and a Masters degree. In 1982 he joined LDP's Special Weapons and Tactical (SWAT) Unit as a SWAT Officer and eventually rose to Training Coordinator, where he remained until 1991. During that time he served as a Detective investigating physical and sexual abuse of children, as well as homicides and sex crimes. He was promoted to Detective Sergeant in 1987, where he supervised district and robbery detectives until his promotion to Lieutenant in 1991. In 1991 he supervised a uniform patrol for the district until 1993, when he achieved the rank of Major, Assistant Chief of Police. During his time as a Major from 1993–1999, he was the Commander of the Criminal Investigation Section, which is responsible for multiple units and squads. In 1999 he was promoted to the position of Lieutenant Colonel, Associate Chief of Police. He held that position and was the Chief of Investigations until his retirement in 2003.

Barbara Warman holds a Masters Degree for Administration of Criminal Justice from the University of Louisville. She served LDP for 25 years, beginning as a Police Recruit in 1977, and then she became a Patrol Officer in 1980. In 1989 she was promoted to Sergeant, a rank she held until she was promoted to Lieutenant in 1991. Upon her retirement from LDP in 2003, she took the role of Coordinator of Internal Security at JCPS.

Warman is a seasoned police officer with a wide range of responsibilities. She was a Patrol Officer for three years, a Homicide Detective for six years, a Sergeant with the communication section for two years, and a Lt. Street Platoon Commander in two different districts for a total of three years. She then performed many duties, such as working on special projects and updating and writing policies and procedures while she held an Administrative role with Staff Services for four years. She left Staff Services to serve as Adjutant to the Chief of Police, where she assisted the Chief of Police in the daily operations of the police department. She spent the last three and a half years of her career as the Assistant Commander of the Louisville Jefferson County Crimes against Children Unit (CACU) where she supervised Sergeants and Detectives assigned to investigate physical and sexual child abuse.

Stephen Cheatham had over 26 years of law enforcement experience before coming to JCPS. He began his career with JCPD in 1977 as a Patrol Officer. He rose through the ranks to achieve the position of Lieutenant in 1999 and held that rank until his retirement in 2003. He was the Assistant Commander of JCPD's David District from 1999–2000 and the Assistant Commander of the training section from 2000–2002 until he took he the position of Coordinator for Homeland Security. He held a "Secret" security clearance with the FBI, and before being promoted to Lieutenant he was a Sergeant with the Internal Affairs Unit from 1996–1999.

Danny Harrell has a Bachelor of Science degree, and he is a graduate of both the Southern Police Institute and the FBI National Academy. He was a member of the LDP for 26 years, and, during his time with the department, he worked as an investigator in multiple units, including the Robbery and the Crimes against Children units. He also taught Criminal Investigative Classes for the Department of Criminal Justice Training for three years. After he retired, Harrell accepted employment with JCPS in 2002 as a Security Investigator.

D. Keith Kiper has a Bachelors degree in Police Administration, and he worked at Jefferson County Youth Center, a detention center for minors, from 1984–1988. He joined the JCPD in 1988 and worked the Patrol Division until 1993, when he became a Detective with the department's CACU. He remained there until 1995 when he transferred to the Robbery unit where he stayed for nearly five years. In 2000 he joined the Polygraph unit where he stayed until his retirement in 2005. He was hired by JCPS shortly after his retirement.

Mike Mulhall attended the Police Academy and joined the Shelbyville (KY) Police Department in 1979. He was hired by JCPD in 1989 where he spent two years on patrol and 16 years as a detective with JCPD's CACU. He has over 1500 hours of training from the FBI Academy at the Southern Police Institute, and he joined JCPS in 2005 upon his retirement from the LMPD.

Jim Hearn, Jr., holds a Bachelors degree, and he was the only investigator who had not been employed by a metropolitan police department; however, he did complete the state's police academy training during his tenure with JCPS. He initially began with JCPS in 1984, and he has held several positions involving security, such as Security Shift Supervisor and Security Investigator. He has held the position of Coordinator of In-School Security since April 2005.

It is clear that the investigators responsible for JCPS's investigation into the circumstances surrounding Max Gilpin's death were not some "Barney Fifes" plucked out of Mayberry. These were seasoned investigators, several with command level experience that included a former Associate Chief of Police. They worked in units such as Robbery, Homicide, and CACU that regularly had to deal with some of Louisville's most heinous crimes. Considering many were once with the Crimes Against Children Unit, it is hard to believe any, let alone all of the people involved in this investigation, conspired to cover up Jason Stinson's responsibility for Max Gilpin's death. People who would suggest or say it was a cover up obviously did not do their homework. But many were commenting on issues and people they had not thoroughly vetted. Such behavior was starting to become a theme, and JCPS, its investigators, and its investigators' stellar backgrounds were not immune.

The legal battles were really starting to heat up. The Commonwealth Attorney's motion to exclude the JCPS report was not the only motion being considered. Defense attorneys Butler and Dathorne had filed a motion asking the court to exclude evidence entered by the prosecution.

An article, titled "Stinson's attorneys ask judge to prohibit testimony about water breaks and running," stated the following:

> Attorneys for former Pleasure Ridge Park football coach Jason Stinson want a judge to keep out testimony from his trial that players were denied water or ran more than normal at a practice last year where sophomore lineman Max Gilpin collapsed and later died, saying the allegations are not relevant to the teen's death.

The article, written by Jason Riley and published in the *Courier-Journal* on August 4, went on to explain the defense's request.

In a motion filed Wednesday, defense attorneys Alex Dathorne and Brian Butler claim the Jefferson CAO doesn't have a medical expert opinion stating that water deprivation or excessive running at the Aug. 20, 2008 practice caused Max's death.

"Unbelievably, the Commonwealth did not consult with a medical expert, including the Kentucky Medical Examiner's Office, prior to indicting Jason Stinson," Dathorne and Butler wrote in a motion to Circuit Judge Susan Schultz Gibson, adding that investigators also didn't "get an autopsy to prove how the teen died."

Defense attorneys contend that statements from several players and witnesses claiming Stinson denied players water and punished them by making them run more than usual should be excluded, because they do not prove how Max died and would only be used by the prosecution "to paint Mr. Stinson in a poor light" and anger jurors.

"Otherwise, the trial becomes much like the investigation and indictment; a witch hunt based upon pure speculation," the motion says.

Assistant Commonwealth Attorney Jon Heck said prosecutors had not received the motion and will respond "fully" in court proceedings.

If Gibson agrees with the defense, the decision would undermine the prosecution's case against Stinson.

We knew if Judge Gibson threw out that evidence, the case would be over for sure. Without the water evidence and the excessive amount of running evidence, there would not be much left for the CAO to go on. The defense wanted to block what it considered prejudicial evidence, and the prosecution wanted to block evidence that the defense claims exonerates Stinson. The decision on these two motions would surely decide if this trial moved forward. It was totally in the judge's hands at this point.

I was driving down the road I live on when my cell phone rang. It was August 11, and, with the trial less than three weeks away, preparing for it was a daily task. To no surprise, it was Jason on the other end. After our customary greetings, Jason asked me if I was sitting down. I told him "yes," because I was driving my car. He said he would wait until I was no longer driving because he thought I might be shocked.

I began to smile, because this was the call I had waited for. I just knew Coach Stinson was calling to tell me it was all over, and the CAO had dropped the charges.

"OK, Jason, I'm pulling into my garage right now. What's so big that I need to be sitting down?"

"I just got indicted on a new charge of wanton endangerment."

That was not what I was expecting to hear. It was like someone had just punched me in the stomach.

"What! You've got to be kidding me. How many counts?"

"One."

"One! For who? Antonio Calloway?"

"No, for Max," Coach Stinson answered.

"For Max? How is that possible? I thought wanton endangerment applied if the event did not result in the person's death. I said all along I thought they might charge you with wanton endangerment for Antonio and the players who threw up. But I never thought this. What is Brian saying?"

"He's pretty fired up right now. This was a real cheap shot. He said he would call me back, but he's steaming right now. What does all of this mean?"

"I am not totally certain, but I sure didn't see this coming."

I began to conclude that this new charge had something to do with the new prosecutor who had been assigned to the case. His name was Jonathan Heck, and he typically prosecuted child abuse cases. He was assigned as Dave Stengel's replacement after Stengel stepped down as prosecutor of Stinson's case, citing he needed to deal with some issues in his 19-year marriage.

It would make sense to assign someone like Heck to this case. There was probably no one better in the CAO to vilify a person as a child abuser than Jon Heck. He did not prosecute armed robberies or drug trafficking cases; he prosecuted crimes against children every day, so surely he knew how to attack someone.

"Man, this dude is in it to win it," I told Jason. The more I thought about it, the more it seemed to make sense to me. Jason's attorneys had just filed a motion a few days earlier asking to keep out testimony from his trial that players were denied water or ran more than normal at the August 20 practice. If Judge Gibson ruled in favor of Stinson's defense, there would be nothing left to the prosecution's case. Securing this new indictment was the only way the CAO could guarantee to hold onto the denial of water evidence and the excessive running evidence.

The Commonwealth's Attorney could not prove that dehydration or excessive running killed Max Gilpin, so there would be no reason to allow that type of evidence. It would be strictly inflammatory and would only make Coach Stinson look bad. It would not prove that he was responsible for Max's death, so there was a good chance the judge would throw out all of that kind of evidence. However, in a case of wanton endangerment, it would be very appropriate to keep the evidence in. Denial of water and excessive running were very relevant if you were looking at behavior prior to Max Gilpin's collapse.

This was an onside kick, I told Jason. An onside kick is what you do when you're afraid of your opponent, or you're desperate and need an upper hand because you cannot win straight up. You need an edge, so you run a trick play in hopes of gaining an advantage.

In the game of football the ball is live and is anyone's ball on a kickoff once the ball travels at least 10 yards or is touched by a receiving player. An onside kick occurs in football when the kicking team only kicks the ball 10 yards in an attempt to recover it. It is rarely recovered by the kicking team, so that is why it is considered to be a trick play. The element of surprise greatly increases the chances of success with this type of play. (If you watched the Super Bowl between the New Orleans Saints and the Indianapolis Colts, you saw how a surprise onside kick can completely change a game. New Orleans' onside kick took the ball away from Indianapolis, leaving Payton Manning on the sidelines where all he could do was watch.)

Much like New Orleans' onside kick, the Commonwealth Attorney's trick play could be a real game changer. By securing the indictment on the second charge, the CAO greatly increased its chances of some sort of conviction. Wanton endangerment is a felony and carried the same penalty as reckless homicide, so to Jason Stinson there was not much difference between the two.

The new charge definitely changed things, because Stinson's attorneys had been preparing to defend a homicide case. With less than three weeks before the case went to trial, they would have to retool their defense to include a defense for wanton endangerment. The evidence did not change with the new indictment. There were no new revelations that brought about the new charge. It is not like the prosecution was turning over rocks and said, "Oh look, here is new evidence against Jason Stinson. We can file a new charge."

It didn't happen that way, because there was no new evidence. From early on there was the theory that prosecutors had something that most others did not know about. We had mockingly surmised that Stengel had a "*Zapruder film*" showing Jason in some incriminating or compromising position, and he was going to break it out at the last minute. It would take something spectacular like that to make sense of this prosecution. However, the *Zapruder film* never showed up.

For whatever reason, the CAO didn't seem to see anything wrong with filing a charge so close to trial. In fact, John Heck, the new prosecutor on the case, stated that it was not uncommon for a new charge to be filed right before trial. He was sure the situation would be the same if we were to pull cases that Brian Butler or Alex Dathorne had prosecuted when they worked for the Commonwealth Attorney's Office.

Jon Heck's review of the case did not turn up anything new, so why wasn't this charge filed when the homicide charge was filed? Is this a reflection on the original team of Stengel and Hulbert? Did they miss something that Jon Heck did not? Stengel is a seasoned prosecutor, so it would seem he would have a tight grasp on the fundamentals of a case he personally took to the grand jury.

In an article titled "Ex-Coach indicted on second charge in player's death" that appeared on July12 in the *Courier-Journal*, Jason Riley wrote:

> Jason Stinson was indicted by a Jefferson County grand jury Tuesday on a charge of first-degree wanton endangerment in the death of sophomore lineman Max Gilpin, who collapsed Aug. 20 and died three days later at Kosair Children's Hospital, after his body temperature had reached 107 degrees… Assistant Commonwealth Attorney Jon Heck said it is not unusual to file additional charges after further investigation in a case, which is what happened with Stinson.
>
> "My detailed review of the case prompted me to put it back before the grand jury," said Heck. "The investigation does not stop when the charges are filed… It's an ongoing process up through and into the trial."

Heck would not discuss specifics of the new charge against Stinson.

The indictment accuses Stinson of wantonly engaging in "conduct which created a substantial danger of death or serious physical injury to Maxwell Gilpin."

The onside kick undeniably left Stinson's defense scrambling to recover. The attorneys immediately began to fight the new indictment, and like most everything else with this case, it appeared vulnerable. Once again Stinson was not allowed to testify or present testimony to the grand jury on his behalf.

CHAPTER 13

LAST-MINUTE MANEUVERS

The action-packed week of August 10–14 ended with a bang as Butler and Dathorne recovered the Commonwealth's onside kick. Just as soon as Stinson's attorneys learned of the new indictment, they set out to have it dismissed. They were successful three days later when Judge Gibson threw out the latest indictment. (Judge Gibson's ruling could have been considered an "illegal procedure penalty" against the Commonwealth. Unfortunately, unlike the game of football where the illegal procedure penalty would end the play, it appeared the Commonwealth might still get another chance.)

A *Courier-Journal* article titled "New Stinson charge dismissed" was written by Jason Riley on August 15, 2009. It stated:

> A Jefferson Circuit judge on Friday dismissed a felony wanton-endangerment charge against former Pleasure Ridge Park High School football coach Jason Stinson in the death of a 15-year-old player who collapsed from heatstroke during practice.
>
> Judge Susan Schultz Gibson agreed with Stinson's attorneys that prosecutors improperly failed to tell the grand jurors who indicted Stinson that the coach wanted to testify before them.
>
> The Jefferson Commonwealth Attorney's Office immediately told Gibson that they would seek to re-indict Stinson next week, this time asking jurors if they would like to hear from the former coach.
>
> But prosecutors may have won a bigger battle Friday when Gibson said she would allow testimony that contends players were denied water and ran more than normal when Stinson's trial on a reckless-homicide charge begins Aug. 31.

Defense attorneys Alex Dathorne and Brian Butler had argued that prosecutors don't have a medical expert's opinion stating that water deprivation or excessive running at the Aug. 20 practice caused Max's death, meaning those allegations were irrelevant to the homicide case.

Max collapsed at practice and died three days later at Kosair Children's Hospital, after his body temperature had reached 107 degrees.

But Gibson noted that prosecutors have recently filed notice of at least one witness who will testify that Stinson's actions that day led to Max Gilpin's death.

Dr. Doug Casa, director of athletic training education at the University of Connecticut and a national leader in heat-stroke prevention, will testify that Stinson created an environment where Max believed he could not stop running "even if it was medically necessary to do so," which caused the massive heatstroke that led to the teen's death three days later, according to court records.

Gibson warned prosecutors, however, that their experts will have to prove that Stinson's actions led to Max's death or the case may never make it past a "directed verdict," the point in the trial where the prosecution has finished and the defense asks that charges be dismissed for lack of evidence.

It was unclear how Dr. Doug Casa could be considered a medical expert since he is a PhD and not a medical doctor. Kentucky law clearly states that only medical doctors can render an opinion on a cause of death in Kentucky. Besides, how could Casa opine that Max believed he could not stop running "even if it was medically necessary to do so?" How would Casa know that?

There was an additional matter put before Judge Gibson—the JCPS report that prosecutors wanted blocked. In the same *C-J* article, Riley reported the following:

Also on Friday, the judge heard arguments, but did not make a decision, on a motion from the prosecution to exclude from the trial a school district report on Max's death that concluded neither Stinson nor his assistants violated state rules or district policy at the practice.

125

Assistant Commonwealth Attorney Jon Heck said the report contains summaries of witness statements that have been altered by the school district or selectively chosen to clear Stinson of wrongdoing.

"It's unbelievable what is omitted and what is changed," Heck told Gibson. "... These are not reliable findings. To put it politely, they are ridiculous."

Heck said the school system's "tortured interpretation" of the heat rules was that water should always be available, but not that players should be allowed to take a drink when they desire.

Butler, however, said it would be "absurd to have a practice where players willy-nilly go wherever they want to go" whenever they want. He added that it would have been in the school district's best interest to find that Stinson was a "rogue" employee who violated regulations—and thus was himself liable in a civil case—but that it wasn't true.

Gibson said she would rule next week on whether the district findings will be allowed at trial.

Earlier in Friday's hearing, Stinson pleaded not guilty to the charge of first-degree wanton endangerment after being indicted on Tuesday.

Gibson dismissed the charge after the defense argued the grand jury that indicted Stinson was not told the coach wanted to testify, even though jurors repeatedly asked questions about what the former coach told police, according to the defense.

Heck said the defense had told prosecutors that Stinson wanted to talk to grand jurors in January, when he was indicted on a charge of reckless homicide. But, Heck argued, they had not renewed their requests for the new grand jury.

Gibson ruled that the initial request by Stinson was sufficient notice and prosecutors should have told grand jurors.

"The rule does exist for a reason," she said. "If it wasn't important, it wouldn't be there."

The Commonwealth made it clear that it would immediately seek a new indictment, so Butler and Dathorne left the courthouse to prepare a motion to block the prosecutors. Monday morning they filed that motion, and a hearing was scheduled for 8 AM on Tuesday, August 18 in Mitch Perry's Jefferson Circuit courtroom to hear the defense's motion to block the latest attempt at a new indictment. Stinson's defense contended that the new indictment should be blocked because the grand jury would be tainted by previous testimony on the wanton endangerment charge since its members had already deliberated on the issue.

The hearing was set for 8 AM, but when that time arrived, the only ones present in the courtroom were the judge, bailiff, Stinson's defense attorneys, a couple of reporters, Jason, and myself. The prosecution was late as usual; however, I took a real exception to this because *they* had set the time for this hearing. There was absolutely no excuse why at least one of them could not be there on time that morning. They couldn't claim they were "held over in another hearing" or a required whatever "ran long." (They always had some fabulous excuse for their repetitive tardiness.)

Somewhere around five after 8, Judge Perry stated that if the Commonwealth did not show up soon, he would go ahead and rule without them. I sat there impatiently watching the seconds, then minutes, tick by. (A thought about sending a bill to the CAO for Butler's and Dathorne's time crossed my mind.) When the CAO finally arrived at somewhere between six and seven minutes after 8, Stinson attorneys had sat there for nearly 15 minutes, collectively waiting. Who pays for this time? (It is highly unlikely the CAO would have paid that bill had I actually sent one, but it was still a nice way to pass the time while we waited.)

We actually waited for the prosecution longer than it took for the hearing to be completed. Within a matter of minutes, Judge Perry ruled that he was not going to interfere with the grand jury process, and that the Commonwealth could again present the case to the grand jury. A few hours later, the same grand jury that heard Stinson's case a week before returned a true bill against him. Again his request to testify before the grand jury was denied.

CHAPTER 14

ENEMY OF THE STATE

The next issue was whether or not Stinson's defense would subpoena Dr. William Smock to testify on Jason Stinson's behalf. It was easy to understand that testifying for the defense would put Dr. Smock in an uncomfortable position, considering he was normally the Commonwealth's medical expert. However, as the prosecution got more and more aggressive, it seemed that Butler and Dathorne would have no other choice. Since Dr. Smock was going to be out of the country during the trial, he would have to be deposed beforehand in order for him to testify.

From the very beginning of this deposition, that was closed to the public, it was clear it was going to be unique. For over two decades, Dr. Smock had sided with the prosecution in its theories, but today he was taking the stand for the defense. There was not a judge present, so many questions and answers were objected to without an immediate ruling. One of the main objections was about a meeting in March of 2009 between Dr. Smock and the COA. Apparently the Commonwealth failed to divulge this exculpatory meeting to Stinson's attorneys, which was a gross violation of the law.

Dave Stengel sat in the front row behind Hulbert and Heck, occasionally whispering instructions. He spent most of the morning either staring at the floor or glaring at Bill Smock. The CAO clearly was not going to take Dr. Smock's opinions lying down. They had filed a motion 10 days earlier attempting to limit Dr. Smock's testimony. I was present for that deposition/testimony, so I fully understood why they didn't want his testimony in front of a jury.

Smock almost completely contradicted everything the prosecution was claiming happened that day. He stated that it was his opinion that Max Gilpin was not dehydrated. He also testified to a "Brady violation" when he told of the meeting he had with the prosecutors. He further opined that Adderall® had played a role in Max Gilpin's heatstroke.

It appeared that a man who had been a friend of the prosecution for such a lengthy amount of time was no longer held in high regard. It was clear that Dr. William Smock had now become an enemy of the state. Dr. Smock was set to testify about that March meeting on Monday August 31, and once that happened there would be no turning back.

Jury selection was scheduled to begin the morning of August 31, but it was postponed until after Judge Gibson heard the final arguments on the alleged Brady violation and whether 1,500 pages of evidence would be allowed in. The prospect of the trial actually beginning was a relief for most. August 31 could not come soon enough for Jason Stinson.

Previously, Judge Gibson had ruled that the JCPS report on Max Gilpin's death would not be allowed in as evidence. She had also recently ruled that the two charges be consolidated into one trial, and she refused at least one defense request for a dismissal.

It seemed like there was one hearing after another throughout August. Butler and Dathorne again fought to have the second indictment thrown out, but they were unsuccessful. (It deeply concerned me that they might actually get it thrown out. I was worried that if it was dismissed, the Commonwealth would just get another indictment in September, which would mean another trial. The thought of that left a hollow feeling in my gut. I told Jason that I didn't know if I could raise enough money for two trials. It had been such a burden for us to finance one trial, I did not want to think that we might have to start over again.)

As many of the legal battles came to a head, the *Courier-Journal* was ready to bring everyone the latest. In an article titled "Prosecutors blast defense and criticize key witness in Stinson case" that appeared on the *C-J*'s website August 28, Jason Riley wrote the following:

> [Smock] a professor of emergency medicine at the University of Louisville who has served as a medical expert for prosecutors for more than two decades, testifying in hundreds of cases.
>
> But when Dr. William Smock went to the Jefferson Commonwealth Attorney's Office last March to tell them that PRP sophomore Max Gilpin's death was a "tragic accident" instead of a homicide, he hadn't treated Max, talked to treating physicians,

seen the football practice where Max collapsed or read the accounts from Max's teammates who saw the 15-year-old lineman fall, prosecutors say.

Instead, they say, Smock blamed a prescribed medication for contributing to Max's death, yet "could give no sound scientific basis for his unsubstantiated findings."

Prosecutors criticized Smock—and his conclusions—in a motion Friday that defended their decision not to reveal their meeting with Smock to defense lawyers for former PRP coach Jason Stinson, who will stand trial Monday on charges of reckless homicide and wanton endangerment in Max's death.

Stinson's lawyers had accused the Jefferson Commonwealth Attorney's Office of violating court procedures by not providing the defense information about the March meeting.

Prosecutors contend that Smock's views on the case had already been made public through a *Courier-Journal* interview and through other local and national media, and they had no obligation to turn over the opinions of a "non-treating expert that it never intends to call to trial."

Smock said in an interview he went to see Commonwealth Attorney Dave Stengel as a friend, concerned that Stengel had been given bad medical advice in saying that Max was dehydrated when he collapsed from heatstroke at the Aug. 20, 2008 practice. Max died three days later, after his body temperature reached 107 degrees.

"I explained to them that their assumption that Max was dehydrated was inaccurate," he said. "There was no medical evidence he was dehydrated. None."

Prosecutors accuse Stinson of withholding water from players and making them run extra wind sprints at the Aug. 20 practice, and that he had received training in heat-related illnesses that made him aware of the risks to his players.

Smock said he was subpoenaed to testify by the defense after the *Courier-Journal* asked him in early March to review Max's medical records. Because he will be out of town during the trial, Smock testified in a deposition Aug. 21.

"This is the first time in 25 years that my forensic medical opinion has been contrary to the Commonwealth's evidence," Smock said.

Defense attorneys Alex Dathorne and Brian Butler accused Stengel and his prosecutors Monday of conducting a "secret meeting" with Smock and "willfully" failing to disclose pertinent evidence by failing to turn over information from that hour-long meeting with Smock on March 18.

In a response to a defense motion, prosecutors accused Stinson's attorneys of selectively leaking inadmissible testimony from what "was supposed to be a closed-door deposition" on Aug. 21.

Smock, who also is director of the clinical forensic medicine program at University Hospital, had not treated Max but told the newspaper that his review of the records indicated that Max's heatstroke was not caused by lack of water. He said he believes that Adderall®, a drug used to treat attention deficit hyperactivity disorder, prompted Max's heatstroke.

In Friday's response, prosecutors said Smock didn't provide any scientific studies to back up his claim that "a low therapeutic dose of Adderall® contributed to Max Gilpin's death."

And when prosecutors asked Smock if Stinson was wrong in conducting the practice, he replied, "Hell yah, I think he was wrong," according to the response.

Smock said he doesn't remember making such a statement.

Also, prosecutors noted that Smock could not explain Max's low urine output when he first arrived at the hospital, which is common with dehydration, and said the Commonwealth would need to consult a kidney expert, which the prosecution has since done.

Smock said in an interview that Max could have urinated on himself while he was unconscious, before reaching the hospital. He said tests of Max's blood and urine showed he was not dehydrated.

"No way, no how, was this kid dehydrated," Smock said. "Absolutely zero medical evidence this kid was dehydrated."

When prosecutors asked Smock if he could provide medical proof that Adderall® caused Max's death, Smock told them that if "he wasn't dehydrated, it must be something else. He was on Adderall®, so that must be it," according to court records.

Smock told the newspaper he also provided scientific articles to Stengel regarding the use of amphetamines such as Adderall® and their relation to heatstroke. Prosecutors said none of the articles "linked Adderall® to heatstroke," according to court records.

Max was taking a prescribed daily dose of 20 milligrams of Adderall XR®, according to the medical records.

But those records do not cite Adderall® as a cause or contributing factor in his death, which is listed as septic shock resulting from multiple organ failure brought on by heatstroke. No autopsy was done, because Max's doctors said it wasn't necessary.

This article was one of the more fair articles/editorials of the 100+ that were written about this situation by the *Courier-Journal*, yet the article failed to mention that it would be rare for a medical study to list a brand name of a drug. I told Jason right after we left the deposition of Dr. Smock that the Commonwealth was splitting hairs when it said that none of Smock's articles specifically listed Adderall®. That is like saying, "It was not the acetaminophen that cured your headache; it was the Tylenol® that did it." Every one of those articles listed amphetamines and not Adderall®, because Adderall® is a brand name of a drug.

It is common to list the generic term of a medication in these types of articles to make sure that it is correctly identified. (Medications of nearly the same ingredients can be marketed with many different names. According to the Center for Substance Abuse Research (CESAR), prescription names for amphetamines include Adderall®, Dexedrine®, DextroStat®, and Desoxyn®. Knowing that there are at least four brand names of medications that contain amphetamines, it is understandable to see why the article did not list Adderall® specifically.)

To write an article that lists one brand name drug but does not include the names of the other brand name drugs would be irresponsible. To indentify one brand name and not another could lead a user to believe that one medication containing an amphetamine is somehow safer than the other. Studies on Reye Syndrome will typically list acetaminophen and not Tylenol®, Paracetamol®, or Panadol®. Likewise, articles about amphetamines would not contain brand names nor would they list street names, such as bennies, black beauties, copilots, eye-openers, lid poppers, pep pills, speed, uppers, wake-ups and/or white crosses.

Some people had now begun to speculate what the Commonwealth's new position against Dr. Smock would mean to future cases. Essentially the Commonwealth did everything but call Dr. Smock a quack when they were responding to the defense's claim of a Brady violation.

Defense attorneys in Louisville were salivating at the thought of the Commonwealth ever attempting to use Dr. Smock as an expert witness again. A quarter-of-a-century relationship more than likely went down the drain after the Commonwealth challenged Dr. Smock's ability to opine in the matter of a cause of death. (It seemed that a 25-year "marriage" was about to hit the rocks, and it more than likely did right after Dr. Smock got off the stand on August 31.)

Once Dr. Smock's testimony concluded, Judge Gibson heard more arguments from both sides regarding the alleged Brady violation. Dr. Smock took a seat in the audience section of the courtroom as the banter went back and forth. Judge Gibson gave her ruling, stating that the court would stand in a short recess. As soon as she walked out the door towards her chambers, Dr. Smock cut a path directly toward Assistant Commonwealth Attorney Leland Hulbert. My vision was blocked by Dave Stengel's back as he stood between the two men. I was not close enough to hear what was said, but I can only imagine that Bill Smock told Leland Hulbert that he had ruined a 25-year relationship.

A photo was snapped of that encounter, and it shows Bill Smock's index finger pointing at Hulbert's chest. (It is highly unlikely that he was commenting on Leland's choice of neckwear.) We paid the *Courier-Journal* $175 for rights to publish the picture that I later labeled "the Smockdown." It was worth every penny, because that picture truly was worth a thousand words. When Smock started towards Hulbert, I thought the doctor was going to smack the lawyer. It didn't go quite that far, but I don't think Dr. Smock was whispering sweet nothings into Leland Hulbert's ear.

On September 1, the *Courier-Journal* ran an article titled "Stinson judge throws out 1,500 pages of evidence." Jason Riley wrote:

> A Jefferson Circuit Court judge threw out 1,500 pages of evidence Monday in the homicide trial of former Pleasure Ridge Park High School football coach Jason Stinson, after ruling that prosecutors turned over the information too late to the defense.
>
> Judge Susan Schultz Gibson also chastised prosecutors for

failing to tell the defense about a March interview with a medical expert who said Stinson was not responsible for the August 2008 death of sophomore Max Gilpin.

But Gibson declined to dismiss the reckless homicide and wanton endangerment charges against Stinson, whose trial is expected to last three to four weeks.

Jury selection begins Tuesday and likely will be another battle, because only two of 120 potential jurors questioned Monday said they had not heard about the case.

Gibson warned all of them to avoid further reports of the case which, she said, could be anywhere, from MSNBC to ESPN and all over the Internet.

In throwing out hundreds of pages of medical and training records, statements, and personnel files for Stinson and other PRP coaches that prosecutors have filed with the court since Wednesday, Gibson ruled they "came too late" and cannot be used—unless they benefit Stinson.

If any of the recently filed evidence is relevant to Stinson's defense, his attorneys can present it and prosecutors then would be allowed to rebut that testimony with information from the documents that have been barred, she said.

Gibson also ruled that any other evidence that comes in during the trial—prosecutors said they are still interviewing witnesses—will not be allowed.

Earlier Monday, Gibson ruled that prosecutors violated court procedure by failing to provide information from their March meeting with a medical expert who had asked to talk with them about the case. But Gibson rejected the defense attorneys' request that she dismiss the case because of that.

"I don't think a drastic sanction is warranted in this case," said Gibson, who then told prosecutors to turn over immediately to the defense any other relevant evidence from meetings with experts in the case.

Prosecutors said they had none.

The defense challenge arose after prosecutors failed to turn over information from a March 18 meeting between Commonwealth Attorney Dave Stengel and Dr. William Smock, a professor of emergency medicine at the University of Louisville.

Smock told Stengel that he believed Max's death was not a homicide, but a "tragic accident," according to court records.

Smock testified in court Monday that he went to see Stengel as a friend, so the prosecution wouldn't be "ambushed" when the case came to trial.

"I was afraid he (Stengel) had been given bad medical advice," Smock said, referring to reports that Max was dehydrated.

Prosecutors argued that Smock's views on the case had already been made public through a *Courier-Journal* interview and through other local and national media, and they had no obligation to turn over the opinions of an expert that the prosecution "never intends to call to trial." They said Smock neither examined Max nor consulted records in the case.

Gibson agreed the defense had access to the information through the media or by asking Smock, who the defense has subpoenaed to testify.

"But it's "certainly not 'no harm no foul,'" she said.

Since the trial was going to continue, jury selection was to begin that afternoon. Judge Gibson laid out a very detailed schedule she would like to keep during the jury selection process. Due to pretrial publicity, a *voir dire* was necessary to ensure a fair and impartial jury was selected. A *voir dire* could be best described as the process by which judges and lawyers select a jury from among those eligible to serve, by questioning them to determine knowledge of the facts of the case and a willingness to decide the case only on the evidence presented in court.

Typically a *voir dire* would not be conducted for a class D felony case, but the media coverage was so relentless that this would be necessary. The likelihood of finding 15 people (12 jurors and 3 alternates) in Louisville who had not heard about this was very slim.

Judge Gibson said she had been reading the comments on the *Courier-Journal*'s website, and it seemed that everyone had an opinion on this case one way or another, and some of them were very strong. It was her concern that the court act as fairly as possible when selecting a jury.

The attorneys had a big challenge in front of them: They would have to find people willing to weigh only the facts presented to them during trial.

CHAPTER 15

DAYS 2-4: JURY SELECTION AND OPENING ARGUMENTS

The second day of the trial began with 108 perspective jurors remaining after 12 were excused on day 1. Judge Gibson confirmed an order that the *voir dire* would be closed to the public, including the media. (The day before, she denied a motion to allow people from both the victim's family and the defendant's family to attend the *voir dire*, and she expanded on that ruling by also barring the media.)

She was concerned about pre-trial media coverage making perspective jurors uncomfortable, so she ruled the courtroom closed to the public once the *voir dire* began. The *Courier-Journal's* "court reporter" Jason Riley immediately called the newspaper's attorneys when he learned of Judge Gibson's ruling. Within a half hour, an attorney for the *Courier-Journal* named Kenyon Meyer approached the bench asking Judge Gibson to reverse her ruling. Judge Gibson explained that the *voir dire* could be heard from a live feed to the media room, and no one, including family, was going to be allowed in the courtroom.

Another attorney, Jon Fleischaker, showed up a short time later to argue against the order to close the courtroom. He cited a Supreme Court case ruling that stated this type of order was unconstitutional. Fleischaker cited Press Enterprise 104 Supreme Court 819, decided January 1984, when he pleaded with Judge Gibson to reverse her earlier ruling. He also cited a local high-profile murder case from a few years back where a judge attempted to close the *voir dire*, but the Court of Appeals ordered that the media and family must be admitted into the courtroom.

Judge Gibson ended up compromising to allow one member from the media to attend. She clarified that the fire code limited the courtroom occupants to 117 persons. She began to add up the people required to be in the courtroom. There were 108 jurors, two attorneys for the Commonwealth, two attorneys for the defense, the defendant, the judge, a bench clerk, and a bailiff—totaling 116 persons. These 116 people were indispensible to the courtroom proceedings, so that left room for only one more person.

Judge Gibson ruled that the one seat remaining would go to the *Courier-Journal* since the newspaper filed the motion. She said the media must sit in the jury box, and more could enter the courtroom as perspective jurors were dismissed. She also ordered that no cameras were to be fixed on the panel.

Monica Stinson (Jason's wife) wanted to be present for jury selection, but she was forced to listen to the proceeding from the media room on the 8th floor. We knew Monday afternoon that we were not going to be allowed to be present for jury selection, so we decided to go to the media room the next day.

The 8th floor media room is a rectangular shaped room, approximately 10 feet wide and 16 feet long. The room's outside wall is all glass, with a view of north downtown Louisville and the Ohio River. Every local television station, the Associated Press, a subcontractor from *Tru-TV*, and *Good Morning America* had a reporter, producer and/or camera operator set up for the tedious task of monitoring the jury selection. Some in the media room were definitely surprised when Monica Stinson and I showed up to listen as jury selection began.

Jason Stinson and his family had intentionally avoided media contact, so it was a little weird to have his wife set up shop in the middle of the dragon's lair. A photographer for the Associated Press got up and started taking pictures, and a couple of camera operators followed suit. They settled down once they got their shots, and we were allowed to listen to the proceedings. Once everyone got over the fact that we were sitting in the room, I got up with my phone and started taking pictures of everyone there. It was a nice feeling to make some of the media people uncomfortable as I unexpectedly began taking *their* pictures.

Judge Gibson heard arguments again to permit some of the disallowed evidence. Much as she did the day before, she again denied the request. In addition to hearing arguments about evidence, she had to make a ruling on the Commonwealth's request for a delay.

On September 1 the *Courier-Journal* posted an article titled "Judge denies prosecution's request to postpone Stinson trial." Jason Riley wrote:

A Jefferson circuit judge on Tuesday denied a request from prosecutors for a continuance in the trial of former Pleasure Ridge Park football coach Jason Stinson, saying that both sides have long known that, "barring something cataclysmic," the trial would start this week.

The Commonwealth Attorney's Office sought the delay after Judge Susan Schultz Gibson barred about 1,500 pages of evidence late Monday, saying it had been turned over to defense attorneys too late.

"Things we need to make our case are being excluded," Jon Heck, an Assistant Commonwealth Attorney, told Gibson Tuesday. "Do we want to do this quick or do we want to do this right?"

Heck told Gibson that the evidence being excluded contained important pediatric and prescription records for the 15-year-old who died Aug. 23 after his body temperature reached 107 degrees.

But Gibson declined to revisit her ruling or allow a postponement, which Stinson's attorneys had fought.... Also on Tuesday, Gibson initially ordered the media to leave the courtroom during jury selection. A sheriff's deputy for several minutes also would not let the media into the courtroom to hear motions on evidence, until a lawyer for the *Courier-Journal* intervened.

Jon Fleischaker, an attorney representing the newspaper, asked for a hearing, saying the media has a right to attend jury selection.

"The press is the eyes and ears of the public," he told the judge.

Fleischaker noted the newspaper won a similar argument five years ago when Judge Judith McDonald-Burkman barred the media from the courtroom during jury selection in the murder trial of then Louisville Metro Police Detective McKenzie Mattingly.

Gibson asked for a copy of that ruling, and the court took a break.

Later in the afternoon, she agreed to let a *Courier-Journal* reporter into the courtroom, but said other reporters would have to wait to enter until some potential jurors had been dismissed— only a certain number of people were allowed in the courtroom because of fire codes, she said.

Shortly after 1:30 PM, the jury panel was finally assembled to continue with the *voir dire*. At the end of day 2, eight more jurors were released. Some of these people had very strong opinions one way or another. They were unsure if they could set these feelings aside and only consider evidence presented to them at the trial. Others knew a party involved (or closely involved) in the case.

On day 3, the attorneys began to examine each juror's familiarity with the case. After going through several potential jurors, much to Judge Gibson's surprise, a juror stated that she had absolutely no knowledge of the case. Judge Gibson then said, "Ok, I've got to ask it even though it's not on the script. Where have you been?"

The juror explained that she been on bed rest and was sedated on August 20, 2008, and knew nothing of the case. When questioned further, she again confirmed that she had not read or seen any accounts regarding this case at all.

This individual line of questioning continued into day 4, and finally a jury was able to be selected. The gender make-up of the jurors was 10 men and 5 women, so the Commonwealth challenged that the defense had eliminated some potential jurors because of their gender. (The defense had eliminated 8 women and 2 men, while the prosecution used its ten strikes to eliminate 7 men and 3 women. The challenge based on gender could have been made from either side.) Judge Gibson denied the challenge, and Commonwealth vs. Football was set to begin.

With the jury finally selected and all objections ruled upon, opening arguments were ready to commence. Assistant Commonwealth Attorney Leland Hulbert presented the Commonwealth's opening argument. The following are excerpts of Leland Hulbert's opening arguments. To include all of it would take nearly 20 pages, so only portions are printed in this book. (It can be seen uncut at the book's website www.factorsunknown.com or at www.courier-journal.com.)

> Good afternoon ladies and gentlemen of the jury. On August 20, 2008, a practice occurred on the [PRPHS] field. This is a place where boys ages 13, 14, 15, 16, 17 and a couple of 18-year-olds went to practice high school football, America's game.
>
> There are over a hundred witnesses to this event, so if one person says 5:55 and one person says 5:56, use your common

sense. But at approximately 3:45 or 4 o'clock, people went out on the practice field that day, August 20, 2008. Maxwell Gilpin was one of them....

What comes with being head coach of a football team in the state of Kentucky? Training, lots of training.... You've got CPR training that involves emergency training. You've got rules that you have to follow; there's a medical symposium. We'll talk about a couple of these things.

Coach Stinson was trained in CPR; it's required on a yearly basis. He had his training in July 2007. It is supposed to be a yearly training, but you will find that in August of 2008, he had not renewed his training....

At 94 degrees and under, you must provide ample amounts of water. These are important rules. Water should always be available. Athletes should be able to take in as much water as they desire.

Coach Stinson also attended a medical symposium. It's mandated by the KHSAA, and this is one of the slides they had at that class: How to notice heat exhaustion and how to notice heatstroke. We'll go through these in detail, but we will submit to you that—based on player testimony, coach testimony, and witness testimony—Max Gilpin exhibited many of these signs and not just the ones on heat exhaustion, but also the ones on heatstroke.

Some of the kids weren't jogging back from a water break, so [Stinson's] going to get them on the line and they're going to run. No more practice, it's time to run. Now you'll hear that they ran at practice.... You'll also hear this was the first time they ever ran this early in football practice, and it was the most gassers they ever ran in any football practice the entire year.

On a 94-degree day when kids are fighting for starting spots, it's the most gassers they ran all year, and coach told them to get on the line. He had the big whistle, his little safari hat, his little gray t-shirt. He blows the whistle, tells them to get on the line, and we're going to run until somebody quits.

Stop running and quit on all your teammates and don't come back, or just run and never stop running. That was the choice they had that day.

Coach Stinson put himself out in the middle of a field with a whistle, watched all the kids line up there, and blew the whistle to start a gasser. Then they go back and up and back...

They didn't have any ice out there that day though. It was 94 degrees, kids vomiting, kids falling out, two kids in the hospital, no ice. No ice towels, no ice buckets, no ice, so they had to borrow used ice in a plastic bag to try to help Antonio Calloway.

They're doing up/down, up/down, up/down, and finally, a senior on the team quits. Is he [Stinson] supportive, or does he say something like, "ding, ding, ding, we have a winner"?

Coach Stinson was trained in how to know the signs of heatstroke and how to deal with it. Coach Stinson never got within 10 feet of Max Gilpin the entire time.

Four or five kids tried to get water after running the gassers. Coach goes out of his way to yell at them, "you're not getting any water 'til we have our team meeting."

The cause of Max's death will not be in dispute, but what led to that cause may be. You may have heard of the drug Adderall®. Adderall® is an ADHD medication that Max Gilpin was taking. Adderall® is a type of amphetamine, and what you will hear is that no study in the United States or Europe has linked a low dose of Adderall® to heatstroke.

[Stinson] put competition and winning, winning his first game as a head football coach, ahead of safety.

Who started this barbaric practice? Who made 'em run more gassers than they ever ran all year? Coach Stinson. And who was the one who never helped? [Coach Stinson.] He never helped number 61 that day. He never helped Max."

The following is an excerpt of Brian Butler's opening argument for the defense. It can be seen uncut at the book's website www.factorsunknown. com or at www.courier-journal.com.

I've never said this before. I want each and every one of you to reflect during this trial on what that man just told you, because it was the most exaggerated account of what happened that you will ever hear. Some of it is out-and-out falsehoods; some of it is taken from one player and disregarding the others.

How much time did you hear this man talk about water? Long time, talked for an hour. Max Gilpin wasn't dehydrated when he got to Kosair hospital. Let me repeat that: Max Gilpin wasn't dehydrated. That's just one example of the nonsense that he just told you.

This case—and I want to come back to some of the things he said—this case isn't about whether you like the way Jason coached football or whether you didn't. Mind you, you'll hear lots of kids that come in here who loved Jason Stinson, but it really isn't about that.

Your job as jurors is to decide a criminal case, whether or not they prove beyond a reasonable doubt that Jason recklessly caused the death of Max Gilpin. And I'm going to tell you a little bit about what that means, so you know whether he wantonly endangered the life of Max Gilpin.

On August 20, 2008, there were between 50 and 100 Pleasure Ridge Park football players practicing. There were practices being conducted by public and private high schools throughout Jefferson County and throughout the Kentuckiana area. I suspect that there were people running in parks throughout the Kentuckiana area; I suspect there were people running on the roads. Why is that important? Because tragically, one person died of an exertional heatstroke.

Nobody else did. So all these players who were playing that day, no one else had an exertional heatstroke. Questions to ask yourselves as you process this information: what's different about Max, why Max? Keep that in mind throughout, because no one else died.

Jason would schedule certain things within his practice. He would schedule water breaks. He would schedule different periods and they would actually have—and if you get to know him, he's a little bit anal retentive so they actually have—these things printed out about when things were going to happen.

These players' statements are all over the place. Do your best to try to put together what they say, but they're going to be very different accounts. On average the players will say they had three to four water breaks during this 4:15 to 5:20 time period. You'll hear some that may say it was two water breaks, some that'll say it was five or six, but on average they're going to say it's about three to four water breaks.

You're going to hear different accounts and try to piece it together. During that time, and what was left a little bit out of the opening statement, the Commonwealth—when it presented the case to the grand jury—told the grand jury it was 30 to 40 minutes of conditioning.

So that's what we're talking about, we're talking about 30 to 40 minutes of conditioning. Now—a little bit unclear during [the Commonwealth] opening—during that 30 to 40 minutes of conditioning, each individual player is going to tell you that he was resting half the time. Let me repeat that, during the 30 to 40 minutes of conditioning each individual player was resting half the time.

On average, approximately, these players ran a mile and a half, give or take; a mile and a half. It was 94 degrees. You will hear about these rules and regulations, when it's 94 and below, water breaks are optional under the Kentucky High School Athletic Association rules; optional. You'll see the schedule; they weren't optional at PRP. Jason had them built into his schedule.

So you had some kids like Calloway who were just up and getting it. You have other kids who are literally walking, laughing, dogging it, and that's why they did the up/downs and you have most of the kids that are doing it, they're jogging, they're somewhere in between.

Max's father's there. When Max's not coming around, they call 911. 911 shows up. They begin doing the same things. They begin icing him down, and they load him up and they take him to Kosair Children's Hospital. If you listen to that, you'll just believe the boy dropped on the field and everybody wanted him to die. That is absurd. Everyone went to this kid. Jason didn't even see him go down. Jason's over with the rest of the team.

We went out and got multiple doctors to try to explain this. Let me tell you a little bit about who you're going to hear from, before we go into exactly the factors that contribute. You'll hear from Dan Danzel, chief of the department at the University of Louisville. He is a world renowned expert on heatstroke. He is an emergency room doctor. He's testifying and will testify for free. Dr. Danzel will tell you—and much, much better than I just did—about his opinion that Max Gilpin was not dehydrated.

You will hear from a medical examiner because we are going to call one. You will hear from Dr. George Nichols, formally the chief medical examiner of the state of Kentucky. George started our medical examiner's office. We didn't have one until he came around. Thirty-five years, he worked for all of us, did thousands of autopsies, rendered his opinion as to cause of death thousands of times. In spite of what you heard over here about no autopsy, you know what George is going to tell you? In 35 years, I never remember a homicide case in Louisville, Kentucky prosecuted without an autopsy. Never. You know how much we're paying George? Nothing.

So, how'd this train get rolling? ..... It's a tragedy, but tragedies happen. Some didn't like Jason's coaching style that day and it got reported. Based on that, they launched the largest homicide investigation in the history of Louisville, Kentucky, and they set detectives out with pre-set questions.

Now if any of you have ever known anybody in law enforcement, that ain't the way it's done. Those questions were primarily about water breaks—how much water was given that day and how long they ran. Nobody ever did an autopsy, ever. Nobody ever talked to an expert.

And then they came, from near and far—the cameras. Everybody's watching. It's too late to do the right thing, everybody's watching. It's too late to do the right thing, because they were wrong. They were wrong.

Don't for a second think that this is not a tragedy. This is a tragedy that Max Gilpin died. But what this trial's going to show you, because this is a criminal trial, that it has been nothing but a witch hunt by these people. And when you've heard it all, you're going to come back to this man. We don't have to prove anything to you. Your verdict forms are going to say, guilty or not guilty, because it's their burden. THIS MAN IS INNOCENT!

CHAPTER 16

CROCKETT AND GILPIN TESTIMONY

Day 5 started with the Commonwealth's case. Leland Hulbert had said some really dramatic things in his opening argument the day before. Brian Butler called them falsehoods and misrepresentations of the truth, but where Jason and I come from, we'd just call it a lie. That doesn't mean everything he said was not true, but there were over 30 instances of where the truth was either bent, stretched, or completely violated. I remembered thinking when he was done, "that's real nice; good luck proving that, Leland."

We surmised that the first witness for the Commonwealth would probably be Max's mother, Glenna Michele Crockett. She was going to testify, because she could not attend the trial until she had done so. It made perfect sense that the Commonwealth would call Max's mother and his father, Jeffrey Dean Gilpin, as early as they possibly could. Holding true to what was expected, the Commonwealth began Friday morning by calling Mrs. Crockett to the stand.

Her testimony was emotional, to say the least, but very little that she said was damning to Stinson. Family pictures including Max were shown to the jury. Crockett was asked to identify Max in the pictures, which of course, made her voice tremble with emotion at times.

Assistant Commonwealth Attorney Jon Heck questioned Mrs. Crockett. She testified that Max gained "maybe 20–25 lbs" and "I would say 2–3 inches" when asked if Max had any weight gain or increase in height from the beginning of the 9th grade to the beginning of the 10th grade. During questioning, she also stated Max didn't like to take his medication.

She testified to buying Max the supplement Creatine from GNC in March or April, 2008. She said she had knowledge of his Creatine use starting then. She did not closely regulate the amount of Creatine that Max was taking. She did not say when he discontinued its use, but said she did not buy any through the summer, and in their investigation, the police collected a bottle from her home with several pills in it.

She said when she arrived at the high school, Max's eyes were half open and bloodshot. She remembered Stinson was over with the team when she arrived. With her attention on Max, she first noticed Stinson on the other side of the stretcher after EMS arrived. She recounted that those attending to Max were holding an ice bag to his neck and running water over the ice.

She said [after Max died] she was approached by Deputy County Coroner Sam Weakley, who told her an autopsy was not necessary. When Asst. Commonwealth Attorney Jon Heck asked if she requested an autopsy, she replied "no."

During the defense's cross examination, she testified that she shared joint custody with her ex-husband. She normally had Max on Monday and Wednesday. Max's father had him Tuesday and Thursday, and they alternated weekends.

She stated that Max's use of Adderall® was listed on Max's physical form and was disclosed to PRPHS. She would fill the prescription once a month and give half to Jeff and she kept half at her house. "I never gave it to Max; I always gave it to Jeff. Whenever we exchanged, I would give it to Jeff." She said, "We had to tell Max every morning to take the medicine. He didn't want to take his medicine." Under redirect by Jon Heck, Crockett stated that Max had the amount of Adderall® needed at his father's home. She testified Max did not take Adderall® during the summer because he didn't like the side effects. She also said that he suffered from ADD and not ADHD, because he didn't have the hyperactive problems. She said Max began taking his medication again on August 7.

She described Jeff and Max's relationship as good and healthy. She recalled that Jeff encouraged Max to lift weights and play football. She said Jeff was very interested in Max's football activities. She recounted that Max was proud of his weight gain, lifting weights and playing football.

It was not unusual for Jeff to attend practices, and he was at the practice field when she arrived. She didn't think he would be there since he was supposed to be going out of town.

She was excused from the witness stand, and the Commonwealth asked the court for permission to allow Mrs. Crockett to remain in the courtroom. This was not met with any objections by the defense. There were three other witnesses who testified between Mrs. Crockett and Mr. Gilpin, and their testimony is detailed in the next chapter.

Day 6 began with Max's father, Jeff Gilpin, taking the stand. His testimony should have lasted only an hour or so, but it extended well past lunch because of arguments over his testimony. Apparently he had given answers to a sworn interrogatory in March 2009 that did not match his current testimony, and Stinson's defense attorney Brian Butler took exception to that.

Jeff Gilpin was called to the stand by Leland Hulbert, and he described Max's history with sports. He stated that Max played tee ball, baseball, soccer and basketball, and that he played youth league football during 5th and 6th grades. He went on to say, "Before his freshman year, he came to me and said he wanted to play football. He came to me in the 8th grade, the winter right after Christmas, and said he wanted to start going to the gym."

He testified that he and Max worked out two to three times a week, for four to five months, for an hour to an hour and 15 minutes a day "on the nights I had him." He stated that Max grew from 6' to almost a little over 6'2." He weighed almost 220 when he died, and "he gained approximately 27–28 lbs." He stated they never worked out every day together.

Gilpin recounted telling Max about his own personal (ages 22–27) use of steroids and how he had told Max he didn't want someone telling him, "These are a miracle." "I didn't want him to buy into these. If he had any questions, I wanted him to ask me, his mother, or one of his aunts who worked in the medical profession."

In talking about a scrimmage on August 15, 2008, he told about watching Max play. "I had never seen him play really good like that. I was pleasantly surprised." He recalled purchasing Max two 32oz. Gatorades® on the way home from the August 19 practice. Max had one of them "emptied" before they arrived home in Brooks, which is about 15 minutes from PRPHS. He stated Max ate fried chicken, mashed potatoes, green beans, and rolls. "I don't think he went back for seconds, but he ate a healthy plateful."

He then testified that they watched TV, and around 8 PM, Max said he had a headache. Gilpin told Max to get a "couple of ibuprofen" and told him to take them with water. "Keep drinking fluids." Max finished his other Gatorade® and then had either iced tea or a fruit punch drink. He went to bed around 9 PM with the drink and a couple of cookies. Gilpin stated he saw Max again the next morning, when he woke him up for school at 5 or 10 minutes after 6 AM.

When he was asked about Max's Adderall® administration at his home, Gilpin stated "Max would usually bring some from his mother's house, usually 8 to 10 at a time. I did not see him take it that morning." He said that they did find some Adderall® up in Max's room. He found seven or eight capsules in Max's sock drawer.

Gilpin recounted that Max ate an egg, cheese, and bacon biscuit along with a pint of chocolate milk before school on August 20. Gilpin testified that Max said his headache was gone, and he didn't see anything wrong with Max that morning.

Gilpin stated that he arrived at practice "after 5," and that he was wearing shorts and a tank top. "I didn't even have my phone with me." He was watching practice from the south end of the field, under the tree behind the bleachers. He said he would look up every once in a while and "I remember seeing Max bent over throwing up. Max kinda wiped himself off and at some point they took off their helmets and shoulder pads."

He stated that Dale Hibbs nudged him to say that Max was cramping up, and that Max was about 75–80 yards from them at this time. He was trying to make it to the sideline. He was pretty much down to a slow trot. That's when Stinson said, "Ding, ding we have a winner." Max turned around and started heading back. As soon as he crossed the line, he went down on all fours. "I kinda froze. He staggered, tried to get back up, but went back down. That's when two kids tried to carry him; they got under each arm. He was unresponsive; his feet were dragging, his toes were dragging. They might have carried him 15–20 yards. That's when they waved, and we ran out there."

Gilpin said he thought Max would "shake it off," or that he was just a little dizzy or something. He didn't realize how serious it was, even when he got to him. Max was making a loud moaning sound on exhale, very loud. "His eyes were rolled back in his head; you couldn't even see his pupils."

He also described Max as "a little warm," but not as hot as he expected him to be. He said Max was sweating a little, and his face was pale. A minute or so went by, then Craig Webb pulled up on the Gator™. The coaches put an ice pack on Max, and they loaded him up on the Gator™ and took him to the water station, which was 75 yards away.

He went on to explain at the time of Max's death he didn't blame the coaches, because he was in shock. "It takes a while to absorb what happened."

Gilpin told the news stations he didn't see anything wrong at that point, because he didn't see the coaches point a finger at Max or deny him water or anything like that. He said he attended PRP football games after Max's death because other kids and players were his only connection to Max. As the season went on, questions started to arise that he didn't have answers for. He said when the reports started coming out, he still believed the coaches had done no wrong.

Under cross examination by Brian Butler, Gilpin testified that Max never took Creatine around him, and Max said he quit taking it around mid May. When asked if he recalled telling Sgt. Butler that from November 2007 through January 2008 Max used premixed Creatine under his supervision, he replied, "I don't remember telling him that." He stated that he knew that some drinks the gym sold had Creatine in them. They would occasionally get one of those that were fruit flavored. He was asked again, "Did you tell Sgt. Butler that from November 2007 to January 2008, Max used premixed Creatine under your supervision?"

He answered "Yes, but I don't think that is an accurate statement, the way you phrase it." He said he didn't recall making that statement and that his son had just died.

Gilpin attended practices on 8/18 and 8/19. He also attended the August 20 practice, even though it was not his night to have Max. He was going out of town on a business trip, and he wanted to swing by and see how practice was going, and he didn't even think Max knew he was there.

Using Gilpin's phone records, Butler established that Jeff Gilpin arrived at the practice at 5:37 PM, and Gilpin agreed. Butler confirmed that Gilpin saw all of the coaches present that day.

Butler asked Gilpin if he recalled speaking with the police, giving two interviews to WHAS-11 TV, and answering sworn interrogatories. Gilpin said he remembered each situation. Butler asked, "At any of these times, did you ever mention you saw your son throw up that day?" Gilpin answered, "I can't remember. I don't know what I spoke of back then."

Butler asked, "You're not familiar with ever saying that before, are you?"

Jeff Gilpin replied, "I thought I did. I know I talked to other family and friends about it, because there were several kids throwing up that day."

Butler then showed Jeff Gilpin his police interview and his answers to the interrogatories. "You didn't mention that in the court filing or in your interview with the police, did you?"

Gilpin replied, "No, I don't think so."

Butler then asked, "Mr. Gilpin, when Max collapsed, did you believe Coach Stinson witnessed that collapse?"

Gilpin testified, "I don't know how he could not see him."

"Did you in the answer to interrogatories say Coach Stinson did not notice Max had gone down?" asked Butler.

Gilpin said, "I don't know if I said that or not. I don't remember a lot of things I said back in September right after my son died."

Butler fired back, "I'm showing you interrogatories that were filed in March of 2009."

Gilpin just said, "Okay."

At that moment, Jon Heck tried to come to Gilpin's rescue with another objection. An extensive argument began as to whether Gilpin's interrogatories were admissible for the purposes of impeaching Gilpin. An agreement could not be quickly achieved, so Judge Gibson put the court in a 10-minute recess. As the jurors filed out, Alex Dathorne requested to discuss the issue without the witness present. Judge Gibson agreed by dismissing Jeff Gilpin from the witness stand.

Ten minutes went by and still no agreement could be reached, so it was suggested that everyone break for lunch in order to give both sides time to prepare their arguments as to whether this document was admissible or not.

Upon returning from lunch, Judge Gibson heard brief arguments from both sides, and then she ruled in favor of the defense. "Based on everything that I have read, I think that these statements may be used as prior inconsistent statements to question or impeach the witness."

Butler picked up where he left off with his questioning of Jeff Gilpin. Heck objected again. After a brief bench conference, his objection was overruled and Butler was allowed to continue.

"On April 21, 2009, did you not swear that when Coach Stinson called for the players to stop running, he did not notice Max had gone down?"

Gilpin replied, "I believe I stated that, but how was I to know if he noticed him or not? He didn't acknowledge Max going down; let's put it that way."

Butler continued to pick Gilpin's testimony apart. He then asked, "Is it fair to say—prior to August 20, 2008—that you had seen your son run harder in hotter weather?"

Jeff Gilpin explained, "I did make that statement and I think they have practiced in hotter weather, but I don't think he ran nearly as long or as hard."

Butler then asked, "But you do acknowledge that you told the police on September 4th that he'd run harder in hot weather and that you didn't know what happened?"

Gilpin dryly replied, "Right."

Attempting to set the record straight, Butler brought up the WHAS-11 TV interview. "On that particular day, do you recall telling Renee Murphy the coaches didn't do anything wrong?"

"I don't remember saying that in those exact words. That may be well what she reported, but..."

"Do you recall saying on October 15th, nearly two months after that, that Max had run further in hotter weather for longer?"

"I believe I did say that, yes."

"Do you recall telling Renee Murphy that the coaches did everything they could, that I would have done?

"Yes."

"Do you recall telling her that Max was never denied water?"

"I didn't see anybody deny him water while I was there. That's correct."

Butler then asked, "Do you recall telling her you didn't see anything wrong with practice?"

"At that point, yes."

Butler inquired, "And those statements were all made five days short of two months after this happened, correct?"

"Correct."

Butler asked his last question, "And give or take you were at this practice from around 5:37 PM until EMS arrived and left, correct?"

"Right. I left when EMS did."

Once Butler sat down, Hulbert decided he would like to redirect Gilpin. They spoke about Max's diet, and then Hulbert mentioned Gilpin's phone records. He asked what the team was doing when he arrived. He then wanted to make sure he asked again, "And I'm asking you now what specifically you saw. Did you see your son throw up on the field that day?"

"Yes, I did," replied Gilpin.

Brian Butler was given the chance to ask Gilpin some additional questions. "I want to go back to some of the statements you made. You're saying you saw your son throw up. At that point you didn't go intervene, did you?

"No," Gilpin said.

Butler then went for the jugular. "Can you explain why, on August 20, you called the doctor's office—Haller, Hazlett and Adams—three times during that day?"

Once again, Heck sprang into action with an objection. He argued that it was beyond the scope of the redirect, and Judge Gibson agreed by sustaining Heck's objection.

The bell could not be "un-rung," so Heck asked to have the question struck, but Judge Gibson declined.

Brian Butler said he did not have any more questions for Gilpin, so the judge excused him from the stand.

CHAPTER 17

Days 5–6: The Commonwealth's Case

After Michele Crockett testified, the Commonwealth filled the rest of day 5 with individuals who had trained Jason Stinson or who were responsible for the Kentucky High School Athletic Association, Stinson's governing body.

One witness was Tom Steltenkamp, a certified athletic trainer and practice manager employed by Ellis and Badenhausen. He taught the required medical symposium that Jason Stinson attended in June 2008. He testified that with heatstroke, you should dial 911 as soon as possible and when asked again in a little different way, he agreed that 911 should be called immediately.

Steltenkamp is considered the "go-to guy" for training in the local area. He stated it is easy for a professional to miss a heatstroke and that a few hours of training every few years doesn't make coaches experts. He testified that the Kentucky Medical Association and the KHSAA require head coaches to attend medical symposiums once every two years. Coaches are taught five different subjects during their three-hour symposium. He further stated that only ten minutes of the symposium covers heat illnesses, and that coaches are not trained enough.

Steltenkamp covered three different stages of heat illness: Stage 1—heat cramps, Stage 2—heat exhaustion, and Stage 3—heatstroke. He said diet, caffeine, supplements, lack of sleep, and medication including amphetamines all can contribute to heatstroke. He also covered the signs and symptoms of heat exhaustion, and stated that an affected athlete should be moved to a cool shaded area. He further stated that heat exhaustion is very common, but heatstroke is entirely different, and it can happen without warning. He also testified that heatstroke can occur without dehydration.

Brian Butler conducted the cross examination and asked if a heatstroke could be overlooked by the most trained professional. Steltenkamp answered "yes." He added that a coach doesn't have a fraction of the experience or knowledge of a certified athletic trainer, and he stated only a few of the schools have certified athletic trainers.

Steltenkamp had heard about teams practicing as much as nine hours in a day, but he believed PRPHS's practice on August 20, 2008 was only two hours. He said many areas with much hotter weather do not have the restrictions that Kentucky has, and that 30–40 minutes of conditioning is not considered excessive. He was not aware of any rules that stated high school athletes cannot run 30–40 minutes. He would not stop practice or a game for one or two players experiencing breathing problems; he said he would treat that individual.

Another witness was Tim Amshoff, a high school physical education teacher currently teaching at Iroquois High School. Amshoff taught the CPR/AED class Jason Stinson attended on July 25, 2007. He stated that in the particular class Jason Stinson attended, he does not teach the importance of dialing 911. He teaches coaches to secure the scene first, and then he describes the "check, call, care" procedure.

When questioned by Jon Heck, Amshoff said the KHSAA requires American Red Cross CPR training for laypersons or coaches every year. He stated that the American Red Cross has a 30-day grace period for renewals. He stated that the certification of anyone who attended the July 12, 2007 symposium would have expired by August 20, 2008, if he or she had not renewed it by then. When Amshoff was shown the July 12, 2007 class attendees list at PRPHS, he could not find Jason Stinson's name on this sheet. When he was shown the July 25, 2007 class attendees list at Waggener High School, he found Jason Stinson's name. He stated that would mean Jason Stinson was properly accredited on August 20, 2008.

The Commonwealth spent a great deal of time trying to prove Jason Stinson did not have a valid CPR certificate on August 20, but all it did was prove he *was* certified. (It turns out that the prosecutors just assumed that since Jason didn't attend the class held annually at PRPHS in 2007 or 2008, he must not have gotten recertified. They didn't bother to check into whether he may have possibly attended the class somewhere else. (That must have been a very humbling feeling when Dathorne proved the prosecution's whole argument false and used *their* documents to prove it.)

After witnessing most of his argument torn to shreds, Heck redirected with a line of questioning that intended to have Amschoff agree that 911 should be called immediately. Heck presented several scenarios that he believed Amschoff would answer "dial 911," but Amschoff would either answer "no," or reply he wasn't comfortable answering that question. He then stated that a person—people who are drunk, not wanting to participate, or even having a panic attack—could present false symptoms. He stated there are times when someone has collapsed that may not be an emergency situation.

A third witness was Julian Tackett, the Assistant Commissioner who has been with the KHSAA for 26 years. He covered training requirements that all head coaches must complete. He told the jury that "ample amounts of water" didn't mean you have to stop a drill or game. He also stated that it did not break any rule to condition for 30–40 minutes.

Upon questioning by Leland Hulbert, Tackett stated that under 95 degrees, all heat play rules are "optional," but 95 degrees would require a 10-minute water break every 30 minutes. He stated "safety first" is the policy of KHSAA. When asked if competition should ever be put ahead of safety, he answered "no."

During cross examination by Brian Butler, Tackett stated that, by rule, a coach would not have to schedule in any water breaks at 94 degrees and did not break any rules if he conditioned athletes for 30–40 minutes. He stated that PRP could have held two four-hour practices on August 20, 2008, without violating any rules.

The Commonwealth didn't have any more witnesses to call that day, so court was put into recess a couple hours early on day 5. It was the Friday before Labor Day, so no one objected.

Day 6 began with Max's father, Jeff Gilpin, taking the stand. (His testimony was detailed in the previous chapter.)

> **Kentucky High School Athletic Association Heat Guidelines under 95°**
>
> Provide ample water. This means water should alwasy be available, and athletes should be able to take in as much water as they want. Provide optional 10-minute water breaks every 30 minutes. Ice down towels for cooling. Monitor athletes carefully.
>
> KHSAA REG. 1-2-21

His testimony was followed by the testimonies of Brian Bale and Joann Gayle, two witnesses from the soccer game. (Bale and Gayle were two of the five witnesses quoted in the *Courier-Journal* regarding water denial allegations.) The day ended with two players, Ben Bickett and Antonio Calloway, taking the stand. (Calloway was the player transported to the hospital along with Max Gilpin.)

Jon Heck called Lawrence "Brian" Bale to the stand for the Commonwealth. Bale testified he was at PRPHS on August 20, 2008, to watch his daughter play soccer for Waggener High School (WHS). Bale said he arrived around "20 to 6 or 5:35 PM, somewhere around there." He testified to eventually turning his attention from the soccer game to the football practice. He stated that he heard a coach reprimanding a player for asking for water. He did not hear the player ask specifically.

He testified that the running continued for an hour. He said he didn't see Max Gilpin go down, and he believed the ambulance arrived about the time he was leaving the soccer game. Bale was shown an e-mail he wrote, and Heck asked him why he wrote it. Bale stated, "I thought that the practice may have been a little excessive, and I thought somebody should know." The e-mail said, "Kids were verbally reprimanded for asking for water, and they needed somebody to quit before the running would stop."

Alex Dathorne handled the cross-examination for the defense. Bale agreed that he just saw a small snapshot of the practice that day, and he wouldn't have known if the players were given water breaks before he arrived. Bale was not certain who was doing all the yelling, but he did see Stinson yelling a few times.

Jon Heck next called Jo Ann Gayle to the stand. She testified that she and Bale arrived at "5:30ish" and the football players were running sprints with their equipment on. Heck then asked her if there was a coach in the middle of the field, and did she remember what he looked like? She testified, "I don't know what he looked like. I know he had on a floppy hat." Heck showed her a picture, and she said, "That's the floppy hat."

She recalled, "I saw one kid vomiting. The others were bent over, gasping and spitting. They were sweating so much, I couldn't tell if they were crying. Actually I think they were just sweating a lot. . . ."

Gayle further testified, "They ran the whole time that I was there, until right before 7:00." Media coverage of the situation was then discussed. She stated, "We had seen some news coverage and found a lot of the statements made by an athletic director and principal were incorrect and I felt kind of like, you know, somebody needs to know the truth about this because this isn't how it went down. So we just thought that someone needed to know."

Heck thanked her for her time, and then Alex Dathorne began his cross examination. She described seeing Gilpin with bags of ice around him on the cart. She estimated there were probably three or four bags on each side.

Gayle confirmed that the players ran until around 7:00 PM. She said they ran for about an hour and a half. She said the ambulance arrived around 7:00 PM. Dathorne went back to Gayle's timeline and asked her if she could possibly be mistaken. She didn't believe so, because she got there around 5:30 PM and she knew she was still there about 7:00 PM, to a quarter after 7:00. When Dathorne confronted her with the fact that the ambulance was called at 6:17, she stated, "I was wondering why it was taking so long for an ambulance to get there. But no, I was not aware that one was called."

The court stood in a short recess, and it was confirmed that the media was not supposed to show any of the children's faces while they testified. (The issue was brought up because the Commonwealth planned to begin calling players after the recess.)

After the recess, Jon Heck called Benjamin Bickett to the stand. Ben Bickett was a 16-year-old junior on August 20, 2008. He is currently a senior and said he has played football since the 6th grade, with the exception of his sophomore year. He testified that he is a 6-foot, 3-inch defensive end. Bickett then detailed for the jury what a "gasser" was and how it was performed. He said ten gassers would usually be the maximum amount they would run in a day. Bickett later described the August 20 practice. He said Coach Stinson had gotten a little angry with them, and he didn't let them go get water after coming out of the team drill. He stated they went straight to gassers.

He remembered Stinson saying that they were not hustling enough and that Stinson told the team to "get on the line." He knew that meant the team was about to start running. He said he ran 20–25 gassers. Bickett stated Coach Stinson said the running would stop when somebody quit or at 6:15. He said David Englert quit—that he just took off his helmet and walked off the field. Bickett said that was when Coach Stinson said, "Ding, ding, ding, we have a winner!"

Bickett stated that he had never run that hard before in a football practice. He also stated he couldn't spit, but "other than being thirsty, I was okay."

Brian Butler cross-examined Bickett, who stated he had at least three water breaks during practice. He testified that the running began shortly after the soccer game started. Bickett said the team usually runs every day there is practice, which is typically 4 to 5 days a week after July 15.

Bickett testified that the gassers where not timed that day, but Coach Stinson was removing players from the run who were trying hard. He agreed that as a player he knew the running would stop at 6:15 regardless, because some players had to catch an activities bus home. He also agreed that players were running from a full sprint to jogging. He said Coach Stinson made the ones walking and laughing do "up/downs."

Day 6's final witness was Antonio Calloway. He was called to the stand by Jon Heck. He was an 18-year-old senior wide receiver on August 20, 2008, and as mentioned earlier, he was transported to the hospital along with Max Gilpin. He stated that the team was just walking around, so Coach Stinson made them run gassers.

He testified that, after his collapse, the first thing he remembered was being on the back of the Gator™. He had a water bottle in his hands and some ice packs on his back. He said he remembered getting into the ambulance and the ride to the hospital.

It seemed Antonio suffered from what I jokingly call "police induced amnesia, or PIA." PIA occurs when a police officer shows up asking a bunch of questions. Something about the officer's probing must trigger a self-defense mechanism in the brain of the person being interviewed. This type of reaction usually is accompanied by phrases such as "I didn't see anything," and "I don't remember what happened." Calloway also didn't recall being told players would have to run until someone quit the team, but he explained that "things tend to be said" at football practices.

Alex Dathorne handled the questioning of Antonio Calloway for the defense. Calloway testified that the team would run 10–12 gassers on a normal day. He explained that he was running as fast as he could since he (Calloway) was angry with the team because everybody had been slacking and he was trying to set an example for the rest of the team. He admitted to being a little upset that he was not one of the first players pulled out of the run for good effort.

He recalled coaches saying things like "we're going do this until somebody quits" since playing youth football at age 10 or 11. Calloway agreed that coaches have said all kinds of things to him throughout the years to motivate him. He also agreed that coaches were not trying to hurt him by doing this.

In an attempt to be brief because it was so late in the day, Dathorne wrapped up his questioning, but Heck decided to go further. (That was probably a mistake because Calloway didn't respond like Heck probably thought he would.) Heck asked if the kids in Little League had to run until one of them quit the team, and Calloway replied, "Sometimes." Heck was surprised and then asked Calloway if kids leaving the field had been kicked off the team. Calloway explained they didn't actually get kicked off; it was just a saying to make them run.

After the court broke for the day, the defense went to the back room to reflect on the past couple of days of testimony. One attorney not representing Stinson, but who was present, stated. "You could not be doing much better at this point." He was absolutely correct with that assessment. Between the botched attempt at proving Coach Stinson's CPR certification had expired, Tackett stating that water breaks are optional at 94 degrees, and Bale and Gayle failing to get their timelines straight, things were not going so well for the prosecution.

As well as everything had gone over the last two days of testimony, there was still a reason to remain cautious. The Commonwealth still planned to call more players and soccer parents, in addition to a few medical experts.

CHAPTER 18

DAYS 7-8: THE COMMONWEALTH'S CASE CONTINUES

Day 7 was the day with the most witnesses. The morning began with Susan Fife, the parent who ran the soccer concession stand and witnessed Jason Stinson tell four players to get out of the water and go to a team meeting. In addition to Fife, the Commonwealth called nine players and a student manager who were in attendance that day. If at times it seems the testimony of a player is brief, it is because the testimony becomes repetitive.

Susan Fife is the parent of a PRPHS soccer player. She was at the complex on August 20, 2008, to work at a concession table set up for the soccer parents and players. She arrived around 5:45 to 6:00 PM, and she recalled Antonio Calloway's breathing difficulties. She then testified to seeing six to eight players going to the water area. She said Stinson came after them, yelling and saying they were a bunch of babies; they would never win at anything because they couldn't follow directions. She believed the players went to the meeting from there. She testified the assistant athletic director from PRPHS came over to get ice from her.

Alex Dathorne, who questioned Fife for the defense, mostly went over what she had testified to moments earlier. She said she could not see what was happening on the practice field, but she could hear Stinson yelling.

The next witness was Christian Vincent, a junior defensive tackle at the August 20 practice. He said he knew Max, and he would help him with his weight lifting in the weight room. He testified Max was trying to get stronger so he could get a starting position his junior year. He said he was involved in extra instruction before the last water break, and he did not receive a water break. Instead, he went straight to gassers. He recalled that after he got sick, Coach Stinson allowed him to stop running. He stated he began running again on his own after taking two or three gassers off. He said Stinson had called him a coward, and he seemed disappointed in the effort the players were exhibiting. He recalled Coach Stinson telling players they could not get water until after the meeting.

Upon cross-examination by Alex Dathorne, Christian Vincent agreed that gassers are usually timed, but they were not timed on August 20. The players were running at their own pace, and no one made him start running again after he stopped. He explained whenever Stinson would call somebody a coward, he was just saying they were afraid to challenge themselves past their normal limits.

The second player of the day to be called for the prosecution was Daniel Farris. He told Leland Hulbert that he was a junior on the PRP football team on August 20, 2008, but he did not participate in the conditioning portion of the practice. He explained that he was feeling dizzy during a drill, and Coach Webb told him to go sit under the shade tree. He said the coach had put a bag of ice on his neck that he kept there until Antonio Calloway came off the field. Farris testified that one of the coaches took the ice from him and didn't give him another ice bag because by that time he was fine.

Brian Butler only had a few questions for this witness. Farris agreed that his coaches had told him on numerous occasions to tell them if he did not feel well. He also agreed the coaches had said they wanted to know if something was wrong, and he didn't suffer any consequences from the coaches because he asked to sit out that day because he didn't feel well.

David Englert, a senior on the PRPHS football team on August 20, 2008, was called to the stand by Leland Hulbert. (Englert is the player who quit during the up/downs, invoking the "Ding, ding, ding... we have a winner!" comment from Coach Stinson.) He said the players just weren't running like they were supposed to. Many players were walking around, and they weren't going to drills "like we were supposed to." Englert stated that he ran over 30 gassers, and then Coach Stinson had him doing up/downs. He testified that Coach Stinson was going off on him, so he ended up quitting the team. Englert said he came back to the team a few days later and then quit again later in the season because he was not getting any playing time.

During cross-examination by Brian Butler, Englert agreed that August 20 was not the hardest practice he had ever attended, nor was it the most he had ever run at a practice. Englert had apparently quit the team in the years before also, and it was always Coach Stinson who encouraged him to rejoin the team.

The next witness to be called by Jon Heck was Cordell Watts, a junior defensive end for PRPHS on August 20, 2008. He stated that he had been playing football since he was six years old. He said that after the gassers he went to go get water, but Coach Stinson told him to come back. He testified that he didn't run all of his gassers, and when it was his turn, he would just stay back.

Alex Dathorne handled the cross-examination for the defense. Watts stated that the players were allowed to go at their own pace, and the gassers were "not as intense as they usually are." He agreed that he didn't "hide" when he took off every other gasser. He just didn't go, and he was not punished for doing that.

Leland Hulbert next called 15-year-old Brandon Kitchens to the stand. (On August 20, 2008, he was an eighth grader from Conway Middle School participating with PRP football team practices.) He testified, "I guess coach got mad, and we had to run gassers about 30 minutes." He thought about 4 players quit, and that the team ran a total of 30–31 gassers. He testified that he asked to get water, but another coach said not to until Coach Stinson said so. Kitchens went on to elaborate that he wasn't allowed to get water. He said his body was completely numb and "my mouth was dry."

He recalled "Ding, ding, ding, we have a winner" was the phrase Coach Stinson used when the running stopped. He testified that he was diagnosed with ADD, and he has taken a 30 mg dose of Adderall XR® for 9 years. He reported that he had played soccer while on the medication and had not had any side effects related to heat illness.

Under cross examination by Alex Dathorne, Kitchen confirmed that all of the coaches were out on the field. They went over what a gasser was, and he again said they ran 30–31 gassers in 30 minutes.

Another player, Charles "Chase" Sweat, was next called to the stand by Jon Heck. Chase stated he knew Max from football. They went to Conway together, and they hung out in the morning. He guessed they ran about 30 gassers, stating the team "ran a lot more than normal." He recalled that Max was one or two people away from him during the run. He said as the run continued, he (Sweat) got sick and threw up. He testified that he saw Max Gilpin and Blake Johnson vomit once or twice. He stated Max collapsed about 15–20 minutes after he got sick.

Sweat gave a very disturbing and graphic account of how he remembered the 30–35 minutes of conditioning. He said, "We helped Max stand up, and then he would go down and then run a gasser." He also claimed that he and David Thompson were the two players who held Max up after he collapsed.

Brian Butler questioned Sweat for the defense. During questioning, Sweat agreed that when they start training, players usually throw up. He stated he was fine the next day and that he had no health problems other than being tired. He recalled that they went to water before gassers. He didn't remember the gassers being timed.

The next witness was a football manager/trainer named Trae McFarland. (He claims he tapes players and gets water and ice ready for practice and for games.) When recounting the beginning of the gassers on August 20, he stated Coach Stinson got mad and made the players start running. He stated he went and bought Antonio Calloway a bottle of water after he started experiencing breathing problems. He said, "Coach held Calloway's head back to drink, but he didn't drink it; he spit it up." McFarland saw Max go down and went to the field to help. They put him on the Gator™ and drove him to water until the ambulance arrived. He recalled two to three coolers full of ice water and one cooler full of ice.

The defense chose not to challenge Trae McFarland on his testimony. (They declined to cross-examine him because they felt it was a no-win situation: let him go, or jump on him and get it straight. Either way, there was nothing to gain. In fact, many of us were appalled that the prosecution put Trae on the stand to begin with. He had been in an accident a few years earlier and suffered a traumatic brain injury. The Commonwealth may have found it acceptable to exploit this young man, but the defense team was not comfortable with such tactics.)

David Thompson was the next witness called for the prosecution. He stated he only played football his senior year. Thompson explained that the team is supposed to jog wherever they are go, but everyone was "walking around." He saw "Cookie" get sick, and he said his friend Justin was crying. He testified that he could see people crying all the way down the field. He said 6–10 gassers would be normal, and he estimated they ran more than 20 gassers that day.

Thompson further testified that he and Justin were carrying Max after he collapsed, and he was "really heavy." He stated they got about half way to the shade tree when Coach Donnelly told them to put Max down. He recalled Max had white stuff around his mouth, and his face was pale blue.

He also testified that when he came back from running his last gasser, Max Gilpin didn't go on the last one and was on his hands and knees.

During questioning from Alex Dathorne, Thompson stated that gassers are usually timed. He stated the team ran 30 minutes to 1 hour, but he did remember telling police 20–25 minutes. He confirmed it was Justin Agrue who was on the other side of Max. He was 100% positive, and he was also positive Sweat wasn't the one who helped him.

Another witness was Aaron Shelton, a sophomore running back for PRPHS on August 20, 2008. He testified the team ran 25–30 gassers. He recalled some players were not running very hard. He stated about 10 players, including himself, had to do up/downs towards the end. He said they had run about 10 gassers, and "I wasn't going hard for real." He said he wasn't trying hard, and that David Englert was kind of laughing and playing around. He testified Englert quit when Stinson started getting on him for playing around. He stated Englert was the last person to finish every time. Shelton said Coach Stinson called the players who went to the water instead of the meeting "cowards," and he (Stinson) said, "Did I tell you all to go get water?"

When Brian Butler questioned him, Shelton agreed the coaches let him stop and go get water. He also agreed that when the running stopped, he was supposed to be going to a team meeting and not getting water. He said the meeting lasted five minutes. He agreed a lot of players were not running hard, and he could not recall hearing anyone crying.

DeAndre Cole was the next witness called by Hulbert. Cole stated they ran 15–20 gassers, the most they ran all season. He said he threw up somewhere between gasser number 7 and number 10. He testified that Stinson saw him throw up, and Stinson let him "sit one out" because he was still throwing up.

Alex Dathorne questioned Cole for the defense. Under cross-examination, Cole explained he threw up because he drank too much water. He stated that the team received four–five water breaks, and the team had water right before the gassers.

That was the last testimony for day 7.

On day 8, the Commonwealth called four doctors and Max Gilpin's maternal aunt, Teresa Crask, to testify. (Three out of the four doctors are medical doctors who treated Max, and the fourth is a PhD specializing in heatstroke.)

Teresa "Terri" Crask was the first witness for the prosecution that day. She stated she is Michele Crockett's younger sister, and she has been employed at Kosair Children's Hospital as a MRI technologist since 1995. She then testified that Stinson said at the hospital, "I called the boys to the huddle; they did not get there quickly. I got mad, so I made them run a lot. We were going to run them until someone quit."

Crask said she would check on Max Gilpin several times throughout the day. She was scheduled to work on Friday, but she did not work because Max's condition started getting worse. She told who was present right before Max Gilpin died, and then she told about the coroner's visit and the ultimate decision not to have an autopsy performed.

The next witness called to the stand was Dr. Douglas Casa. He is an associate professor at the University of Connecticut. His area of research and expertise is heat and hydration issues with athletes. He has been a certified athletic trainer since 1993. He has been involved in many aspects of treating and avoiding heatstroke. He described many actions that could be taken to help prevent heatstroke, such as being aware of the temperature and humidity, acclimatization, and the removal of equipment.

The 911 tape was played for the jury. Dr. Casa said that submersion in a tub of ice would guarantee survival of a heatstroke. He testified Stinson probably did not know about this technique, and he agreed EMS didn't mention it either when instructing Steve Deacon. He estimated that Max Gilpin's body temperature climbed to over 109 degrees. He stated that all high schools should have athletic trainers. He agreed that 10 minutes of training on heatstroke every 2 years is not enough for coaches. When pressed by Brian Butler about the level of care Max Gilpin received from the coaches, Casa stated, "I would have never for a second thought that they didn't care. I imagine they cared tremendously. They treated him like their own son."

Dr. Casa testified that he was a paid expert for the prosecution, as well as the civil attorneys suing the coaches. He stated that the Commonwealth currently owed him $22,500 for 75 hours of work at $300 an hour. He said he wasn't contacted by anyone in the Commonwealth Attorney's Office until July 2009, which was less than 60 days before the case went to trial.

The first medical doctor to take the stand for the prosecution was Dr. Leslie Greenwell. (She is employed by the University of Louisville and works at Kosair Children's Hospital. She has been practicing pediatric emergency medicine since 1996.) She described how, upon Max's arrival at 6:59 PM, they worked on his A, B, C's (airway, breathing, and circulation). Once they addressed those concerns, they took his body temperature and began cooling him. She testified how they had to put a large tube into his stomach. They started rinsing his stomach with ice saline by squirting in a few ounces and then taking it back out. They would then squirt in a few more ounces and also take it back out. This was done to cool Max because external cooling methods were not working.

Greenwell said that Max's blood was drawn for testing by a nurse at 7:06 PM, when IVs were attached. They also took a urine sample when a catheter was inserted at 7:14 PM. She stated it was not very concentrated urine, so it suggested that he was adequately hydrated. She said initially they started looking at dehydration, hypovolemia, and inadequate volume, but 10 minutes into it, it became apparent that the real issue was Max's temperature. In order to raise his blood pressure, they gave him between two and three liters of IV fluids.

Under cross examination by Brian Butler, Dr. Greenwell went over the lab results. She explained there were multiple factors used from the lab results to determine that Max Gilpin was not dehydrated. She testified she was not contacted by the police or prosecutors until March, 2009.

Under redirect, Heck began multiple attempts to discredit his own witness. He went over all of the areas a doctor would look at and asked if each individually would suggest someone was hydrated. Heck then attempted to get Dr. Greenwell to validate his next witness by implying Dr. Potter would somehow be more qualified to read the lab results. Greenwell eventually explained that it took "all of those readings," and collectively they suggested Max Gilpin was adequately hydrated.

The Commonwealth's second medical witness of the day was Dr. Katherine Potter, who has been a pediatric intensive care physician for two years. She was initially contacted around 8:00 PM on August 20, 2008, by Dr. Greenwell because Max's blood pressure had become very high. She stated he was transferred to her care at 11:10 PM. After a physical examination, she determined Max was suffering from shock, dehydration, and heatstroke. She testified that the kidneys function to help clear toxins and metabolites from the bloodstream and to make urine. She stated that there is no one number from the lab results that would point to or away from a diagnosis of dehydration. She said Max needed four liters of fluid to slow down his heart rate. Based on his elevated creatinine level, she contacted Dr. McKenney, a kidney expert. She also stated she did not believe Max Gilpin was suffering from a viral infection. She turned over Max at 8:00 AM on August 21, 2008, to the care of one of her partners, Dr. Melissa Porter.

Brian Butler handled the cross-examination for the defense. He immediately began questioning Dr. Potter on her relationship with Terri Crask. She agreed that they were friends who knew one another from Kosair. He then began to pick at her diagnosis of dehydration and the factors she used to make that determination. She agreed that all of the factors mentioned by Butler would suggest Max Gilpin was not dehydrated. She said she had been an ICU physician for 14 months when she had treated Max Gilpin, and as of September 2009, she has treated 3 heatstroke patients.

The last witness for day 8, Dr. Melissa Porter, was questioned for the prosecution by Jon Heck. She has been employed as a pediatric intensive care physician at Kosair Children's Hospital since 2006. Her testimony was very brief, and she stated she had no reason to believe that Max Gilpin was suffering from a viral infection. She also stated that Adderall® is a common drug.

Brian Butler immediately went to the issue of increased lymphocyte count, pointing out the elevated number from the lab results. Butler handed Dr. Porter a resident's daily note dated August 22, 2008, from the medical records, and he asked her to read it. She stated, "It says, new history, that patient may not have been feeling well on day of collapse."

She confirmed the note would have been written by Dr. Jett, who was a resident who had treated Max Gilpin. Dr. Porter had talked with Michele Crockett, who reported Max was feeling fine on that morning. Dr. Porter stated she did not discuss Max's morning with Jeff Gilpin.

A bench conference began after testimony on day 8, because the defense felt that another Brady violation had occurred. It was clear that Dr. Greenwell's opinion was that Max Gilpin was not dehydrated. The defense felt the information was exculpatory and the prosecutors should have turned it over to the defense. The Commonwealth argued that it was a surprise and that they had no idea that was going to happen. The prosecutors claimed they had no memory of Dr. Greenwell opining that Max was not dehydrated.

Judge Gibson ultimately said, "You are all officers of the court, and I would expect that everything you say here is to the best of your recollection."

Alex Dathorne wanted to make sure this alleged violation was on the record. Gibson stated, "You have made a record. And at this point, I don't think the fact that Dr. Greenwell said something different on the stand today contrary to the memories of the interviews is sufficient for a sanction."

And so ended day 8.

CHAPTER 19

Days 9–10: The Commonwealth's Case Concludes

Day 9 started with more "soccer witnesses" who were in attendance at PRPHS on August 20, 2008. Much like the football players' testimony, these witnesses became very repetitive, so some testimony found in this book may seem somewhat thin. In fact, the day started with an objection from the defense that any further testimony from the "soccer witnesses" was cumulative testimony. The objection was heard, but was not ruled upon. Day 9 also included the deputy coroner, a kidney doctor, the lead detective in criminal investigation, PRPHS' athletic director and his supervisor and finally a couple more "soccer witnesses."

The Commonwealth's first witness of the day was Brian Bratcher, who was at PRPHS on August 20 to watch his niece play in the soccer game. He stated he was located at midfield of the soccer field, and he was standing right next to where Max Gilpin was standing. He testified to watching Max begin to have trouble. Bratcher said Max stumbled and had trouble keeping his balance. He stated that Max went down into a three-point stance to keep from going all the way down, and then he ran another lap. He recounted seeing Max struggle to run the last lap, and as Max was returning, the running stopped. He stated that Max returned to the sideline and collapsed.

Bratcher stated he played football from the third grade all the way through high school. He didn't see anything wrong with the yelling, and he stated, "It's just—that was football."

Under cross examination by Alex Dathorne he explained further what he meant by, "that was football." He stated, "If you don't do things right, you know, I've had coaches get in your face…. It's football." He continued, "You never know what's going to come out of some people's mouths, because it's a very high intense environment at that time and things happen."

Bratcher testified that he watched Max for quite some time, but he never did see him throw up.

Phil Compton was the next witness called. He attended the soccer game with his wife and two daughters, one who plays soccer in middle school. Shortly into Compton's testimony, Alex Dathorne objected to the judge again about cumulative testimony. The witness was already testifying, so nothing was done about it this time. However, the judge did put the prosecution on notice that she would sustain the objection for any cumulative witnesses.

Compton stated he had arrived around 6 PM. He witnessed the meeting after practice and the incident where Stinson told players not to go to water and, instead, get to the meeting. He testified that he believed Coach Stinson may have said, "Get your asses back over here," and he recalled Stinson being very upset with the team. The defense had no questions for this witness.

Greg Smith took the stand next, and the defense again objected to the witness on the grounds of cumulative evidence. The prosecution argued that he could offer a vantage point from the parking lot, and he also had established times based on cell phone calls he made. The objection was overruled, but the prosecution was warned that the witness could only testify to new information.

Leland Hulbert asked Smith to testify as to why he was at the sports complex that day. He said his daughter was playing goalie for Waggener. He had another child in the car who had fallen asleep, so he remained in the car with the air conditioning running. He was parked outside the fence, just a few feet from where his daughter was playing. He stated he had made a cell phone call at 5:58 PM, the same time Antonio Calloway was at the water being cooled off. He said his wife then came over, wanting to use his phone to make sure 911 had been called.

Then Hulbert asked the witness a question that was in defiance to the direct order the judge had given moments earlier. Again Dathorne objected, but this time he went a little further. He pleaded with Judge Gibson, "I'm up here objecting again to something we just talked about, and I'm looking like a dirty defense attorney. If you want to talk about prejudice, they just go back and defy this Court's order. When they don't like your order, Judge, they just run right through it. If they don't like it again, they ask you to reconsider it 14 times. This is absolutely ludicrous."

After a lengthy discussion at the bench, Hulbert was told *again* what was not acceptable, and after all the fuss and commotion, Hulbert ended with the question, "Mr. Smith, is it true that you referee basketball games?" After Smith replied "yes," Hulbert said he had no more questions.

Dathorne kept his questions brief and essentially went over what Smith had already testified to in an attempt to further solidify the timelines.

The next witness was one from whom many had waited to hear. Sam Weakley was the deputy coroner from the Jefferson County Coroner's Office who told Max Gilpin's family an autopsy would not be necessary. Jon Heck handled the questioning for the prosecution. He revealed that Weakley's primary duty as deputy coroner was to come up with a manner and cause of death. Weakley estimated he has performed over 7,000 death investigations in his 15-year career as a deputy coroner.

Weakley stated he completed a formal document called the Coroner's Investigation Report (CIR). He stated the death certificate listed septic shock, multi-organ failure and heatstroke as the cause of death. He stated he spoke with Dr. Donna Stewart at the state medical examiner's office, and they did not feel as though an autopsy was needed. Weakley testified that, on the CIR he completed for the death of Max Gilpin, he listed the manner of death as an accident. He explained, "I knew of no malfeasance involved in the situation. I just thought it was a horrible accident, and that's the way I classified it."

Alex Dathorne cross-examined Sam Weakley, and they discussed the 12 reasons why the coroner should be called after someone's death. After covering those, Dathorne mentioned the 19 regulations that a coroner must follow when deciding whether or not a postmortem examination is to be completed. Since Max Gilpin's death was an accident, and he was under the age of 40 with no previous medical history, was a postmortem exam performed? Weakley answered, "no."

Weakley also answered "no" when asked if he was aware of any prosecution for a homicide that did not involve an autopsy. Dathorne gave multiple ways someone could die, including a gunshot to the head or being hit by a car, and he asked the coroner if an autopsy would be appropriate. He answered "yes" to each scenario, and he later explained he didn't order an autopsy because Max had been in the hospital for three days.

Jon Heck then called Dr. Daniel McKenney to the stand. Dr. McKenney is a pediatric kidney doctor employed by the University of Louisville, and he also works at Kosair Children's Hospital. He stated there are only three pediatric nephrologists in Louisville, KY, and Larry Shoemaker is their division head. McKenney stated he treated Max Gilpin, but Shoemaker did not. He was first contacted to treat Max on August 22, 2008, when Max developed problems with his kidney function as well as a significant volume overload from a large amount of fluids that he had received to help his blood pressure. He stated in his review of Max's lab results he had noted his creatinine level was 1.9, and that someone Max's age and weight should have a creatinine level somewhere in the 1.0–1.1 range.

McKenney explained that numerous events, such as dehydration, kidney damage, or muscle breakdown could cause a number that high. He also said it could be an indication of prior kidney failure. When it was the defense's turn to question Dr. McKenney, Brian Butler only wanted to confirm that he became involved in Max's treatment on August 22, 2008.

Following the lunch break, Detective Terry Jones was the first witness for the prosecution. Questioned by Jon Heck, Jones said he retired after 23 years with LMPD. He was a detective, and he worked the final 21 years in the homicide division. He explained the hierarchy of the homicide unit, and that he was assigned this case on August 28, 2008, because he was the next up in the rotation. His original plan was to approach the school board since it had already started an investigation. He was able to collect numerous records and documents, as well as the hygrometer used by Coach Stinson.

He said there were witnesses interviewed from the soccer game, spectators of the football practice, players, coaches, and a concession stand worker. Det. Jones said the players who did not have parents present were interviewed individually in a police car. He said the police would take that particular child, while still on school property, to an area of the parking lot, and they would conduct an interview of the player. Jones testified he personally conducted over 80 interviews, and the players' interviews took his whole platoon over a week to conduct. He also stated there were over 120 interviews total, and the investigation took months to complete.

In the defense's cross-examination, Alex Dathorne questioned Detective Jones about who had been consulted during the investigation. Det. Jones was not aware of any medical expert (including Dr. Smock) being contacted. He also said he was not aware of anyone contacting the medical examiner's office or the coroner. He stated the coroner notified LMPD that the victim had died of heatstroke, so "that's the information I ran with."

Then Dathorne asked a question many had wondered about. He asked Detective Jones, "In your 21 years as detective, as a lead detective in a homicide case, have you ever not testified in front of the grand jury when it was your case?" Jones answered, "No, sir." As the lead detective, he had always been the one who presented a case to the grand jury. He said he learned from some other detectives that the Stinson case had been presented and indicted. During his 21 years as a homicide detective, he could not recall a homicide case without an autopsy.

The first JCPS official to be called to the stand by prosecutor Leland Hulbert was Jerry Wyman. Wyman is the director for activities, athletics and academic competitions. He stated he normally has weekly contact with all the athletic directors (AD) throughout JCPS. He testified that after Max Gilpin's collapse, he went to PRPHS to collect several documents, including physicals of Calloway and Gilpin, proof of insurance, the heat index measurement sheet and a timeline generated by Coach Stinson that was faxed to the school from the hospital. Wyman stated that JCPS expects all coaches to follow KHSAA guidelines.

The next official from JCPS to be called was PRPHS's athletic director, Craig Webb. Webb told Leland Hulbert that he supervises the activities and athletics of the school, and he oversees the coaches and the students as well. He testified that he passed on an e-mail from Jerry Wyman to Coach Stinson that stated: Be very aware of heat index readings and continue to record these as required by the KHSAA. He testified to forwarding other communication from Wyman to Stinson. He was then asked about the day's activities on August 20, 2008. He described seeing Max Gilpin collapse on the sideline, and he stated he did not see any ice towels that day.

During cross-examination by Brian Butler, Webb testified that there was about a minute delay from when Max Gilpin went down and when he drove the Gator™ over. He said that several coaches came to Max's aid, and at no time was he ever ignored.

Next, when the Commonwealth called Rhonda Barnett to the stand, the objection to cumulative testimony was raised again. According to the Commonwealth, there were two more soccer witnesses and each of them had something new to add. Eventually Judge Gibson excluded Barnett from testifying, but she included the testimony of Tim Moreschi. Once the Commonwealth had a ruling on Moreschi, prosecutors disclosed they had one more soccer witness after him. Of course that was met with another objection, but it was agreed that the objection would wait until after the next witness.

Leland Hulbert called Tim Moreschi to the stand as the Commonwealth's final witness of the day and week. Moreschi testified he was at PRPHS to watch the girls' soccer game because, "I had two little girlfriends who played on the field that day." He stated his oldest son graduated from PRPHS in 1999, and he had helped coach youth league football and basketball for Panther Youth. He said his home is so close to the PRPHS girls' softball field, that he can sit on his porch and watch the girls play.

He claimed he arrived at 5:31 or 5:32 PM, and the players were already running with their equipment off. He testified he heard Coach Stinson ask who was going to quit or some variation of that, at least a dozen times. When Moreschi would answer a question, he would turn to the jury and answer in a very dramatic "over the top" way. Then Moreschi began to lay it on thick when he stated, "'What's that coach's name that's abusing you boys?' That's what I hollered. And I pointed at him. I was hoping to draw his attention that I was watching him." He continued with his unique version of events when he said, "I told him, I said, you're out of the drill. I placed myself between him and the coach."

It was my concern that the jurors might actually believe this guy until he made a very crucial mistake. Everyone paying attention during this trial could tell you that "ding, ding, ding... we have a winner" is what Coach Stinson said when Englert quit and the running stopped. However, Moreschi said, "And all of a sudden I heard Stinson say, 'that's it, that's it, he quit,' and he cleared the field." Moreschi also testified that he told the player who quit, "You did the right thing, he was abusing you boys. "I said, 'you're the only man out on that field. Thank you, son, thank you for quitting.'"

Under cross-examination, Alex Dathorne only wanted to know one thing from Moreschi. Did he tell the police that the practice on August 20 was typical training, typically what you'd see on any football field? Finally Moreschi admitted, "I said it was training you might see on any football field."

To think this witness was described by Leland Hulbert as one of his best witnesses during a bench argument is absolutely unfathomable. However, in an argument to get Moreschi's testimony allowed, he told Judge Gibson, "He's probably one of our best witnesses. That's why we're saving him until the end."

Day 10 began much like day 9 ended. The defense again went in front of the judge, objecting to cumulative testimony. The prosecution argued that its next witness spoke with Stinson and heard him say something to which no one else had testified. Ultimately, the prosecution was allowed to call this witness.

So Leland Hulbert called Kathleen Smith to the stand. She is married to Greg Smith who testified the week before, and she described many of the same events that Greg described. She testified that Stinson was yelling things to push the players and then he said, "Come on, who's going to be the sacrificial lamb?" She testified to a conversation with Stinson in which she asked if 911 had been called. Stinson responded "yes," and he said the player would be fine and he was just suffering from heat exhaustion.

Sgt. Denny Butler took the stand next. He told Leland Hulbert that he is a supervisor of a platoon of detectives, and one of his detectives had been assigned the case. He stated that Detective Terry Jones opened a death investigation at the request of Dave Stengel. He said he met with Michele Crockett at LMPD headquarters on September 2, 2008. She had provided him with some names of people who had contacted her directly. He said he met with Dave Johnson and Craig Webb at PRPHS to work out the logistics of investigating 80 football players. He stated he also wanted to put the PRPHS administrators on notice that they were conducting a criminal investigation. All the players were to be considered witnesses, and they should not be tampered with in any way. Butler stated that all of the interviews, except for those with Michele Crockett, Jeff Gilpin, and Terri Crask, were tape recorded. Sgt. Butler said he had taped an interview with Jason Stinson, and Leland Hulbert asked the court's permission to play it for the jury.

We were not quite sure why the prosecution would play that tape, since Coach Stinson had explained in it many of the misconceptions about that day. (Playing that tape insured that the defense would not put Coach Stinson on the stand. The defense would not need to, because the jury was about to hear Stinson's recollection of the day's events.) After playing the Stinson interview, Hulbert and Sgt. Butler went over the evidence collected and opened each package for the jury to see. The evidence contained several items, including the hygrometer used that day and a bottle of Creatine pills.

The defense had planned on cross examining Sgt. Butler, but after a short break, it was decided it was best to move on. Asking Sgt. Butler any questions would just open the floor back up to Hulbert for a re-direct, and frankly, it was not worth it. Sgt. Butler's time in the spotlight ended when Brian Butler said, "Your honor, no questions, thank you."

Leland Hulbert next called Joseph Bratcher to testify. Bratcher has been working with Emergency Medical Services (EMS) for 10 years, and he stated he has been employed with the Louisville Metro EMS for the last five years. He said his position with the Louisville Metro EMS was as a paramedic. When asked if he remembered August 20, 2008, he said he remembered everything about that day.

He stated that the ambulance was dispatched at 6:18 PM. They were en route at 6:19; they arrived at 6:27, and at 6:30 they made it to the back field where Max Gilpin was located. Bratcher then said they remained on the scene for 10 minutes, departing for the hospital at 6:40 PM. They arrived at the hospital at 6:58 PM.

Upon arrival at the practice field, Bratcher believed it would be a "load and go" situation, because Max was so critical. He stated once Max was loaded, his EMS partner went to check on Antonio Calloway. He described Max's skin as hot to the touch, like he had a fever. He stated they treated him with icepacks to the neck and armpits to cool the blood as it pumped through the body. They also administered 250 cc of cold fluids through an IV. He didn't recall any ice bags in use. He said that statement did not mean ice bags were not in use; he just didn't remember seeing any.

Under cross-examination by Brian Butler, Bratcher stated that when he arrived on the scene, bystanders were trying to cool Max by pouring water on and fanning him. He agreed that what the coaches and bystanders were doing to treat Max was absolutely appropriate.

The Commonwealth's final witness was Dr. Lawrence Shoemaker. Dr. Shoemaker is a pediatric kidney doctor, and, just like Dr. McKinney, Shoemaker is on the faculty at the University of Louisville. He stated he also works at Kosair Children's Hospital.

Dr. Shoemaker spent nearly two hours explaining how many of the symptoms from heatstroke would cause multiple organs to fail, explaining his calculations and drawing charts and graphical representations for the jury. He did an excellent job of explaining some very complicated issues to an average lay person, but it is unclear how much of this information really applied to Max Gilpin. When confronted with timelines that didn't match his, Dr. Shoemaker admitted that all of his figures might be wrong.

Dr. Shoemaker appeared to be very nervous, and he earned the nickname of "Dr. Microphone" because he would adjust the location of the microphone every time he answered a question. He would pull it to him and then push it back. Eventually he even knocked the protective cover off the top of the microphone.

Jon Heck went a long way to stress that the bacteria found in Max Gilpin's blood probably did not exist until after his collapse. Dr. Shoemaker also stated that a muscular high school student could have a creatinine level of 1.6 and the kidneys would still be functioning normally. He testified that he was amazed that Max was as large and muscular as he was. He then said, "Maybe 1.6 is too high, and maybe 1.5 would be more appropriate."

During questioning by Brian Butler, it became clear Dr. Shoemaker had no idea when the lab specimens he used for his calculations had been drawn. His miscalculations turned out to be problematic for the prosecution, because most of what he testified to was not correct. He stated that he has treated two heatstroke patients in his career.

Once the Commonwealth had rested its case, Judge Gibson heard the defense's motion for a directed verdict. A directed verdict is ordered by a judge when the prosecution rests and it is abundantly clear the prosecution has not proved what it was alleging. Brian Butler cited several cases where reckless homicide convictions had been overturned because the circumstances did not rise to the level of reckless homicide. Butler pleaded, "So in each one of the cases I've cited to the Court, there was a law in place to avoid the harm that occurred; in each case the defendant violated those laws. His conduct directly caused the death. And in each of those cases, the Kentucky Supreme Court and/or the Kentucky Court of Appeals said the conduct did not rise to the level necessary for these charges."

Judge Gibson heard the Commonwealth's side, and she ultimately ruled in its favor by denying the motion for the directed verdict. She felt the case law was very specific, and it did not apply in this particular situation. After stating multiple reasons for denying the motion, she stated, "So taking all the evidence in the light most favorable to the Commonwealth, I do believe that at this point it survives the directed verdict motion."

The court was put in recess until 9 AM the next morning, when the defense would begin calling their witnesses.

2008 PRPHS Panthers running to the locker room after warm-ups.
COURTESY OF JEFF JENNINGS

2008 PRPHS Panthers entering the field against Doss High School.
COURTESY OF JEFF JENNINGS

177

Doss vs. PRPHS team captains and Coach Jason Stinson wait for the coin toss. Pictured from left to right: #12 Dave West, Jr., #8 Willie Northington, #7 Marcus Brown, #22 William "Fuss" Thompson and Coach Jason Stinson.

Courtesy of Jeff Jennings

2008 PRPHS Panthers vs. Doss Dragons

Courtesy of Jeff Jennings

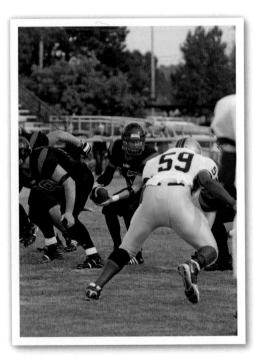

The "Black Hole" Student Pep Section
COURTESY OF JEFF JENNINGS

#12 Dave West, Jr. eluding Doss tacklers.
COURTESY OF JEFF JENNINGS

*2008 PRPHS Head Coach
Jason Stinson*
COURTESY OF JEFF JENNINGS

*Pastor Joel Carwile offering
support to the 2008 PRPHS
Panthers*
COURTESY OF JEFF JENNINGS

2008 PRPHS Cheerleader
Katie Watkins
COURTESY OF JEFF JENNINGS

2008 PRPHS Dance Team
Member Kayla Revell
COURTESY OF JEFF JENNINGS

Rally for Jason Stinson at PRPHS.
COURTESY OF JEFF JENNINGS

Live auction items from the JSLDF benefit dinner/auction.
COURTESY OF PAT MEURER

Silent auction items from the JSLDF benefit dinner/auction.
COURTESY OF PAT MEURER

SOS Fun Run
COURTESY OF PAT MEURER

JSLDF benefit concert/picnic.
COURTESY OF ANNE SULLIVAN

GMA appearance
Left to right: Ann Daugherty, Ashley Butler, Rodney Daugherty, Brian Butler, Diane
Sawyer, Monica Stinson, Jason Stinson.
COURTESY OF ASHLEY BUTLER

John Deere Gator™
COURTESY OF MINDY ELLIS

"The Smockdown"
Left to right: Dr. William "Bill" Smock, Commonwealth's Attorney R. David Stengel,
Assistant Commonwealth's Attorney Leland Hulbert.
© COURIER-JOURNAL

Aerial picture of PRPHS and Greenwood Elementary School.
From bottom left: 1- football practice field; 2 - soccer game field; 3 - baseball field;
4 - tech building; 5 - football game field; 6 - gymnasium and football locker room;
7 - PRP High School; 8 - Greenwood Elementary School.
COURTESY OF EVIDENCE PHOTOS

Aerial picture of PRPHS football practice field and soccer game field.
COURTESY OF EVIDENCE PHOTOS

186

Lengthwise picture of PRPHS football practice field.
COURTESY OF EVIDENCE PHOTOS

PRPHS football practice field's shade tree and bleachers.
COURTESY OF EVIDENCE PHOTOS

View across PRPHS' soccer game field.
COURTESY OF EVIDENCE PHOTOS

PRPHS tech building with view of PRPHS soccer goal.
COURTESY OF EVIDENCE PHOTOS

PRPHS' watering area.
COURTESY OF EVIDENCE PHOTOS

Aerial picture of PRPHS football practice field and soccer game field with dimensions.
COURTESY OF EVIDENCE PHOTOS

THE COMMONWEALTH OF KENTUCKY
Jefferson Circuit Court, Criminal Division
09 CR0207-12

<u>JANUARY</u> Term A.D., <u>2009</u>

THE COMMONWEALTH OF KENTUCKY

Against

DAVID JASON STINSON

⎫
⎬
⎭

RECKLESS HOMICIDE
KRS 507.050 CLASS D FELONY 1 TO 5 YEARS
KRS 534.030 FINE OF $1000 - $10,000 OR DOUBLE
THE DEFENDANT'S GAIN, WHICHEVER IS GREATER
UOR 09210
ONE COUNT

The Grand Jurors of the County of Jefferson, in the name and by the authority of the Commonwealth of Kentucky, charge:

<u>COUNT ONE</u>

That on or about the 20th day of August, 2008, in Jefferson County, Kentucky, the above named defendant, DAVID JASON STINSON, committed the offense of Reckless Homicide when he recklessly caused the death of Max Gilpin.

AGAINST THE PEACE AND DIGNITY OF THE COMMONWEALTH OF KENTUCKY

A TRUE BILL

FOREPERSON

Wit: Det. Denny Butler, LMPD

R. David Stengel /ts
Assigned Assistant Commonwealth's Attorney

20_____
**RECEIVED FROM THE Foreman of the Grand
Jury in their presence and filed in open Court.
ATTEST:** DAVID L. NICHOLSON, Clerk

By_____D.C.

TRUE BILL-COUNTS   /

Indictment sheet of Coach Jason Stinson for reckless homicide.
COURTESY OF RODNEY DAUGHERTY

THE COMMONWEALTH OF KENTUCKY
Jefferson Circuit Court. Criminal Division

09CR2319-12

<u>AUGUST Term A.D., 2009</u>

THE COMMONWEALTH OF KENTUCKY

Against

DAVID JASON STINSON

WANTON ENDANGERMENT I
KRS 508.060 CLASS D FELONY
1 TO 5 YEARS
KRS 534.030 FINE OF $1000 - $10,000 OR DOUBLE THE DEFENDANT'S
GAIN, WHICHEVER IS GREATER
UOR 13201
ONE COUNT

The Grand Jurors of the County of Jefferson, in the name and by the authority of the Commonwealth of Kentucky, charge:

<u>COUNT ONE</u>

That on or about the 20th day of August, 2008, in Jefferson County, Kentucky, the above named defendant, DAVID JASON STINSON, committed the offense of Wanton Endangerment in the First Degree when, under circumstances manifesting extreme indifference to the value of human life, he wantonly engaged in conduct which created a substantial danger of death or serious physical injury to Maxwell Gilpin.

AGAINST THE PEACE AND DIGNITY OF THE COMMONWEALTH OF KENTUCKY

A TRUE BILL

TRUE BILL-COUNTS____1____

_____
FOREPERSON

Wit: Det. Denny Butler, LMPD

Leland Hulbert
Jon Heck
Assigned Assistant Commonwealth's Attorneys

8-11_____20 09
**RECEIVED FROM THE Foreman of the Grand
Jury in their presence and filed in open Court.
ATTEST: DAVID L. NICHOLSON, Clerk**

By _____ D.C.

FILED IN CLERKS OFFICE
DAVID L. NICHOLSON, CLERK

AUG 1 1 2009

BY _____
DEPUTY CLERK

Indictment sheet of Coach Jason Stinson for wanton endangerment.
COURTESY OF RODNEY DAUGHERTY

Defense Attorney Alex Dathorne and Coach Jason Stinson
COURTESY OF RODNEY DAUGHERTY

After a hard fought battle, they can finally smile.
Pictured from left: Defense Attorney Alex Dathorne, Author Rodney Daugherty,
Coach Jason Stinson and Defense Attorney Brian Butler.
COURTESY OF JASON STINSON

CHAPTER 20

DAY 11: THE DEFENSE'S CASE BEGINS

Day 11 began with the defense opening its case. A classmate and four players, including one of Max Gilpin's best friends, were called as witnesses. The day ended with two medical experts, one who was the former Chief Medical Examiner of the State of Kentucky.

Alex Dathorne started the defense by calling Logan Vardeman to the stand. Vardeman stated that he was one of Max Gilpin's best friends, having first met Max in kindergarten. He testified to seeing Max take a Creatine capsule one to two weeks before his collapse. On the way out to the practice field on August 20, Max had said something to him about "not feeling good." Vardeman described the day's practice where the players were told to run gassers. He said he was allowed to stop running early for putting forth effort, but not all players were going all out. He stated he went under the shade tree, and he briefly recalled Antonio Calloway's episode. He said Calloway was sitting on the front row of the bleachers when Max went down. Vardeman testified they ran out to help Max, and he remembered Max just kept saying he didn't feel well. "And then he just stopped altogether," said Vardeman.

Since Vardeman stated who ran out there with him, Dathorne asked him if he knew Chase Sweat. Vardeman testified that Sweat did not help carry Max off the field. Vardeman answered "no" when asked if Sweat was a starter on the team or a super athlete. He described Sweat as a "jersey wearer" who was only on the team to be known as a football player.

He testified to Coach Steve Deacon putting ice under Max's armpits. He testified that he was still friends with both Max's mother and with Coach Stinson, and "yes" he felt like he was in the middle. He then testified to meeting with both Hulbert and Heck on separate occasions, and he said he told them the same things he just testified about. Dathorne thanked him and said he had no more question for him. Then Logan Vardeman asked the judge, "Ma'am, may I have permission to speak freely?" Judge Gibson explained there were rules, and he could only answer questions asked of him.

Leland Hulbert handled the cross-examination for the Commonwealth, and he opened with, "Are there any other comments you would like to make about that day?" That may have been a question he wished he hadn't asked.

Vardeman answered, "Yes, sir, there are. Max was one of my best friends, you know. You've got to realize, he was like a brother to me. If I believed that Coach Stinson did anything wrong, I'll be the first person to say it. If I believed that man right there did anything to intentionally hurt somebody, then I would be the first person to tell anybody. But he didn't."

The next witness to be called was Justin Agrue, but before he could make it to the stand, Judge Gibson told Alex Dathorne to excuse his witness. (He was wearing one of the t-shirts that had been made in memory of Max Gilpin.) After removing the shirt, Agrue returned in a white t-shirt to testify.

Agrue was running next to Max Gilpin on August 20. He stated that they ran for about 30 minutes, and he didn't see Max have any issues while running. He said after the run Max was bent over, so he and David Thompson put Max's arms around their shoulders and they helped him walk to the shade tree. Agrue testified they were heading in that direction because practice was over, and they always have team meetings after practice. He said they were walking when "Max just dropped in our arms." He also stated Chase Sweat was not involved in carrying Max at any time.

Under cross-examination by Jon Heck, Agrue answered "no" each time he was asked if he had seen a particular person vomit that day. Heck went through a number of names—Max Gilpin, Christian Vincent, DeAndre Cole, Blake Johnson, and Dalton Duff—and Agrue said, "I don't remember anybody vomiting." He also testified that he ran 15 to 30 "extra gassers." He confirmed twice that it was Coach Donnelly, and not Coach Stinson, who told him to lay Max down.

David Keown was the next player called to the stand by Alex Dathorne. Keown said he was currently a student athlete playing football at Kentucky State University. He described many of the same events that had already been testified to, such as the players were "goofing off," so they had to run gassers. Then some other players who were still playing around were made to do up/downs. Then David Englert and Chris Bryant quit.

Keown said he was in the same group as Max Gilpin. He recalled, "He (Gilpin) was a little off.... He just wasn't Max, you know." He testified that he received four water breaks, and Max was with them when they came back from the water break right before the gassers began. Keown stated he was running in the same group and close to Max, and he did not see him have any problems during the run.

Leland Hulbert handled the questioning of David Keown for the prosecution, and he started off by asking him if he remembered telling him that Coach Stinson was like a best friend to him. He replied, "Yes sir." Then he said he didn't remember if he told LMPD or JCPS that Max was not himself.

Dathorne decided to re-direct David Keown after Hulbert opened the door about his friendship with Stinson. Dathorne asked him about the relationship, and Keown stated, "Well, since I came into PRPHS, me and Coach Stinson have been real close. In my life, I have had a lot of hard problems. I have had kind of a rough life. But Coach Stinson has always been there for me. When I needed stuff, when I didn't have any money for food, he was there. When I needed somebody to talk to, he was there. He always told me if I needed someplace to stay, his place was always open for me. I wasn't always the best student, but he never gave up. He was always there. And it wasn't just me. Every kid in that school building he was willing to help."

It was at that moment that the first *real* emotion entered the courtroom. Hulbert objected to the testimony being given, and at the bench Dathorne reminded him that he opened the door. The prosecution inferred Keown may have been biased, based on their friendship, so Dathorne said he wanted to clear that up. He then asked Keown if he would lie for Coach Stinson, and he replied "no."

Kelsey Schmidt was called next by Alex Dathorne to testify for the defense. She stated she was a classmate and friend of Max Gilpin. Schmidt stated she attended a second period chemistry class with Max, and he seemed fine at that time. However, when she saw him again at lunch, he wasn't really talking as much as he usually would. She said he put his head down on the table, which was odd because normally he would be talking with everyone at the table. She testified that she did not see him again until after school. She said, "And after school I saw him and he didn't talk; usually he would run up and be like, 'Hey, what's up?' I asked him what was wrong, and he

195

said he didn't feel good." She said that when Max left, he said he was going to football practice.

Under cross-examination by Leland Hulbert, Schmidt agreed she had told him Max didn't feel well. He didn't want to go to football practice, and she saw him walk off with Chelsea Scott.

Cody Keown was the last player called to the stand for the defense. Alex Dathorne immediately asked if he was related to David Keown, and he answered "no." He testified that he participated in the individual drills with Max Gilpin. Max was towards the back during the blocking drill, so Coach Cook asked him why he wasn't getting in. He said Max didn't answer Coach Cook, so he [Keown] asked Max if he was okay, and Max said he wasn't feeling well. Keown said during the last water break, Max Gilpin was there across from him. He had looked up and had seen Max drinking water. He said he ran in the same group beside Max, and towards the end, Max had become angry that he was running because of other players' actions.

Under cross-examination, Leland Hulbert asked Keown if they had ever spoken to one another. He answered "no," and he agreed it was probably because his father, Tim Keown, would not let him. He said he was aware that his father was a financial supporter of Coach Stinson. He recalled telling LMPD that it seemed like they ran 30 gassers.

The first medical expert called to the stand by the defense was Dr. Dan Danzl, Chair of the Department of Emergency Medicine at the University of Louisville School of Medicine. He has been a member of the U of L faculty since 1979 and the Department Chair since 1991. He also has been a treating emergency room physician since 1991. He was one of the editors of, and authored some chapters in, *Rosen's Emergency Medicine*, the emergency room textbook used in "essentially every medical school across the United States."

Butler covered Dr. Danzl's extensive history with heat illness, including books and literature he either authored or edited. Dr. Danzl teaches University of Louisville medical students about heat illness, and for the last 20 years he also has given lectures to different medical groups regarding heat illness—the diagnosis of heat illness, as well as the treatment of heat illness.

Dr. Danzl gave a very detailed description of what heatstroke is and what happens to the body to cause it. He explained how heat exhaustion and heatstroke were distinctly different. He clarified how heat exhaustion can be treated and the patient released, because the body has not lost its ability to maintain a temperature at which it needs to stay. Heatstroke, however, is entirely different because it is life-threatening and has a high mortality rate.

Dr. Danzl testified, "We admit all of them (heatstroke victims) to the intensive care unit and monitor them to make sure they don't have other organs that have been damaged." He said that people do not go from heat exhaustion to heatstroke, because if they did, doctors could predict heatstrokes. He then said the only way to prevent exertional heatstroke was to never exert yourself in the heat.

He enlightened the jury about how unpredictable heatstrokes can be. Dr. Danzl said, "It's very tricky and very subtle, and depending on what the risk factors or contributory factors to the heatstroke were, sometimes you just can't predict who or why certain patients go into heatstroke."

He then explained the procedure that is performed "100% of the time" when a patient who is in serious condition enters an emergency room. He stated that a "rainbow" of tubes is drawn when the IV is inserted. Hospital personnel do that because they don't know how much blood they will need. He then stated that you could not put a Foley catheter in a patient without drawing urine, because it must be ensured that the catheter reached the bladder before blowing the balloon up. Failing to follow this step could result in rupturing a patient's urethra. He said urine was obtained at this time, and he said the collection of urine in an emergency room was done every time a Foley catheter was entered.

He testified that, per standard operation procedure, Max's blood was drawn at 7:02 PM, and his urine was obtained at 7:14 PM.

Butler later asked Danzl how he got involved with the case. Dr. Danzl replied, "I got a phone call from Mr. Mark Fenzel saying he represented the school district. I said to him, 'I've read something about this in the paper. I really don't think you want to talk to me, because you're really not going to like what I have to say'—because I mistakenly assumed that this was going to be another obvious severe dehydration exertional heatstroke case. Fenzel said, 'No, would you please look at it? The school district wants to know, and I'm representing the school district.'"

Dr. Danzl said he conditionally agreed to look at the case. He stated, "I felt I had an ethical obligation as a professor of the medical school in this community who's an expert on environmental emergencies to do an 'academic' review. I would not agree to be an 'expert witness'—as I define an 'expert witness'—not that anything is wrong with expert witnesses, but that I was not going to be compensated; I was just going to testify to the facts medically as I saw them."

Danzl said he had not been paid anything by Jason Stinson, JCPS, or anybody in relation to this case. He also explained why he did not wish to be compensated. "That was a condition of my agreeing to review this. As I would not be compensated, I would consider myself an academic reviewer."

He then explained what data he had used to offer an opinion that Max Gilpin was not dehydrated. Butler then asked him about Max Gilpin's 1.9 creatinine level. Dr. Danzl said, "It told me something was wrong, very wrong. In fact, all the heatstroke patients I've seen, that's what their creatinine is 8 or 12 hours later, after their kidneys have shut down and then that builds up in your blood. The creatinine level should not be that high on *arrival* to the emergency department. There are only a couple options. The patient had preexistent kidney disease, extremely unlikely, really, or he's taking something that will increase the serum creatinine. And there are two things that do that commonly. One is Creatine, which is metabolized into creatinine, and it's in every textbook that I've ever looked at. And the second is extreme high protein."

He explained how 2.7% of volume loss did not reach the required 5% of depletion to be considered moderately dehydrated. If an infant was treated in the ER who was 2.7% dehydrated, the doctors would order oral hydration therapy and *not* start an IV. He then explained that Max Gilpin was given so much fluid to raise his blood pressure and that it had nothing to do with rehydrating him.

He explained there was medical evidence to dispel any notions that Max Gilpin was run to death. Dr. Danzl stated, "There's multiple laboratory evidence. If you exercise too hard, you get acidotic; you build up acids in your blood. Max's initial pH was 7.4, which is normal. So his total body hadn't been exerted to the point that he was acidotic.

"There's an acid we measure called lactic acid, which builds up very high in patients who are extremely exerted. Max's was 1.6, which is the high range of normal, but consistent with exercise.

"Thirdly, there are studies that show, in college football players with twice-a-day practice, their CKs are in the 5,000–10,000 range. I've seen patients in the ER over a hundred thousand.

"If you exercise a normal person—for example, you (jurors) sitting here—pretty hard, the range would seem high (5,000–10,000), and the reading would be 223. But it would not be considered high if you had just jogged five miles. So 333 (Gilpin's reading) is low in this picture."

Dr. Danzl stated, "It tells me that not only dehydration *wasn't* a contributory factor, but extreme exertion was *not* a contributory factor." He then explained in detail how Adderall® could cause problems regulating body temperature. He testified it was his opinion that amphetamines were a risk factor for the onset of heatstroke for Max Gilpin.

He testified to how he believed Max Gilpin probably suffered from a viral illness and had an abnormally elevated serum creatinine level prior to practice on August 20. Those factors coupled with amphetamines were the contributing factors to Max Gilpin's heatstroke. He testified that heatstrokes are not 100% preventable. He stated, "The only way they are 100% preventable is if you don't exercise in the heat." He then said that heat exhaustion is 100% survivable, but 100% of heatstroke patients need to go to the emergency department, and "100% either die or get admitted to the intensive care unit. Otherwise, by definition, the heatstroke was misdiagnosed."

Dr. Danzl testified that placing a heatstroke victim in a tub or pool of ice is not only dangerous, but is a less effective method of cooling the patient vs. using lukewarm water and fanning the patient.

Dr. Danzl then testified that Antonio Calloway was hospitalized because of a heart murmur. His body temperature was normal; he suffered from heat exposure and his heart murmur had nothing to do with his heat exposure or the football practice. He then testified that Calloway's CK reading was a little higher than Max's, but still in the normal range with a reading in the 500's.

Butler wrapped up by having Dr. Danzl to explain why an autopsy would have been so helpful in this case. He answered, "The reason in medicine that we do autopsies is we're often surprised, and we're often trying to learn. And you might find other things that would explain which of the contributory factors were preventable and which weren't, and what we can learn from a tragedy like this."

Cross-examination by the prosecution and redirects did not reveal very much that was new. Dr. Danzl had solid evidence for his opinion that Max Gilpin's death was not caused by the exercise from the football practice.

Instead, it was "a perfect storm" of contributing factors, such as Creatine, Adderall® and a viral infection that triggered the heatstroke.

The next medical expert for the defense was Dr. George Nichols, and his testimony mirrored Dr. Danzl's. In order to avoid repeating the same medical evidence, the summary of Dr. Nichol's testimony will be brief. Dr. Nichols told Brian Butler he is currently employed as a consulting forensic pathologist, and before that he was the Chief Medical Examiner for the State of Kentucky for 20 years and 2 months. When asked to explain what "forensic medicine" means, Dr. Nichols stated, "Forensic has two major meanings. For our purposes today, it means 'law applied.' So I'm a forensic pathologist. Theoretically, anything having to do with the law and human disease is what I have studied."

Dr. Nichols then explained the procedures of an autopsy. He stated he could only recall one homicide case prosecuted without the benefit of an autopsy during his 20+ years as a medical examiner. It was the case of serial killer Donald Harvey where many of his homicides were not detected until decades later.

He stated that he had reviewed Calloway's and Gilpin's EMS and medical records, as well as the entire case file including all the interviews LMPD conducted. Based on all the information available, it was his opinion that Max Gilpin's death was an accident and not a homicide.

Nichols testified he did not think Max Gilpin's volume loss was 2.7%; he believed it was even less than that. He said that would be the equivalent of a long-haired 62-year-old man mowing his grass in 90° heat. The man would be thirsty, but in no danger. Nichols also covered the role that amphetamines, specifically Adderall®, play in heatstroke. He stated a clinical trial published by the manufacturer stated that 2.4% of the people who were on a 4-week trial of Adderall® developed a fever. He stated that if the deputy coroner had done his job and collected the fluids from the hospital, they would have been able to analyze the data further. However, the deputy coroner did not.

When asked if heatstroke is 100% survivable, Nichols replied, "There's nothing that's 100% survivable. I've literally seen someone die from an ingrown toenail." He stated the mortality rate from heatstroke varies from 50–80%, depending on the medical center studied. He also stated there is no continuum that goes from muscle cramps to heat exhaustion to exertional heatstroke.

Jon Heck handled cross-examinations for the prosecution. Heck asked Dr. Nichols if they had spoken to one another about this case, and he said, "I think I told you on the phone exactly what I just told the jury. Mr. Heck, if you want to know in a criminal case what my conclusions are and why I came to those conclusions, please ask me so you can better prepare your case." He believed there was nothing excessive about the football practice on August 20.

Under redirect from Butler, Dr. Nichols stated that Stinson had not done anything wrong by not treating Max, because he was being attended to by others. He also stated that Max Gilpin's heatstroke could not have been foreseeable, based on the control group of soccer players and the high school and pee-wee football players at PRPHS that day. He testified, "It's highly unlikely that Max, given any type of treatment after his collapse, was going to survive intact."

CHAPTER 21

DAYS 12–13: WHITE FLAG, DR. SMOCK, AND CLOSINGS

Day 12 saw the last of the "live" witnesses. Lois Gilpin was the first witness for the day, but before she could make it to the stand she was involved in some controversy. While she was waiting to be called to testify, Leland Hulbert entered the room she was waiting in and told her he would like to talk to her. When she stood up, I intervened and asked Hulbert if he had talked to Brian Butler. Hulbert began saying something about he didn't have to talk to Brian, so I turned to Lois and said, "This is Leland Hulbert, one of the prosecutors. You don't have to talk to him if you don't want to. She expressed that she didn't wish to talk with him, so I told her to sit down. Hulbert was talking about something when one of the people in the room kicked the door closed on him. I was aware that blocking him from Lois Gilpin was not illegal, so I didn't think much more about it until her cross-examination from Hulbert.

Brian Butler called Lois Gilpin to the stand. She testified that she had been Max Gilpin's stepmother since he was five years old. She stated that he would spend half his time at the home she shared with his father Jeff Gilpin. She recalled how, when Max was younger, he was not crazy about football, but that changed when he started high school. She testified, "So when Max was showing interest and starting to grow, Jeff would take Max to go work out as many times as Max would come to our house. They drank their protein shakes; they ate a lot of proteins and big diets. But Max enjoyed that. Jeff would go work out with Max every night."

She stated that on the evening of August 19, 2008, Max went to bed earlier than usual and he did not feel good. She said, "He went to bed with no dinner that night. He said he had a headache, and he said that he had a belly problem when he was in the bathroom." She then recounted what happened the morning of August 20 before Max left for school.

She testified, "I asked him if he wanted juice. He was to take his medicine, his Adderall® that morning. He was cranky. I leaned over and kissed his head, and he told me he had a headache, that he was sick and he was hot.

"Jeff walked in and told him, 'We're going to be late; you need to get up. You need to get your butt in gear, and you need to get to school.'"

When asked did Max want to go to school that day, Lois Gilpin answered, "He just said he didn't feel good; he had a headache. He didn't talk back to his dad. When I kissed him, I told him he was hot. You know, I imagine he would have liked to have stayed home. I wish he would have stayed home. But he did what his dad said."

Gilpin stated she and Jeff talked about how Max didn't feel well the night before. She said she relayed that information to everybody, including doctors and Michele and Aaron Crockett. She said they talked about his belly problems the night before his collapse. She also stated how he was hot in the morning the day of his collapse, and that he had gone to Greenwood Elementary School after school that day to lie down. She testified it was she and Jeff who told the doctor Max was not feeling well the day he collapsed. She stated she and Jeff joined Jason Stinson's church after Max's death, and she was never contacted by the LMPD for an interview.

Leland Hulbert handled the cross-examination for the Commonwealth. Hulbert asked Lois if he had tried to set a meeting, and Gilpin answered, "You did." She then explained, "I told you that I wanted to think about it. Then I told you I didn't have anything to say, and I didn't wish to speak with you."

When asked if she had shared the information about Max being sick with Michele Crocket, she answered, "Absolutely. Jeff and I both did, beginning at the hospital that first night when we were called there, continuing through the funeral home, in private moments we had at their home and in private moments we had during the visitation."

During Lois Gilpin's testimony, Michele Crockett got up from her seat and stomped out of the courtroom in anger. She was pounding the keys of her cell phone, and I surmised she might be calling Jeff Gilpin. (Jeff could not be in the courtroom during Lois' testimony because of an Emergency Protective Order (EPO) she had against him.) At least three jurors watched Michele Crockett charge out of the courtroom, and at that moment I finally believed there would be a "not guilty" verdict.

Hulbert wanted to make sure the jury knew he had made multiple attempts to contact Lois Gilpin, and he wanted them to know I interfered with him talking to her just prior to her testimony. In an apparent attempt to attack her credibility, he went after her because she attended the same church as Jason Stinson. He attacked several aspects of her religion, and she shot each one of his theories down. (Her answers had to be coming from her heart, because no one had ever discussed with her the notion that the prosecution would attack her affiliation with the same church as the defendant.)

Under redirect from Butler, Lois stated that Aaron and Michele Crockett were talking about filing a lawsuit at the hospital.

Next, Alex Dathorne called Robbie Sample to the stand for the defense. Sample is retired from Ford Motor Company and is currently employed by JCPS as an In-School Suspension Coordinator. He stated he also referees soccer and basketball games as a hobby. He stated he was at PRPHS on August 20 to officiate the soccer match between WHS and PRPHS. He said he arrived about 5:00–5:10 PM to inspect the field and the area, and he then stated he went to PRPHS's Athletic Director Craig Webb for a heat index reading around 5:15 PM. He testified it was 94° and what rules would be in place for that temperature. He said he had a meeting with the other officials, and they agreed they would not be stopping for a water break since it was not required. He then testified to meeting with the coaches and team captains before the game to inform them of the same thing. He stated they understood this action was taken because it was under 95 degrees.

He recalled that at least two midfielders ran the whole soccer game, which totaled 80 minutes. He testified that he is an EMT and first responder, and he had noticed Antonio Calloway, so during the break he went to see if the football coaches needed any help. When he saw they had it under control, he began the second half of the soccer game. He said he had a player in the second half suffer an asthma attack, and she threw up on the field. He stated he didn't consider stopping the game. He heard Coach Stinson say they were going to run "until someone quits," but he didn't find that odd or out of the ordinary.

Under cross-examination by Leland Hulbert, Sample stated he allowed the soccer players to drink water during the first half while an injured player was leaving the field. He said he is a friend of Stinson and would see him at church every Sunday, but they did not always speak to one another. He testified that he attended a vigil for Coach Stinson, but he did not attend any fundraising events, nor had he contributed to Stinson's defense.

The first coach called to the stand for the defense was Steve Ellis. He told Alex Dathorne, "I am a heavy equipment mechanic. I travel and repair large pieces of equipment." He stated he was a youth league coach with Panther Youth for nine years and he helped out from time to time with the PRPHS football team. He testified about what practice consisted of on August 20, and he remembered Coach Stinson calling for the players to begin conditioning. He spoke of Stinson having the players remove their helmets and shoulder pads, and then he said he went to help Antonio Calloway. He said when he took the ice bag from Daniel Farris, Farris had been sitting there awhile and was fine. He said there was other ice available, but he took it from Farris because he was right there.

Ellis stated that once he got Calloway's breathing controlled, he was walking him back to the bleachers when he noticed a kid with "rubbery legs." He said at the time it did not concern him because it was common to see kids who had pushed themselves. He figured the kid just needed to come to the tree. He said he noticed Craig Webb go by on the Gator™ behind Coach Stinson, and then he realized the player had gone down. Ellis said Stinson had his back to the situation, but he (Ellis) ran out at a dead sprint to assist. He said as soon as he arrived, they put Max in the Gator™ and took him to the water.

He testified to the treatment given to Max Gilpin, and how he thought they were going to be able to cool him and bring him back around. He gave probably the most detailed recollection of the treatment of Max because he had his hands on him the whole time, except for the moment he went to get the hose. Ellis said he was yelling at Max to open his eyes, and that Max was trying, but then "they just started to close again." He said that was when he realized Max was in trouble. He knew 911 had been called, so all he could do was try to cool him.

Ellis then explained how the boys could have only run 12–14 gassers that day, based on the amount of time they ran and how fast they were running. He painted an excellent picture of what was going on that day, especially regarding how long it would take each to finish a gasser. He said it was mathematically impossible for the players to have run 20–30 gassers. He then testified about a 300 lb. player who ran every gasser Max ran. He said this kid was not in good shape and that he could stand to lose 120 pounds, but he ran every step Max did.

At this point, it is important to note that the witnesses in this trial did not agree on the number of "gassers" the players ran that day. Witnesses said the running lasted anywhere from as little as 20 minutes to as much as an hour and a half. From its beginning, the criminal case against Jason Stinson focused on water breaks and the number of gassers run during the August 20 practice. It was repeatedly termed "excessive running" by the Commonwealth Attorney's Office, but according to the evidence, it doesn't appear excessive at all.

Both Jefferson County Public Schools (JCPS) and Louisville Metro Police Department (LMPD) conducted independent investigations concerning the events of August 20. (The LMPD and JCPS investigations were initially conducted jointly, but JCPS was asked by LMPD to operate independently from the police department's investigation during its very early stages.) There were at least two meticulous inquiries about the day's events. In addition to these investigations, at least two other inquiries were completed, one by the Commonwealth Attorney's Office. The conclusion of these four investigations cast great confusion about what *really* happened on August 20, 2008. The reason for the different conclusions seems to lie in the different methods used by the investigators. The criminal defense and JCPS used several tools and factors that the Commonwealth Attorney's Office chose to ignore. The three most glaring factors were the use of forensic science, math (used to determine a window of possible gassers run), and common sense. (Common sense indicates that there is no way the players ran only 20 minutes, just as there is no way they ran 90 minutes.) What was the truth? Steve Ellis' testimony set the record straight.

Based on numerous factors that could be proven, Ellis estimated that the run lasted at least 30 minutes and no more than 45 minutes. With that stated, a time frame was established (using 30, 35 and 40 minutes) to determine how many gassers each player ran. (Every investigative team who bothered to do the math determined that 12–15 gassers were about all that would be possible. It would be utterly impossible for two groups to run 20–30 gassers in 30–40 minutes, considering each gasser is a total of approximately 213 ⅓ yards (640 feet). This comes to a grand total of 9,200–12,800 feet for each group to run.)

Considering there are 5,280 feet in a mile, this would mean each group ran between 2.4 and 3.6 miles in 15–20 minutes. The following chart shows 1.5 miles (12 gassers), 2.4 miles (20 gassers) and 3.6 miles (30 gassers), along with the estimated times that each group ran. The chart reflects 15-, 17.5- and 20-minute timelines.

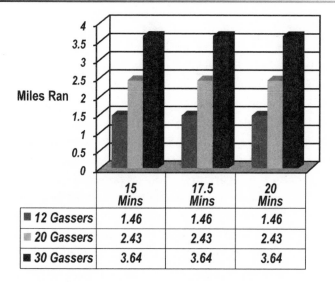

	15 Mins	17.5 Mins	20 Mins
12 Gassers	1.46	1.46	1.46
20 Gassers	2.43	2.43	2.43
30 Gassers	3.64	3.64	3.64

The next graph shows how many minutes it would take to run each mile. Estimates range from 4-minute miles to nearly 14-minute miles.

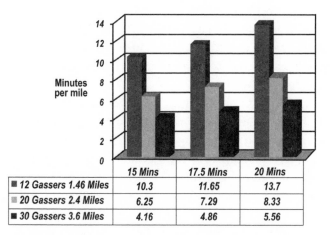

	15 Mins	17.5 Mins	20 Mins
12 Gassers 1.46 Miles	10.3	11.65	13.7
20 Gassers 2.4 Miles	6.25	7.29	8.33
30 Gassers 3.6 Miles	4.16	4.86	5.56

On a day when gassers are timed, the "little guys" (the faster and skilled positions such as backs, receivers and linebackers) typically run their gassers in about 42–52 seconds, while the "big guys" (the offensive and defensive linemen who are typically larger in size and slower in speed) usually turn in a time of about 52–60 seconds. On August 20, 2008, the gassers were not timed, and by most accounts many players were doing everything from running at full speed, to jogging, to briskly walking. The second team cannot begin the next gasser until every player from the previous group has finished. The reason for this is safety; after all, allowing 50 players to sprint while one or two are going against the grain would surely get someone hurt.

It is estimated that the "little guys" were taking about 60–80 seconds and the "big guys" were taking 60–95 seconds to complete each gasser. It is widely reported that the last gassers without equipment were taking up to 1.5 minutes for the "little guys" and over 2 minutes for the "big guys." On August 20, the players were told after gasser number 10 to remove their shoulder pads. It is certain that at least one minute was lost during this event. (It easily takes 30–45 seconds to get shoulder pads off and that's when you are in a hurry.) When equipment removal is factored in, the window of time becomes even smaller.

It is important to prove definitively how many gassers were run that day, because the players' recollections kept growing larger and larger. (Commonwealth Attorney R. Dave Stengel and LMPD Sgt. Denny Butler testified before the grand jury that the players ran 12–15 gassers, yet Assistant Commonwealth Attorneys Leland Hulbert and Jonathan Heck allowed players to testify at the subsequent trial that they ran 20–30 gassers. A few days after the August 20 practice, several stories as to what happened emerged, and a few witnesses actually stuck with their implausible and nearly impossible accounts under oath at trial.)

Given all of the information, it is *possible* the players could have run 15 gassers, but 12 seems more likely. It is also very clear that 35 minutes is about the amount of time the players ran (5:30–6:05 PM).

Under cross-examination by Jon Heck, Ellis confirmed these numbers. Ellis was also able to explain to the jurors that the conditioning was not a punishment. He stated the coaches were not pushing the kids, and they were allowed to run at their own pace. When given names of players who had vomited, Ellis said he recognized Duff's name from youth league, and he stated Duff would throw up every day. He said it was not uncommon to have four or five kids hanging on a fence throwing up.

The next coach to testify about the August 20 practice was Steve Deacon. Deacon told Alex Dathorne that he is employed as a teacher by JCPS at Kammerer Middle School. Deacon explained what an assistant coach's role is, and he briefly described what he witnessed that day. He stated he went to the locker room around 5:45 PM to treat injured players, and he returned around 6:05–6:10 PM. He stated he was at the bleachers treating Antonio Calloway when he heard a player call for him, saying Max needed help. As he jogged to Max, Max was still walking on his own with a player on each side assisting him, and then he went down. He said they assessed him and quickly decided to put him on the Gator™ to transport him to the water. He said he sent a couple of players for the ice bucket, and he explained that they had ice, as well as ice bags, in the cooler that day. He stated that they attempted to cool Max down until EMS arrived.

Jon Heck cross-examined Deacon and went over many of the same things. They also went over when it is appropriate to treat a player experiencing problems, and they discussed support in the PRP area and high school for Stinson. There was a redirect and then another cross of rapid-fire questions that left Deacon very happy to get off the stand.

Day 13 brought about an abrupt end to the trial because of an agreement between the prosecution and the defense the day before. A suggestion was made that the defense would only call Steve Deacon and play Dr. Smock's testimony in exchange for the Commonwealth agreeing not to call any rebuttal witnesses. The defense was willing to give up its toxicologist, plus some other witnesses to end the trial.

Brian Butler stated during a bench conference that he had been doing this long enough to read a jury, and he thought they were ready to be done. Dr. Bosse was not the only witness the defense had standing by ready to call, but by the time Steve Ellis left the stand *everyone* knew it was over. There were multiple character witnesses prepared to testify for Coach Stinson, including a retired Kentucky Supreme Court Justice. Anyone who had been paying attention knew this was over, and there was no need for the defense to go any further. Butler and Dathorne had completely crushed the Commonwealth's case. The prosecutors must have agreed, because they took the deal and waved the white flag.

Dr. Bill Smock's pre-recorded deposition was played for the jury. By prior agreement, several portions were edited out. I drew the short straw on who was going to edit the video, and about half way through the video, the issue arose. Apparently there were two different papers being used for editing, so approximately a minute was not cut and a shorter exchange was cut. The uncut content was skipped over and the cut information was read to the jury. Dr. Smock's testimony mirrored Dr. Danzl's and Dr. Nichols', with the exception that Dr. Smock was normally a paid expert for the Commonwealth Attorney's Office.

Once the deposition ended, the defense rested its case. Instructions were read for the jurors, and the closing arguments began. Much like the opening arguments, the closings are summarized here for the sake of brevity.

Alex Dathorne reminded the jurors they had a decision to make, and they were talking about a football practice that no experts said they would have stopped. Dathorne explained, "You've got a man looking at prison time for being a football coach. Jason Stinson, on August 20, 2008, did absolutely nothing different than every coach—in this county, in this Commonwealth, in this country—was doing on that day. Football players get sick. They vomit. It is a violent sport. You don't have to like it; you don't have to watch it; you don't have to go to it, and you don't have to play it. But you have to understand that it exists."

He stated that "this situation got out-of-hand when the *Courier-Journal* printed a series of articles. It quoted witnesses who said the players were denied water. They said, 'It was awful.' You heard from those witnesses. Soccer parents came in here. They, too, said, 'It was awful.' They were denying those boys water. Even Dr. Danzl believed what he was reading in the newspaper, and he assumed water denial would be the cause of the heatstroke. However, after reviewing the case, he realized dehydration was not the cause at all."

Dathorne next described how the LMPD investigation was woefully incomplete. He stated the deputy coroner ruled Max's death an accident, and neither the police nor the prosecutors bothered to talk to him. In fact, they didn't consult any medical experts before indicting Stinson, nor did they bother to talk to the ER doctor who treated Max. Dr. Greenwell said Max was not dehydrated. Then, in March, their own expert told them it was not a crime. Prosecutors, however, did not dismiss. Dathorne stated that could not happen because "all the cameras showed up." He didn't blame the media for coming because, after all, it was the first time ever a coach had been charged for doing what coaches do every day.

Dathorne further emphasized how the prosecution had struggled "since day one" to hold this case together. The prosecutors were "playing games" when they say that Adderall® is not an amphetamine. Dathorne stated, "That's the kind of stuff that smacks of desperation." He reminded the jury how many of Hulbert's comments during his opening statement were proven false. He pointed out how the prosecution failed to prove Stinson's CPR certification was expired. Dathorne said, "They are so sure and arrogant of themselves that they don't even look at their own paperwork." He even reminded the jurors how the prosecutors had argued with their own witnesses when they would not say what they wanted them to say. Dathorne elaborated, "If they can confuse you enough, they're hoping you'll convict this man."

He continued to expose more "facts" Leland Hulbert said would be learned at trial but were never quite developed. Dathorne repeated Hulbert's opening statement, "The reason why the coach was out there acting like a jerk was because he had the big game with Valley coming up.' You didn't hear any of that on the stand. That's all nonsense." Dathorne reminded jurors about Hulbert going on and on about Coach Stinson blowing his whistle. That didn't happen either, but it sounded good, and it helped paint Stinson as a drill sergeant, a commandant, or even a Nazi. He recalled how David Keown cried on the stand when he told about Coach Stinson helping him when he needed it.

Dathorne reminded the jurors how the defense called the medical examiner, who testified for free. The Commonwealth Attorney's Office could have called a medical examiner, but they did not. He went to explain how it was never proved that Max Gilpin was run to death. He said there was something different about Max that day, and it was amphetamines, a viral illness and his irregularly high creatinine level. He asked the jurors to remember what Jeff Gilpin said, and then how Lois Gilpin came in and disputed most of his testimony. He also wanted the jurors to recall how many times Jeff Gilpin's story changed and how, for several months, he said the coaches did nothing wrong. After ripping the prosecution's case wide open, Dathorne closed with, "So that's what it is, ladies and gentlemen of the jury, and I ask you to convict football, not Jason Stinson."

We went to our conference room, and everyone began sharing hugs because we knew Alex had knocked it out of the park. Jason thanked Alex, because he said it was the first time all of this madness had ever been fully explained.

Of course, the Commonwealth still had its closing statement. Jon Heck opened by saying, "I have found myself in the difficult position of trying to bring order out of the last two weeks, at 10 minutes to 2 o'clock in the afternoon when you have not had a lunch break." He then explained how he saw August 20, 2008. He stated, "A child died on a football field. He was run to death. He needed a break. He's dead, folks. He's dead. And this is why we're here." He continued, "I hope I don't have to go any further into this. I hope there's no more explanation needed. It doesn't matter if Max was dehydrated or not. An exertional heatstroke, by its definition, is the exertion that caused it. It's what happened leading up to the collapse; what Max was being subjected to, what was he being told, what symptoms was he manifesting. That's the only thing this case is about." He said the defense failed to mention what this case was about and that was Stinson's conduct. He stated, "They can't have free rein over our children; to say what they want and to do what they want, because it's football."

He asked what character was built for David Englert and his buddy when they walked off the field because they quit the team. Was this the NFL? What lessons was Stinson teaching those kids? He pleaded, "I think the evidence is very clear; that David Jason Stinson in 2008, 364-and-a-half days out of the year, was a model citizen. He was probably a fantastic teacher, a man of strong moral character, who loved these kids. I don't think there's any doubt in my mind that that is true."

Heck continued, "But like most criminal cases, at least a lot of them, we don't indict or charge people for what you did those 364-and-a-half days. It's the day you took a risk, the hour you took a stupid risk, and there was a real consequence. It's just the way it works. To tell kids they have to run until they quit, that's so wrong. That's wrong on every level. I don't care if you're a football fan or not, but it happened.

"David Thompson said he saw people crying, and the best athlete on the team started having problems. At what point do you stop it? The running continued another 10 to 15 minutes. Now we have a crime. This is your crime, folks. Stinson had all these factors.... The fact that he deprived them of water—let's be clear on that—what it tells us is his state of mind. Despite all that, is it any wonder that only four players wanted to get some water afterwards? Despite all that, we're not done yet. Then he holds a team meeting.

"Stinson was in complete control of this situation. How could he not see six to eight players throwing up and Max's stumbling, but he sees four going to get water? How is that possible? Unless it isn't. This is your crime."

He then explained how none of the soccer parents had an agenda, and their credibility should not be challenged. However, Lois Gilpin should not be considered credible, because she wouldn't talk to prosecutors. "She goes to Stinson's church. They pay her mortgage. What's it going to be like when she goes back to church if he gets convicted? Why in the world wouldn't you tell the police or the prosecutors about this, unless you wanted to set them up for failure? When you let us know, we can look into it. If you don't let us know, we can't.

"When you compare that response of those coaches with the response of Coach Stinson, the difference is extraordinary, because he did nothing. He failed to monitor the athletes. The rules say, 'monitor athletes carefully for necessary action.' Is there any doubt in your mind he failed that one? Is there any doubt in your mind that he put competitive preparation over safety? What we have is an exertional heatstroke. We have a child who suffered exertional heatstroke, August 20, on a practice field who was given an ultimatum: Run until someone quits the team. And we had a child who had the character that wouldn't allow him to quit."

In closing, Heck explained that if the jurors could not find Stinson guilty of reckless homicide, there was the charge of wanton endangerment they could fall back on. "The mechanism is there. I ask that you go back, and I wish you the best in reviewing all this evidence."

CHAPTER 22

THE VERDICT AND ITS AFTERMATH

Less than 90 minutes after the jurors were sent to deliberate, the phone call came in to let everyone know the jury had reached a verdict. (We had gone to a sandwich shop a couple blocks from the courthouse for a late lunch, and we had just returned when the call came in.) In my mind, this was very positive. It was my belief that the jurors could not have convicted Stinson that quickly given all of the evidence, so the quick decision must have meant an acquittal.

The security in the courtroom was quadrupled for the reading of the verdict, and Judge Gibson made sure the gallery knew that a perceived threat or outburst would not be tolerated. (It was explained to me by one of the sheriffs that this is normal protocol when a verdict is read. The court just called for more officers because the courtroom was nearly full.)

Once the preliminary instructions were complete, Judge Gibson called the jury back into the courtroom. She asked the foreperson if the jury had reached a verdict, and he replied "Yes, Ma'am." With no delay, she read the verdict.

"Under instruction number one, reckless homicide, we, the jury, find the defendant David Jason Stinson not guilty. Under instruction number two, wanton endangerment in the first degree, we, the jury, find the defendant David Jason Stinson not guilty."

Judge Gibson asked the jurors if this was indeed their verdict, and the foreperson confirmed it. She asked both the prosecution and the defense if either wished a poll of the jury. Once they both stated "no," Judge Gibson thanked the jurors for their service and released them. And with that the longest year of my life came to a close.

As soon as the jurors left the courtroom, Monica Stinson burst into tears. She got up and headed towards Jason, who was sharing a hug of relief with Brian Butler. She later recounted at that moment it felt like the world was lifted off her shoulders.

As happy as Coach Stinson supporters were, it appeared that Max Gilpin's family was equally disappointed. Michele Crockett had previously stated that she did not want Max's death to be in vain, so maybe she believed the criminal trial would see to that. It didn't happen quite that way. The prosecution fumbled and bumbled its way through 13 days of a trial that many times it just did not seem prepared for. As a matter of fact, they were so unprepared, by the end of the trial they still had not filled out the jury instruction sheet. When Brian Butler saw this he told the court, "This speaks volumes… here it is the day before this goes to a jury and they haven't even filled out their jury instruction sheet yet. This should have been done long ago." Crockett did not get the conviction she was hoping for, but she was at least satisfied that the trial brought about awareness of heatstroke.

Her statement made me feel that we raised nearly $100,000 for heatstroke awareness. Actually, we raised the money to defend Coach Stinson from a frivolous prosecution, but in the process we were able to help fund a heatstroke awareness campaign. Couldn't we have raised awareness about heatstroke in a much more appropriate way, one that would not have been so costly to the taxpayers? Imagine all the good that could have come if the money spent on Stinson's trial had been used another way. (When we wrote the first $20,000 check for his defense, Coach Stinson said that much money could have bought defibrillators for every high school in the entire county.)

Many residents of Jefferson County and the Commonwealth of Kentucky have failed to realize that their tax dollars funded this entire charade. Jason Stinson's legal defense is the only exception to that statement. No taxpayer dollars were spent defending Coach Stinson in his criminal case. In fact, all the professional witnesses who testified on Coach Stinson's behalf did it for free. We didn't have to hire an out-of-state expert, because the leading local experts testified at no charge.

The cameras were huddled around the courtroom door looking for comment, and practically everyone but Jason Stinson obliged. Assistant Commonwealth Attorney Leland Hulbert stated, "I do think more good will come from this trial. If every coach steps on a football field and now thinks about what he is doing a little bit more—maybe thinks about water a little more, or watches his players a little bit more—we are all better off for having this case."

A reporter asked Alex Dathorne, "What do you think contributed to the verdict?" Dathorne simply replied, "The fact that Coach Stinson didn't do anything wrong or illegal. Max's death was unfortunate, but we are satisfied with the jury's verdict, and we are all happy to be moving forward."

Brian Butler was not so coy with his comments. He stated, "I think it was a witch hunt that included nobody ever bothering to check with any medical doctors. We had some of the best people in Louisville come forward for free and tell this jury what really happened. This was a tragedy, but it wasn't a crime. It never was a crime and, had it been investigated [properly], it wouldn't have been prosecuted."

The local media was scrambling for interviews from all involved, and Dave Stengel was ready to go on camera. If I ever wondered if this guy was a jerk or not, he helped clear it up with his interviews following the trial. The first hint that he was making out of bounds statements was when WLKY-32 TV's reporter Ben Jackey called me, seeking comment on some of the remarks that Dave Stengel had made the day following the verdict. Apparently, when asked if he thought the events of the last year had changed Jason Stinson's coaching philosophy, Stengel replied, "I don't know him well enough to say that, but from what I have seen, I don't think he listens very well." My official comment to that was "Wow! Obliviously Dave Stengel does not know Jason."

My thoughts on it were somewhat different. After I said, "Wow," there was a slight pause for a couple of seconds. That is because my initial thoughts probably would not have been appropriate for the six o'clock news. The first thing that went through my mind was that Stengel had some nerve to say he didn't think Jason Stinson listens very well. That is the pot calling the kettle black. I also thought that Dave Stengel should shut up and go away at this time. Please stop talking, and for your sake do not give any more interviews about Jason Stinson. We have heard enough from you. We have heard all of the allegations levied against Jason Stinson. Your office had their chance in a court of law to prove these allegations, and you failed miserably.

If Stengel were to say anything at all, I believe he owed an explanation to the residents of PRP and the taxpayers of the city of Louisville and the Commonwealth of Kentucky as to why he pursued this case with absolutely no scientific evidence to support his theory. If he cannot explain his actions then perhaps his last words on this subject should just be an apology.

If anyone has proven they do not listen very well it is *you* Mr. Stengel. It is *you* who didn't listen to *your* own expert Dr. William Smock when he tried to warn you. He came to your office because he was afraid you may have been given some bad advice, and he didn't want to see you get "ambushed". If someone from the Commonwealth's Attorneys Office had bothered to call Dr. George Nichols, he would have told them the same thing. In fact he did, the Commonwealth's Attorneys Office was given access to all of the defense's medical experts prior to the trial.

That could have been considered a very unusual move on the part of defense team, but Butler and Dathorne thought after the prosecutors heard from the leading experts they would drop the charges. They didn't listen, or if they did all they heard was they didn't have a case. Instead of dropping the charges, they went out and secured a new indictment a few weeks later. Did Stengel listen to what these doctors told him when they informed him that Max Gilpin's death was a terrible tragedy and not a crime? I don't know him well enough to say that, but from what I have seen, I don't think he listens very well. Does that sound familiar? Perhaps Stengel was instead reflecting on his own character when he made that remark.

Stengel obviously has some issues with Jason Stinson that exceeds the normal prosecution vs. accused relationship. Otherwise, he would do what most prosecutors do when they are thoroughly defeated and embarrassed in court. They stand in front of the media and explain while they believed their case had merit, but the jury didn't see it that way. They usually state they respectfully disagree with the jury's verdict but justice has been served and it is time to move on. They generally don't go out and verbally attack a former defendant who has just recently been acquitted. Many times Stinson's prosecution seemed to be more a personal vendetta than the pursuit of justice. Even though I state Stengel pursued this case because he believed a crime had been committed, I have to wonder if it had anything to do with unresolved issues Stengel may still hold fifty years later regarding football coaches. Thomas Lake with *Sports Illustrated* touched on this when he recounted how Stengel stated Stinson reminded him of his old football coach. Apparently, according to Lake, Stengel was mistreated by his coach in high school, and Lake implied the sour relationship may have influenced Stengel's judgment.

Two jurors granted interviews to the media following Coach Stinson's trial. The first one was an alternate who had heard the entire body of evidence. (He and another man were chosen as alternates at the end of the trial by jurors' numbers being drawn at random.) In a WDRB 41-TV interview on September 18, 2009, the alternate juror shared some enlightening information with reporter Stephan Johnson. He was surprised it took his fellow jurors an hour and a half to reach a verdict. "I would have voted to acquit Coach Stinson on both charges," the juror stated. "I was not surprised at all by the verdict." After nearly three weeks of testimony and dozens of witnesses, he said it was actually testimony from expert witnesses for the defense that convinced him. Dr. George Nichols (pathologist and former Kentucky Chief Medical Examiner) and Dr. Daniel Danzl from U of L Hospital had said other factors likely played a role in Gilpin's death. The juror said, "Their testimony seemed to provide more than reasonable doubt about the case, especially since they're leaders in their field."

On September 21, 2009, a second juror appeared on WHAS 11-TV. He was interviewed by reporter Chase Cain. He called the decision a "no brainer." He said, "Thirty-five minutes, that's about tops. The rest of it was eating and waiting to go back to the courtroom. I was amazed that we were all on the same page. There were older people, younger people, middle-aged people, and we all must've heard the same thing in that courtroom. The evidence was just overwhelming. I don't feel like the coach did anything wrong to hurt Max Gilpin."

Following the verdict, Jason and Monica Stinson, and Brian and Ashley Butler, along with me and my wife Ann, flew to New York City on Monday, September 21. The producers of ABC's *Good Morning America* (*GMA*) flew us there, so Jason and Brian could appear on the show the following morning. In addition to appearing on ABC, interviews were granted to FOX News, ESPN's *Outside the Lines*, and the *Mike Gallagher Show*. An interview with *Inside Edition* was cancelled for no other reason than it made me feel uncomfortable, and an interview scheduled with CNN for September 23 had to be cancelled because Coach Stinson was experiencing back pain from a car wreck he was involved in months earlier.

They were all primarily the same interview, except the interviewer at Fox became somewhat aggressive. However, Jason handled her with class, and he was never sucked in. The *GMA* interview was by far the longest, but it was not confrontational at all. However, a question was asked that we didn't expect to hear until a scheduled appearance on CBS the next morning. A clip was run of an interview conducted a day earlier on CBS' *The Early Show*. In an interview with Harry Smith, Michele Crockett said that "she's yet to hear the words 'I'm sorry' from Stinson." Asked whether he'd apologized, Crockett said, "Not personally, no. During the funeral and all that, of course he did offer his condolences and those kinds of things, but as far as an apology, no."

"Do you want an apology? Smith asked in his interview of Crockett. "Yes, I would like one. I want him to take responsibility for what's happened. That's the bottom line. At this time, I feel he hasn't stepped up to the plate."

After watching that clip, Diane Sawyer asked Coach Stinson, "What do you want to say to her this morning?"

Stinson replied, "I understand her loss. She's lost her son. It is a terrible tragedy that I can't begin to comprehend because I still have my children at home. There was a fair-minded 12-person jury that sat down and decided in 35 minutes that I was not guilty. There was an independent School Board investigation that came back and said I violated no policies or procedures. There was also a letter from the Superintendent that said I am allowed to go back to coaching and teaching with no stipulations. I cannot sit here today and take responsibility for something I am not responsible for."

That quote from Coach Stinson couldn't have summed up the last year any better. First Mrs. Crockett said she wanted answers. Then she wanted the truth. After that, she desired anyone responsible for Max's death to be held accountable. In a *People Magazine* article published September 7, 2009, she then said, "Now I want to see him [Stinson] do time." And finally, she wanted an apology from the person she believed responsible for her child's death. Perhaps she is looking in the wrong place. The ones who know the facts of the case are no longer willing to accept that Coach Stinson's practice methods killed Max Gilpin. An illness, a body building supplement, and a prescribed amphetamine all mixed together were the most likely causes of Max's death, and the monitoring of the aforementioned all begins at home.

Would an apology have ended this? That is highly unlikely, but it would have indeed helped Mrs. Crockett with her final request. In a wrongful death civil suit brought against the coaches, Michele Crockett and Jeff Gilpin are seeking over $19 million in damages.

To be able to say who or what was definitely responsible for Max Gilpin's death would require an autopsy. However, after consultation with a deputy coroner, Max Gilpin's parents declined an autopsy. Would an autopsy have been helpful or hurtful to the civil case? We can always speculate to what that answer might be, but we will never *really* know for sure.

Jason Riley wrote an article titled "Stinson says he is not responsible for terrible tragedy," which appeared on the *Courier-Journal*'s website Tuesday,

September 22, 2009. The story detailed the exchange between Crockett and Stinson via early morning national news programs, and the story also included some comments from Dave Stengel.

> Also on Tuesday, Jefferson Commonwealth Attorney Dave Stengel said in an interview with the newspaper that he has no regrets about taking the case to trial.
>
> "We accept a 'not guilty' verdict, but that doesn't mean innocent," Stengel said. "We saw it as a reckless homicide. We still see it as a reckless homicide."
>
> Stengel said in an interview that his only regret was not having an autopsy performed on Max, a point repeatedly stressed by the defense and its experts during the nearly three-week trial. Stengel said Max was buried by the time an investigation began, and doctors told the prosecution that the three days the teen spent in the hospital after collapsing at practice had provided vast amounts of information about Max's death.
>
> "The prosecution made a decision that 'We'd just as soon lose the case than put the family through the horror' of exhuming Max," Stengel said.
>
> Initially, after Stinson was indicted, Stengel said he would be handling the Stinson case with Assistant Commonwealth Attorney Leland Hulbert. But Stengel said he asked another assistant, Jon Heck, to take his place because he was having problems in his marriage. In addition, Stengel said the case was a massive undertaking and that he had only tried one case in the last several years.

If the lack of an autopsy is all Stengel regrets, then he probably doesn't have a conscience. If there had been an autopsy, there would have been no criminal case. Secondly, it was convenient how Stengel bailed out, once the ship started sinking. The only thing that might have been worse than starting a gigantic brawl and then leaving others to handle it would have been criticizing the ones who actually stood and fought.

The same *C-J* article stated:

> Stengel said the case was never about dehydration, saying that the prosecution knew early on that Stinson did not specifically

deny Max water. The prosecution told jurors that Stinson denied three or four players water after the running, telling them to go to a team meeting first.

Stengel said the case was about Stinson "pushing them beyond their limits and being totally unaware of the results that it caused," arguing the former coach ignored signs of heat illness among players and never attempted to help Max after he collapsed.

But the defense, he said, focused on the water issue, and the case was severely damaged when several defense medical experts testified that Max was not dehydrated.

"The defense did an excellent job of portraying the case as something it wasn't," Stengel said.

It is absurd that Stengel would say this case was not about water. It may be the only thing that I agree with him about, but go back to the beginning and see how many times water was mentioned by the CAO. Like most of his other failures with this case, Stengel looked to blame anyone or anything but himself. Blame it on water, and then don't blame it on water. Blame your subordinates, and then blame the defense. But don't blame yourself, because your only regret is not having an autopsy. Perhaps at the end of the day, it's the defense attorneys' fault because they did their job. Whatever the case might be, it sure wasn't Stengel's fault. Either Stengel was not thinking clearly, or he just could not admit when he was wrong. All Butler and Dathorne did was defend Coach Stinson against erroneous allegations.

Several journalists across the country weighed in about what the Stinson verdict meant, but most of them didn't have the facts correct. In a commentary titled "When high school football turns deadly," Mike Galanos of *Prime News* severely confused the facts. This commentary, posted at CNN's website on September 30, 2009, stated "It was a hot, humid day in August 2008 in Louisville, Kentucky. Max and his Pleasure Ridge Park High School teammates were wrapping up the second of two practices that day. They finished with a grueling round of 'gassers,' or sprints."

Two practices that day is the first mistake in Mike's commentary. There was only one practice on August 20, and the outdoor portion of the practice didn't even last two hours. (In fact there was school that day, so two practices would have been nearly impossible.) It was the irresponsible regurgitation of "facts" like this that spread so many untrue stories.

The primary reason I focus on Mike Galanos is because of a conversation I had with a man in New York City. While we were each waiting for a cab, we began a casual conversation about why each of us was in NYC. It turns out he was there to film an episode of a popular game show, and he was aware of Coach Stinson's criminal case. He immediately began with a statement about two practices a day, and I interrupted him and said, "Not even two hours." He then began on water and how his coach denied him water when he played football, and I again had to tell him water had nothing to do with it either. By the end of our brief conversation, it was clear he really didn't know many facts, even though he had watched several news stories.

I wondered, how does this happen? Doesn't the media have any accountability? I had forgotten about the encounter with the misinformed game show contestant until I stumbled across Galanos' commentary. It said, "Every coach should monitor how hot it is before and during practice. A heat index monitor costs less than $150, and that is a small price to pay for safety."

Thank you for the tip. The "heat index monitor" is called a hygrometer, and Coach Stinson used one that day.

Galanos also stated, "Another thing to consider is how many times a team should practice during the scorching hot, dog days of August. There is usually a 'hell' week in there, when a team practices two times per day. I have no problem with that, as long as a coach is smart about how hot it is out there."

Was he talking about Stinson? That is unclear, but the comments lead the reader to believe he was. The character assault began to wrap up with the statement, "The last thing, and this could be the most important, is to never deny a player water. According to the Centers for Disease Control, one of the best ways to prevent a heat-related illness is through proper hydration. So if a player is asking for a drink, give it to him."

Once again, thank you for that tip. Galanos was probably proud of his water comment, but he should have been ashamed for not doing any homework before saying such things. He did not do much to investigate his sources, or he would have known that at this point even the prosecutor was finally admitting this was *not* about water.

Earlier in the same commentary, Galanos said, "But I think it is a good thing that this trial took place, and I hope coaches across the country now think twice about how they run their practices and whether they are putting our kids in danger."

Galanos closed with these words: "Stinson has said Max's death is a burden he will live with for the rest of his life. I hope his story, and Max's tragic death, bring about needed changes to the game we love."

Maybe we should not be focusing on the game we love, two practices a day, or even water breaks. Perhaps the focus should be on what caused Max Gilpin's death and not what sounds good in a story intended to grab viewers' attention.

It is the aftermath of the verdict that made writing this book necessary. We had dispelled all of these allegations, but many false or irrelevant allegations were still being reported. Apparently the trial did not stop the flow of misinformation; for the most part, this book would be the only real chance to set the record straight.

CHAPTER 23

WHAT WE LEARNED

Throughout this whole process, there were several occasions where we stopped and wondered what the real problem was. We asked ourselves, "Have we become so numb to the game of football that we just cannot see how this practice killed Max?" The answer was "no." In fact, football practices conducted today are no way like the practices conducted a generation earlier. (That generation ran much tougher practices.)

Many practice tactics acceptable in the 70s or the 90s would not be acceptable today. Remember, most people with any experience or knowledge of football said August 20 was an ordinary practice. If there is a problem with football, then change football. Change policies, change procedures, change regulations, change rules or maybe even change some laws. Change can be achieved in many different ways, but using the criminal justice system to bring about change should not be one them.

The football practice was not the cause of Max Gilpin's death; it was merely a catalyst. Given all the factors (medication, supplements and an illness), this tragedy would have occurred under many other circumstances. Max could have been playing soccer that day and not wanted to come out of the game. (One half of a soccer game exceeds the amount of conditioning at PRPHS on August 20, 2008. Some soccer players run the entire game, and in fact, there were soccer players just a few yards away who ran significantly more than Max Gilpin that day.) Max could have been running cross country, or perhaps after-school employment required him to work in the heat. There are many "catalysts" that could be exchanged with the football practice, and the result would end the same. The football practice is an "x factor." Switch the x factor with many other similar activities, and the final outcome would probably be similar.

The three main ingredients in this formula, however, are not optional.

If you remove even one of them (medication, supplements or illness), it is likely this tragedy wouldn't have occurred. Everyone agreed Max died of heatstroke, but what caused the heatstroke? It is hard to say for sure, but we know what didn't cause it.

Once we knew we could prove what *didn't* kill Max (dehydration or excessive exercise), we could begin to focus on what did lead to his tragic death. What we learned is something every parent, coach and player should know. It was not *one single* factor that caused Max Gilpin's collapse. It was a series of multiple events that each made a necessary contribution. Until the combination of these factors is addressed, more children are most surely going to die in a similar fashion.

The first thing to understand is medication. Comparing Max Gilpin's use of Adderall® to others—adolescent football players or anyone else for that matter—is not fair, because the medication was not being taken as prescribed. In the spring of 2009, stories started to circulate about Max's unwillingness to take his ADD medication. There was a letter in the evidence where Michele Crockett notified the coaching staff that Max didn't take his medication during the summer and would not be taking the pills during the team's trip to football camp in early August 2008. She also testified about that note at trial. According to Crockett, the earliest Max would have started back on his medication was August 7, 2008. At the time of his collapse, he would have only been back on his medication 13 days at most. (If he had been back on the medication less than two weeks, and taking it sporadically during this time, he would have been susceptible to a whole different group of side effects that normally would not be present in older and more tolerant users.)

Jeff Gilpin testified that he found seven to eight pills in Max's sock drawer after his death. This could suggest that Max had only taken the medication about half the time since August 7, 2008. Furthermore, in a deposition for the civil case, one of Max's former classmates stated that Max had been selling his medication to another boy at school. This allegation was confirmed by another student in a separate interview. No one is suggesting that Max was on the street corner pushing pills, but there is substantial evidence that he was selling Adderall® to at least one classmate. By all accounts Max was a great kid, so please do not judge him based on one isolated incident. However, it is important to divulge this information because it adds to what may have really *killed* him. (It appears that his infrequent use of the medication, along with a couple of other factors, set off a series of events no one even realized was possible.)

An article posted at the website of the American College of Neuropsychopharmacology details the risk of fatal toxicity from intermittent amphetamine use. The article, written by Everett H. Ellinwood, M.D., George King, Ph.D. and Tong H. Lee, M.D. Ph.D. states:

> Deaths directly attributable to the pharmacological response to amphetamines relate to several phenomena, including: (1) hypertensive cerebrovascular hemorrhage (confirmed pathologically); (2) cardiovascular collapse secondary to ventricular fibrillation, with the majority of these cases in individuals less than 30 years of age with no evidence of pre-existing heart disease; (3) hyperpyrexia in the range of 40°C (104°), and (4) miscellaneous causes, such as septicemia with bacterial endocarditis or necrotizing angitis.
>
> In general, acute fatal drug reactions to amphetamine are more common in the occasional user than in the tolerant, chronic, high-dose abuser. This is particularly true of the hyperthermic and convulsive cascade that precedes many fatalities.

If Max Gilpin was running a temperature from some form of septic shock prior to practice, or if instead he was hyperthermic (which his medical records suggest), then the amphetamine's role cannot be denied. The denial becomes even more difficult, especially if any of these side effects were coupled with other well-known side effects, such as basal constriction. It was stated in trial testimony that Max's pediatrician had moved his dosage up from 20 mg to 30 mg, but Michele Crockett testified that she never picked the new medication up after dropping off the prescription. Typically a doctor will increase a dosage of amphetamines because the user has built a tolerance to the drug. Testimony and witness interviews, as well as other documentation, confirmed Max Gilpin was far from the tolerant category. Like many of the unknown factors, Max's irregular pattern of prescription drug use wasn't entirely confirmed until the trial.

Max Gilpin's irregular use of prescribed amphetamines certainly was a factor in causing his death. If Max had been taking the medication regularly, it is unlikely that he would have gained 35 pounds in thirteen months. (If he had been taking the amphetamine regularly, his weight gain would show that something else was wrong.)

Questions surrounding Max Gilpin's weight gain lead to the second factor: his use of the body-building supplement Creatine. This supplement is sold at many nutritional and herbal supplement stores. However, in the Commonwealth of Kentucky, many stores require the purchaser to be at least 18 years of age or older. At different times, both of Max's parents admitted to purchasing Creatine for him, but both claim he discontinued use months before his collapse. However, two of Max Gilpin's friends stated they had witnessed him take Creatine within two weeks of his collapse.

In October 1994, the supplement industry was deregulated by the Food and Drug Administration (FDA). Once the Dietary Supplements Health and Education Act (DSHEA) passed, heat-related deaths began to spike. After Corey Stringer, an NFL player, died from a heat-related collapse tied to a supplement in 2001, the opinions about these enhancers began to change. In an AP article posted on www.espn.com on July 21, 2002, Frederick Mueller (Professor and Chair of Physical Education, Exercise and Sport Science at University of North Carolina), spoke about the spike in heat-related deaths. The article stated:

> Mueller is also the chairman of the American Football Coaches' Committee of Football Injuries and directs the National Center for Catastrophic Sports Injuries, based at North Carolina.
>
> He said 20 football players suffered heat-related deaths since 1995. In the previous five years (1990–1994), only two football players' deaths were attributed to heat. From 1980 to 1989, 13 players died of heatstroke.
>
> "The trend is really up for those, and it's a real concern," he said Wednesday. "Coaches, players and even parents need to remember how to prevent these tragedies, and that's not hard to do."

I contacted Dr. Mueller in May, 2010, to confirm the figures. He reported 14 deaths from 1980–1989, 2 deaths from 1990–1994, 21 deaths from 1995–2001, and 21 deaths from 2002–2009. These figures were almost the same as what was being widely reported elsewhere. According to those figures, 1980–1989 saw 1.4 deaths related to heat per year. Nine out of the 14 deaths in this decade took place from 1980–1984. This was the decade that the need for hydration and water breaks became a top safety issue, and by the end of the decade, most coaches had received the message. This newfound vigilance might help explain the exceptionally low death rate from 1990–1994 when only .4 heat-related deaths per year occurred.

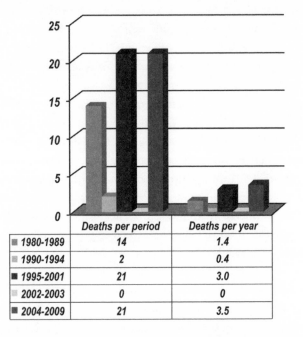

	Deaths per period	Deaths per year
■ 1980-1989	14	1.4
▨ 1990-1994	2	0.4
■ 1995-2001	21	3.0
▨ 2002-2003	0	0
■ 2004-2009	21	3.5

The seven years following the passage of the DSHEA saw a significant spike in these types of fatalities. The period 1995–2001 registered 3.0 heat-related deaths per year, which is over seven times higher than the previous five-year period. The period 2004–2009 experienced 3.5 fatalities per year, yet the period of 2002–2003 is an anomaly because there were no *football* heat-related deaths. (This could be contributed to the negative publicity Ephedra received after NFL player Corey Stringer's death.) A couple of years went by and everyone forgot about Stringer's collapse, so the death rates began to spike again. An additional 21 football players, including Max Gilpin, would succumb to heatstroke during the period of 2004–2009. To find that many heat-related deaths in a 6-year period, we had to go back to 1968–1973 when 32 deaths were recorded.

Whether DSHEA is entirely responsible for this increase in heat-related deaths is impossible to know for sure, but it cannot be ignored that it played a significant role in this case. Max Gilpin's use of a body-building supplement was another smoking gun that the witch hunters wanted to ignore.

With any medication, you should check with your doctor before beginning a regimen of sport supplements, or any other dietary supplements, because there could be side effects that are not commonly known. Whether Max Gilpin's use of Creatine is a minor or major factor in his death may remain a mystery, but something was indeed different that day, and Max's medical records supported that theory.

Tests ran on blood drawn shortly after 7 PM on August 20, 2008, showed that Max had an unusually high creatinine level of 1.9 (normal range 0.3–1.2) at that time. That figure could suggest kidney failure was occurring or was inevitable. (An aspect that is important to know is that it normally takes a minimum of 6 to 8 hours of diminished kidney functions for a creatinine level to rise from the normal range up to 2.0) That indicates Max Gilpin was either overloaded on the body-building supplement Creatine, or his kidneys had begun to fail around lunchtime on August 20, 2008, or maybe even both. It is highly unlikely that a high protein diet accelerated that figure to a number suggesting kidney failure.

With medication and supplements identified as two contributing factors, a pre-existing illness is all that is left to complete the deadly trio of causes. Medical records, doctors' testimony, and eyewitness testimony confirmed that Max did not feel well that day, and more than likely he was running a fever. Jeff Gilpin stated Max had a headache the night before, and Lois Gilpin described Max as hot to the touch on August 20, 2008. Classmates described Max Gilpin as unusually lethargic, including him resting his head on a table during lunch.

It always seemed strange that external cooling methods used by the coaches and the EMS technicians were not able to lower Max's body temperature by very much. In fact, his body temperature did not return to normal until after he was given a blood transfusion. The coaches may have been facing the same problem as the hospital. It appears that Max's blood had some form of bacteria in it that was preventing them from lowering his body temperature. Once the blood transfusion was complete, his temperature began to regulate.

In short, the evidence strongly suggests that a prescribed amphetamine, body-building supplements, and an illness all contributed to Max Gilpin's death.

Like many people, it was my belief that prosecutors are more concerned with conviction rates than they are about what cases they take to trial. A conversation with a friend, an attorney named Tom Denbow, cleared up that misconception. He explained that it is a prosecutor's job to seek justice, and whether he/she obtains a conviction or not is irrelevant.

I have been asked many times by people all over the country: Why prosecute something like this? When I would answer, "the pursuit of justice," most folks weren't willing to accept that. Speculation as to why Coach Stinson really was prosecuted will most likely be debated for a long time, but the most likely scenarios are as follows:

Political Reasons. The most common theory was that politics played a role in the prosecution of Coach Stinson. Many key figures in the prosecution were tied to politics one way or another. The first person who might have had political reasons to pursue this prosecution was the elected official Dave Stengel. Was he thinking about running for mayor? Would there have been any better way to catapult a career politician to the front of the mayor's race? Probably not, especially if—as a prosecutor—he changed football and scholastic athletics forever. Sgt. Denny Butler may very well have also had his eye on public office. His father, Denver Butler, Sr., served honorably for 17 years as a State Representative, and was also an alderman for the City of Louisville before serving the state. Sgt. Butler also has a sister who currently serves on the Louisville Metro Council, so politics appeared to be all around him.

Politics may have played a role in the beginning of this case, but it is hard to believe that it was the reason by the end. The prosecution of a popular football coach became a political nightmare for the CAO. This quickly became an unpopular prosecution; if anything, this whole situation was a political fiasco. Dave Stengel stated that this case was not about politics, and he did not care if there were any repercussions politically. Considering the thorough legal beating his office received, and given the political fallout from that beating, he was probably telling the truth.

Somebody Owed Someone a Favor. This is my favorite theory, but like the other theories, it is nearly impossible to prove. Perhaps a deeper investigation would have found someone willing to tell the whole story. However, conspiracy accusations lead to a slippery slope I was hesitant to travel. It was a known fact that Max Gilpin's maternal aunt, Terri Crask, is married to a detective with the LMPD. The entire deal—Stengel and Sgt. Butler taking this case to the grand jury without the lead detective Terry Jones's involvement—stank. An immediate family member near an investigation always give reason to look closer.

Dave Stengel Really Believed a Crime Had Been Committed. The final theory, which is the most plausible, is that the Commonwealth's attorney really believed Coach Stinson's practice killed Max Gilpin. There are statements from witnesses saying this practice was excessive, yet many of those witness statements did not hold up under scrutiny. In the mounds of evidence, only a handful of people claimed to have witnessed a horrible, barbaric football practice. Along with those statements and a few inexperienced players who had participated in the roughest practice of their lives, a case started to build.

While many factors came together for this situation to get blown completely out of proportion, I believe responsibility partially lies at the feet of Jefferson County Public Schools. It is not what JCPS and its spokesperson Lauren Roberts did; it is what they didn't do. JCPS was very limited with its responses, and when it did respond, it seemed the Board was glossing over a very serious situation. Internal e-mails show the administrative officials were on top of the situation, but publicly it appeared differently. If JCPS had been proactive instead of reactive, it may not have found itself "behind the eight ball" on so many occasions.

At some point, it had to be clear to prosecutors that some of the witnesses' recollections were impossible. Evidence suggested that the case should be dropped, but the prosecutors would not allow it. (Apparently there is some imaginary point of no return with criminal cases, and at some point *Commonwealth v. Stinson* must have passed that mark. It was stated by judges and attorneys alike that Stengel could not drop the case, but none of them would ever really explain why.)

The *Courier-Journal* was probably the final influence that got the ball rolling, but along the way even the newspaper started to give reasons why the case should be dismissed. The *C-J*'s Andy Wolfson called Coach Stinson and asked him about the water denial allegations, but Stinson offered no comment. He told Wolfson to call Dave Johnson. It probably would have been helpful if Stinson had just said, "That is not true," or "That didn't happen." But he did not, because he was relying on JCPS to handle the public relations.

People may not realize the *Courier-Journal* was the primary source of information to the public. Unfortunately, most people relied on whatever was "put on the spoon" by cut-and-paste reporters who rarely delivered a non-biased story. The reason for this either came from a relationship formed between a reporter and Michele Crockett, or the *Courier-Journal*'s pursuit of a Pulitzer Prize.

When does a tragedy get to be just a tragedy? Basically this story snow-balled because of a seemingly endless list of unique circumstances. Since the trial, JCPS—along with other school districts around the country—is try-ing to be proactive. One of the new requirements calls for parents to disclose any supplements used by a student athlete. It also attempts to educate par-ents and students about some of the medical issues that could cause serious injury or even death. However, these new requirements will not matter if the parents do not educate themselves. Until the FDA intervenes or parents understand what risks their children face from mixing medicine and supple-ments, these tragic deaths will continue.

Parents and players need to be honest. They may not realize what their child is ingesting. Distribution of ADD/ADHD medications from one stu-dent to another student for whom it was not prescribed happens more often than most parents realize. Do these children realize that a nontolerant user's body temperature will rise from taking this medication? What if you have a student who doesn't feel good, but wants to get through practice? He gets an ADD/ADHD pill from his buddy to get him through. He doesn't know that the fever he was already running is going to get higher or even worse, once he starts practicing.

There are millions of children who are prescribed Adderall® or similar medications containing amphetamines, and if the medication is not moni-tored, it could lead to disastrous consequences. Many kids mistakenly think if one pill is good, then two have to be better. They must be made aware of the dangers of amphetamines. Popping a second pill to get through the day or a practice could cost a student his life. No one is saying that is what hap-pened with Max Gilpin, but it surely is a possibility.

Parents need to discuss sports and dietary supplements with their chil-dren. If parents purchase these types of products for their child, they should read the labels and warnings closely. They should also let their doctor know, especially if the child is already on prescription medication.

Even if parents do not buy a body-building supplement and perfor-mance enhancer for their child, it does not mean the child is not taking such drugs. Teens can obtain such supplements from other children, or in some cases, they can walk into a store and buy the enhancers on their own. Rules and regulations concerning most dietary and sports supplements vary widely from state to state. Some states have laws regarding purchase by minors, but most do not. Some stores have policies about sales to minors, while others do not. I believe it is time for one standard across the entire country.

In February 2010, the Dietary Supplement Safety Act (DSSA) was introduced before Congress. It would have required all manufacturers of dietary supplements to register with the FDA, among other regulations. It was sponsored by John McCain (R-AZ) and Byron Dorgan (D-ND), but John McCain withdrew his support shortly after he backed the bill. (I didn't feel that the bill would accomplish much, but I was glad it was getting attention. I personally wrote a letter to John McCain offering to share what we have learned about sport supplements, but as of June 2010, neither he nor anyone from his office had responded.)

If we cannot get our lawmakers to do something about this problem, the only effective option is education. At the beginning of each season, if we could have a campaign reminding parents and athletes of the dangers they face, it might make a difference. It might even start putting zeroes back in the column of heat-related deaths. (It has been proven when people discuss how these deaths occur and how to avoid them, the death rate drops dramatically.) It appears we may not be able to get the government to intervene because lobbyists for drug manufacturers and dietary supplement manufacturers own the lawmakers, so we may have to sponsor this campaign ourselves. Much like water breaks in the 70s and 80s made a difference, a continuing awareness campaign could become the way we eliminate medication plus supplement plus heat-related deaths.

CHAPTER 24

THE SOAP OPERA OF IT ALL: ACT I

Most of what you read in the next two chapters did not mean a whole lot to Jason Stinson's criminal defense, but these events happened just the same. It is important that the whole story is laid out, but telling about these incidents earlier may have only added confusion to the case (much like it did for us as these things happened).

This whole drama was a soap opera played out daily. It was said many times by members of the media that PRP was a "divided community." As soon as a phrase like that is heard, it immediately makes many think "divided" means "down the middle or perhaps 50/50." That was not the case, and 50/50 would not have been close. According to several different polls conducted of residents throughout the city, support always seemed to hang around the 90/10 mark favoring Stinson prior to trial. A reasonable person could conclude the distance between those two numbers grew even larger after the all the facts came out.

To some observers, the fringe stories were more interesting than the facts of the case. Max Gilpin's mother, Michele Crockett, works at GES, the elementary school next door to PRPHS, and so does Karen Deacon, the wife of one of the coaches. The fact that they work in the same building, and occasionally in the same classroom, is more than likely very awkward, considering Crockett is suing Deacon's husband.

In fact, Michele Crockett knows Steve and Karen Deacon very well. Max Gilpin and Zach Deacon were very good friends, and Max regularly spent the night at the Deacons' home. The tension at GES was obvious, even though no one would talk about it. That scene of the soap opera was very transparent, and it was played out for all to see. However, there were some things that went on that only a few people knew about.

Two days before Thanksgiving in 2008, Jeff Gilpin left Lois Gilpin.

I sat down for an extensive interview with Max Gilpin's stepmother, Lois Gilpin, and some of the things she shared were staggering to say the least. Prior to Jason's trial, I was very skeptical of Lois Gilpin, and I frequently worried about her and her testimony. I was worried that the things she said were only because she was angry with her estranged husband. I also worried that what she had to say might not be admissible due to spousal immunity. As long as Jeff and Lois Gilpin were married, he could object to evidence given at trial of any marital communication between them.

Some looked at Lois as an ace in the hole, but I was not so sure. Not only did the spousal immunity issues bother me, I was also troubled that Jeff would simply patch things up with Lois. Jeff was subject to return home at any time, and I was afraid Lois would change her story. I had only met Lois Gilpin a couple of times prior to August 2009, but I began speaking to her regularly as the trial approached. She made me worry about many things, but mostly I believed Jeff would get to her at the last minute. She surely felt abandoned, and she appeared to be in a very fragile state. Lois later admitted that she was so sad at the time, that all it would have taken was a sincere apology for her to have forgiven her husband. However, that didn't happen, and Lois and Jeff Gilpin's divorce was finalized in February 2010.

We speculated about what Jeff was thinking when he left Lois. He should have known that Lois would be extremely damaging to the lawsuit if she were to come clean, and as time went on, she certainly did not paint Jeff Gilpin in a very good light. As far as criminal defense is concerned, it is always a good idea not to pick on grieving parents at a trial where they are being forced to testify about the death of their child. For that reason, when Lois Gilpin recounted the events of August 20 at the trial, she left some things unsaid while she was on the witness stand.

Nevertheless, Lois repeatedly described the same event, and her story never changed. She claims that on the morning of August 20, 2008, Jeff emphatically told him to get ready for school. She further claims he told Max "that he had better have his ass at practice, and he would be there to check on him." She told me that story several times prior to trial, but I struggled to believe it. However, after Michele Crockett testified, I doubted Lois Gilpin no longer. Michele Crockett testified that when she arrived at the field after Max's collapse she was surprised to see Jeff Gilpin there. She stated that Jeff had traded days with her because he was supposed to go out of town. Under cross examination by Alex Dathorne she testified, "he had already told me he was going to be out of town. I did not expect him to be there." That sentence tied it all together for me, especially when I considered that she seemed genuinely surprised to find Jeff present upon her arrival at the practice field on August 20, 2008.

Whether Jeff Gilpin was there to "check up" on Max or not, as Lois Gilpin suggests, is only known to Jeff Gilpin. However, any suggestion that Max was trying to please anyone other than his father is unfounded. Lois Gilpin explained that Jeff loved football, but he quit before his senior year. His high school team went on to win a state championship that year (1979). Lois Gilpin has described how Jeff was very involved with Max's football, and the evidence of Max's alleged need "to please someone" points to a very involved parent instead of the coaching staff.

Jeff Gilpin and Michele Crockett were body builders when they were younger, and until recently, Jeff was working out regularly. Jeff had recounted his days as a bodybuilder on more than one occasion, and he brought up the subject of steroids to LMPD investigators and at trial. He said that he was not regularly working out with Max during the season, but Lois Gilpin disputed that in her testimony.

She stated, "He and Max would go to the gym every time Max was here. Jeff was 'getting off' on how big Max had become." She also mentioned all the "stuff" Jeff was giving to Max. She said Jeff and Max were regularly drinking shakes, as well as taking other body-building supplements. She recalled Creatine and Muscle Milk®, but she was not sure of the names of anything else they might have been taking. There were several rumors floating around, and one of them was that Max Gilpin was on steroids. That rumor has been thoroughly investigated, and there is absolutely no evidence that Max Gilpin ever took steroids. Let me repeat that. There is absolutely **NO** evidence that Max Gilpin **EVER** took steroids.

Michele Crockett said she just wanted answers, but according to Lois Gilpin, Michele and her husband Aaron talked about filing a lawsuit at the hospital before Max had even passed away. I recalled mumbling, "there goes millions off any settlement," when Michele Crockett got up and stormed out of the courtroom in anger during Lois Gilpin's testimony. The still-to-come civil lawsuit had been an 800-pound gorilla in the room that no one wanted to talk about, but when Lois Gilpin brought it up, it could no longer be ignored. It was on the tip of everyone's tongue, but no one would publicly say this was all about money. It was almost a relief that someone had *finally* spoken up about the lawsuit, and it was a moment many had longed for.

From the beginning, there were a couple of things that stood out about the lawsuit. First, Christina Spiva had been quoted by Michele Crockett as saying, "Your boy has been down on the ground for several minutes, and I don't think they are moving fast enough to help him." It was implied that Christina was talking about the coaches, but Christina said she was talking about EMS technicians and not the coaches.

Spiva was not the only one to comment on how long it took EMS to arrive. From the beginning, many people who knew the facts commented that EMS and Kosair Children's Hospital should have been the targets of a lawsuit and not the coaches. Upon investigating, it was found that the law firm representing Michele Crockett is primarily a defendant law firm. The website for the firm states, "Thompson, Miller & Simpson PLC ("TMS") provides litigation services to a wide range of healthcare providers and product manufacturers." It would be safe to conclude that healthcare providers and product manufacturers rarely file suits; instead, they are usually the defendant in a lawsuit. Who knows why Michele Crockett chose TMS, other than she had a friend working in their office. If TMS had represented EMS or any of the doctors who treated Max Gilpin in the past, they could not file a lawsuit *against* them now. Who would that leave to sue? JCPS and its $6.5 million insurance policy?

Lois Gilpin agreed with Jeff Gilpin's original claim that he was only part of the lawsuit to get answers. Jeff was very supportive of the coaches, and he stated multiple times that he didn't see them do anything wrong that day. Jeff was so protective of the coaches that he almost got into a fist fight with Michele Crockett's brother-in-law, Mike Crask, at the funeral home. Mike Crask didn't like the fact the coaches were present, and he wanted them to leave. Jeff Gilpin did not feel that way, and it turned into a heated verbal exchange that almost resulted in them coming to blows. The animosity with Crask at the funeral home began at the hospital. Lois Gilpin also said that Terri Crask, who works at Kosair Children's Hospital, was "very involved" during Max's hospitalization, and that she had begun to speak about how Max's death was going to make a difference.

Lois reported that Jeff Gilpin did not ever speak a negative word about the coaches as long as they were living together. She said it was shortly after he left their home that his story began to change.

The soap opera also began to take its toll on another marriage. Jason Stinson's father, Don Stinson, told me of the strain the case put on his 45-year marriage. He said, "I have been married 45 years, and this by far has been the worst year of my marriage." I know the strain this situation put on my marriage as well as Jason's, so I could only imagine the stress it put on everyone else. Between the emotional roller coaster and the physical toll of only sleeping two to four hours a night for nearly a year, this case most surely shaved years off all our lives.

We did many things to raise money for Coach Stinson's defense, but no matter what we did, our first concern was that we act respectfully. About two weeks before a scheduled concert, I received a phone call from Jason who asked what the date of the concert was. He knew the answer already, but he wanted me to say the date out loud. As I mumbled July 19, it hit me like a sledgehammer. July 19 was Max's birthday. Arranging the date for the concert had been my responsibility, and I blew it. I knew when Max's birthday was, but I had just simply forgotten. We didn't realize what we had done until someone from Max Gilpin's family called up and cussed out the people who were holding the event at their home. They tried to reach me, but I was out when they called.

We immediately rescheduled the concert; we held it a week later on July 26. Regardless of the situation, to hold a fundraising event for Jason Stinson on Max Gilpin's birthday would have been insensitive, to say the least. It was never our intention to schedule something on his birthday. No matter what it would have taken, there was never a question about whether to reschedule the event or not.

Coach Stinson and I became creatures of habit when it came to attending court hearings. From March–September 2009, Jason would pick me up at my home, and we would almost always take the same route downtown. We would park in the same parking lot, and we would even walk the same path to the courthouse. There are a lot of "off-center" people in this world, and Louisville, KY, has its fair share. It was always my concern that one of these "off-center" people would end up approaching us on the street. (It was my fear that the newspaper had painted Stinson in such an unfavorable light that he could be subject to some sort of attack while out in public.) When we walked, Jason put his eyes down on the sidewalk and I would sort of scan the area for any potential problems.

It turned out that my hyper-vigilance was nothing more than paranoia.

However, walking back to the car one day, I was not so sure. We were coming from the courthouse, traveling east on Liberty, about half way between Fifth and Sixth streets. A lady caught my attention on the opposite side of Liberty Street. She was originally headed westbound, but it was obvious that she had started across the street making a path directly for us.

"Heads up, eleven o'clock," I told Jason. "She looks angry."

As the woman approached, it was clear she was angry. It turns out, however, that her anger was not with Coach Stinson. She was angry and upset with the Commonwealth Attorney's Office. She told Coach Stinson, "What they are doing to you is wrong." I can't exactly recall everything she said, but I do remember her telling Coach Stinson that she was praying for him, and she hoped everything would turn out all right.

After the verdict was delivered, we ran into this same lady again on the way back to the car. She was on the corner of Fifth and Liberty Streets. It had not been long since the verdict was read, but it seemed like everyone walking the streets already knew. She congratulated Coach Stinson and told him how happy she was for him.

We would frequently have people at random walk by and say things like, "We're behind you, Coach," and "We're praying for you, Coach." Every now and then someone riding by in a car would yell a few words of encouragement. It seemed that the most words of support and encouragement came from inside the courthouse. We would regularly be approached by uniformed police officers telling Coach Stinson they were behind him.

In our usual path to the courthouse, we would also walk past the Commonwealth Attorney's Office, which is located on the southeast corner of Sixth Street and Liberty. We walked past that door many times, but one day was a little different. Jason and I were heading west on Liberty, and we were probably about 20 yards away from the CAO entrance when Jason said, "Wouldn't it be funny if they came out the door right now?"

Sure enough, a few steps later about six to eight prosecutors and assistants came out the door, just in front of us. They looked a little surprised to see us so close, but they had no idea how surprised we were. Jason and I were looking at one another with our eyes wide open and our eyebrows arched. We were trying not to smile about them actually coming out the door within seconds of him making that comment. As we approached Sixth Street and Liberty, we had the "walk" light, so we all crossed Sixth Street together. We would all then need to cross Liberty Street, so we could enter the district courthouse from its Sixth Street entrance. Dave Stengel and his flock headed across Sixth Street, and Coach Stinson went to step off of the curb to follow them. The light was red, so I reached out and grabbed him by the arm. In a tone that was loud enough to be heard a half of a block away I told Jason, "Don't do that. Crossing against the light is *illegal*."

One of the men from the prosecutor's office actually shook his head "no" as they were crossing the street. I don't know if he was saying "no" about them failing to obey a traffic control device or that I had the nerve to say it so loud. Either way, it was extremely funny from my point of view.

On a separate day we were approaching the CAO when Leland Hulbert exited the building. When he noticed Coach Stinson and me coming down the sidewalk, he went around the back of his car. As we were approaching, we could see a parking ticket on his windshield. We reached the front of his car about the same time he reached his driver's side door. I began smiling and Coach Stinson, knowing me all too well, said, "Don't!"

Too late, I said, "Hey, Leland, there's a parking ticket on your windshield."

Through his teeth, Coach Stinson muttered, "Stop it!"

Pretending not to hear him, I went on to rib Hulbert. "I bet you know someone that could fix that ticket."

Once again through his teeth, Coach Stinson said, "Quit!" By that time we were passing the rear of Hulbert's car. He snatched his ticket and got into his car.

Coach Stinson looked at me and said, "You are such a jerk."

Smiling like a cat with a bird in its mouth, I innocently replied, "What?" I couldn't let that golden opportunity pass by.

Referring to my enjoyment of regularly being a thorn in Leland Hulbert's side, Coach Stinson said, "You've got to stop messing with him. You're not the one on trial."

He had a good point. "Agreed," I said.

What Jason probably did not consider when he pulled back on my leash was how much I disliked Hulbert. I didn't want to miss a chance to get a dig in at Stengel or one of his prosecutors. My disdain for Leland Hulbert arose when our phone conversations first began shortly after Coach Stinson's indictment. It was clear he was bent on achieving a conviction against Coach Stinson.

Not knowing my role or anything about me, Hulbert told me that it was the Commonwealth's position that Coach Stinson was angry, out of control, and cussing players that day. He assured me that Coach Stinson would not do any time in prison, and later, several other parents stated that Hulbert approached them with the same claim. He went on to say that the prosecutors seriously considered charging PRPHS Principal Dave Johnson with tampering with evidence for deleting e-mails complaining about the coaches' over-the-top behavior.

Principal Dave Johnson explained that he was not covering up anything, and that he thought the e-mails were a hoax. His e-mail address is easily obtainable, and he receives wacky, off-the-wall e-mails on a regular basis. Hulbert never said whether he believed Johnson or not, but, for whatever reason, the prosecutors chose not to build a case against him. Instead they focused the full power of their office on Jason Stinson.

CHAPTER 25

The Soap Opera of it All: Act II

The second act of the soap opera began with the performance of Tim Moreschi, the "entertainer" of the trial. He was the witness for the prosecution who came into the courtroom with the over-the-top, boisterous behavior. Court records show that several details of his version of events matched no one else's. I asked many times, "Why would he say those things?" As mentioned during his trial testimony, it appeared this guy had an ax to grind against PRPHS, and he was going to use Jason as his grindstone.

When history is needed for something involving PRPHS athletics, "Mama Lou" Nichols is the lady to talk to. She has been a volunteer at PRPHS for 35 years, and has been the president of the PRPHS booster club for several years. She runs the youth league, and in 2007, the PRPHS football field was named "Nichols Field" in honor of the 30-plus years of service Mama Lou and her husband Jim have donated to the school. I wondered what Moreschi's problem was, so I asked Mama Lou if she could shed some light on the situation.

She immediately recounted a story that went back to two head coaches before Jason Stinson. She stated that one of Moreschi's sons was not allowed to play football because of his weight. Apparently he was morbidly obese, and there was some concern about his health. Mama Lou went on to say, "Tim Moreschi always held a grudge against PRPHS after that." There is a counter to that story, which says Moreschi's son quit playing football to pursue some sort of drama training. If Lou Nichols had not told me the story about the boy's weight, I would have probably believed the actor story. If you wonder why I would say something like that, go over Moreschi's testimony. If his son wanted to act, he probably got the acting bug honestly. His father definitely was laying the drama on thick the day he testified.

Since we are on the topic of drama, that leads me back to Jo Ann Gayle. I believe Ms. Gayle was "patient zero" in the "disease" known as Commonwealth vs. Football. As mentioned during her trial testimony and later, many of her recollections turned out to be entirely false. But the reason she makes this chapter is for a very little known reason.

About a month before the trial, Coach Stinson called me and said, "Guess who dated my brother Daniel in middle school?" I answered, "I don't know, who?" He then gave me another hint when he said, "OK; who do you think dated my brother and is also on the witness list for the Commonwealth?" So I guessed, "Who, Jo Ann Gayle?" Coach Stinson replied with his now famous, "Ding, ding, ding... we have a winner!" I wanted to tell him to stop saying that, but instead I blurted out, "Nah, I don't think she's the same one. The one who went to Lassiter spelled her name G-A-Y-L-E, and the one the police interviewed spelled her name G-A-L-E." Stinson retorted, "Someone just sent me a screenshot page from her Facebook page, and I am positive it is my brother's ex-girlfriend."

"*Really*, are you sure?"

"Positive."

"What was the story with her and Daniel?"

"Story??? There was no story. They were boyfriend-girlfriend, and they broke up before they went to Fairdale. They were really good friends, but I think they stopped hanging around together. This woman has eaten dinner at my parents' dinner table."

I was really stunned by what Jason just said to me. Initially I had put Jo Ann Gale's (Gayle's) statement aside, because I didn't think the prosecution would call a witness whose recollections were impossible. (I was wrong about that, as much as I was wrong to think the transcripts from LMPD would not have a witness's name spelled wrong.)

"Let me guess," I said to Jason. "Their relation went sour about the time Daniel started dating his new girlfriend?"

"I don't know, but that would make sense."

"It would, but something isn't right. She said she was not sure if she could identify you. If she was your brother's girlfriend at one time, how could she say that?"

I wonder if Gayle told her current boyfriend just how well she knew Daniel and Jason Stinson. She seems to be at the root of several events that fueled this madness, and you have to wonder exactly what motivated her.

On her Facebook page, she states, "Hopefully, coaches everywhere will pay more attention and use different techniques from now on." We really don't have the answer to what Gayle's agenda was. Maybe she thought she was changing the world.

It was stated many times that emotions ran high with this court case, and regularly there was tension in the courtroom. The tension seemed to be coming from Max Gilpin's stepfather, Aaron Crockett. He had three different outbursts in or around the courtroom, and I believe he had to be warned at least twice by the court about his behavior. The first occasion occurred when Jason looked over his shoulder to see who was coming in the door of the courtroom. Aaron and Michele Crockett were seated in the direction he had to turn to see the door. When Crockett saw Jason look back, he shouted out, "Don't you look back here." The people sitting around him quickly got him to quiet down, before he attracted the attention of the bailiff.

The second time was when the hearing ended. We were walking out of the first set of doors of the courtroom when Crockett started screaming at Jason again. "Tell them how long it took you to call 911," he said. He was in the back row, still some distance from the door. Jason stopped at the threshold so he could hear what Crockett was saying to him. I was right behind Jason, and I pushed him, saying, "GO!"

We immediately went into one of the conference rooms, followed by his attorneys. Jason asked me, "What was Crockett saying? I was trying to hear him, but you pushed me through the door."

"He was saying something about calling 911."

I then asked Alex Dathorne, "Can we do something about that? If Crockett keeps that up, it could be problematic."

Alex Dathorne assured us that the court would not tolerate emotional outbursts, and he (Dathorne) would make sure Crockett's behavior was addressed by the court.

Later that same evening, Jason Stinson visited a local carry-out pizza restaurant, and—as fate would have it—Aaron Crockett walked through the door. He saw Jason sitting in the waiting area, then he immediately turned around and exited the restaurant. If Aaron had something to say to Jason, apparently that was not the time. (Some may have called Aaron's behavior cowardly given his behavior earlier in the day, but in this case I think it was the responsible, if not smart, thing to do.)

At the beginning of the trial, Judge Gibson told everyone in attendance that any type of emotional outburst would not be tolerated. She explained that if anyone were to act out, that person would be subject to ejection from the courtroom. We got through almost the entire trial without any problems, but that came to a screeching halt on day 12. That day, testimony began with Lois Gilpin, and it appeared her testimony really "fired up" Aaron and Michele Crockett.

Upon returning to the courtroom from escorting Lois Gilpin out, I forgot to put my cell phone on "vibrate." During Coach Steve Ellis' testimony, my phone rang, forcing me quickly to leave the courtroom so it would not be a distraction. (It was ironic because I had spent the past two weeks making sure all members of the defense and Coach Stinson's supporters had turned off the ringers on their cell phones before entering the courtroom.)

A few minutes after my return, Coach Ellis wrapped up his testimony. Upon exiting the witness stand, he went to the conference room reserved for the defense, just outside the courtroom doors. I got up to follow him, because I wanted to let him know that his testimony was spot on. (It was my opinion that we had not yet successfully showed the jury what a normal football practice was like, but Coach Ellis' testimony remedied that problem.)

On my way out, Aaron Crockett was standing right beside the door. He said something about how cell phone ringers should be turned off. As I passed him, I said, "Relax Aaron, it will be OK." He continued to go on about the cell phone, and what I said to him at that point is somewhat unclear. (According to one of the sheriffs, Crockett told him I had said, "The phone is on mute like your brain." I honestly do not remember saying that, and I had never before used the word *mute* to describe a cell phone. But I am sure it was something close to what I said to him.) Upon making the "mute" statement, I started into the room Steve Ellis had just entered. Crockett said, "You got something you want to say to me?" I seriously did not see him as a threat, so I stood at the door and told him, 'I said what I had to say, now go away.'"

Then in a much louder tone of voice (which we believe was to attract attention), he yelled, "You got something you want to say to me?" I laughed at him, told him to go in his room which was just a few feet away, and I closed the door of the defense conference room. Inside, I sat down in the seat behind the door because Steve Ellis was sitting in the right hand corner where I would normally sit. As soon as I sat down, the door flew open, hitting me as I sat in the chair. I grabbed the handle of the door and stuck my head around the door to see that it was Aaron. Again he was screaming, "You got something you want to say?"

Still seated, I held the door open. Aaron had now stepped just inside the door, so I told him to come on in and close the door. Steve Deacon, who was sitting inside the room on the other side of the door, said, "Aaron, you need to go."

Aaron's attention was focused on Steve Deacon and me, but we were not the ones he should have been worried about. As I momentarily glanced at Deacon, I noticed Steve Ellis in the corner. Steve had slid to the edge of his seat; he had both hands balled up into fists, and he was leaning forward on the balls of his feet. I immediately wedged my foot and leg against the bottom of the door and placed the rest of my weight against the door with my shoulder. I quickly realized if Steve Ellis punched Crockett, I could be hurt by the sheer force of him bouncing off that solid wooden door and then that door hitting me. My assumption about Steve Ellis' intentions were indeed correct when later that evening he stated, "If he had touched you, I was going to put him through that door."

Fortunately, one of the sheriffs fetched Aaron and moved him along. The same sheriff later pulled me aside and told me that I was now subject to ejection due to the incident outside the courtroom. I assured him that incident was the last thing I wanted, and I promised not to do anything that would further exacerbate the problem. I apologized and told the sheriff that everyone would behave, and indeed the rest of the trial continued with no further problems.

As I mentioned earlier, Jason Stinson and I were creatures of habit. We would travel to the courthouse using the same route, and we would also almost always go home the same way. For whatever reason, on the day the verdict was read, we could not park at our usual place because the lot was full. Instead, we had to park in a lot across the street. (This was the only time that we ever parked in this garage.) When leaving the garage, we were forced to travel back towards the courthouse, since the only way out led us west onto Jefferson Street.

We wanted to travel south, and turning left on Sixth Street would be our first opportunity. We opted against turning on Sixth Street because several news cameras were still set up there, and we would have been stopped by the light at Sixth and Liberty. Our next chance to go south was Eighth

Street, so Jason turned left on Eighth Street. As we were approaching the intersection to make the turn, we noticed four or five jurors walking north up Eighth Street. Coach Stinson pulled over and rolled down his window. He said "Thank you" to the jurors. One of the women simply stated, "They didn't make their case." He then told them that they didn't just put a teacher back in the classroom and a coach back on the football field, they put a Jesus-loving teacher and coach back where he belongs.

We drove away and headed south back to PRP. Instead of our normal route which would take us down Third Street by the University of Louisville, we ended up taking Eighteenth Street back to PRP. As we approached Jason's house, the media was already stationed outside. We stopped for a moment so Jason could be congratulated by Tyler Davidson (one of Stinson's players, as well as his neighbor). There was a helicopter flying around overhead, so instead of getting out of the car, we headed over to my house so Jason could drop me off.

We were sitting in my driveway reflecting on the last year, and both of us were fighting back tears. We quickly ended the conversation, and I rushed to get out the car before I really started crying. As I was about to close the passenger's side door, Jason extended his hand and told me, "Thank you so much for everything." I replied with an obligatory "Sure, no problem," and as we were shaking hands he said, "No, I really mean it. Thank you for everything you did for me and my family." I again told him, "No problem."

I went into my empty home and sat down at my kitchen table. My wife Ann was away working in the concession stand at a football game at PRPHS. My stepson Christopher had left a few weeks earlier for his first year of college at Western Kentucky University, and my daughter Kendall was at her mother's home. Sitting there alone, I began to cry. Throughout the year-long emotional rollercoaster ride, we had been forced to suppress our anger and frustration along with many other feelings. Now that it was finally over, all I could do was cry.

EPILOGUE

As of April, 2010, no coaches who were present during the last thirty minutes of the infamous practice, except Josh Lightle, remain on the coaching staff. Coach Jason Hiser, who had left around 5:30 PM for an appointment, took over the PRPHS football program for the 2009 season, and all the coaches returned for that season except Adam Donnelly. It appears that Jason Hiser will again be the head coach of the 2010 PRPHS Panthers. However, the staff will be significantly different, since coaches Jason Cook, Bobby Deacon, and Steve Deacon did not return.

Jason Stinson is still teaching web design at PRPHS, and he plans to return to coaching very soon. He also is working to advise other coaches and school districts about what to expect if a tragedy like this should occur again.

Michele Crockett has transferred from Greenwood Elementary School to Kerrick Elementary School, and Jeff Gilpin is still employed at the same downtown automobile dealership. Jeff declined media interviews and was literally out of sight until the civil proceedings. Before that, he was last seen after the verdict walking down Jefferson Street alone—carrying Max's helmet. An observer who watched him walk away from the 9th floor window of the Jefferson Circuit Court Building later described it as "very sad."

AFTERWORD

When this book's final edits were completed in June 2010, there were several things directly related to Jason Stinson that had yet to be resolved; however, with one exception that has changed. Not only were most of the loose ends tied up by the end of 2010, but a few other noteworthy events also transpired.

Shortly following his acquittal, Jason Stinson received a letter from JCPS clearing him to return to teaching and coaching, stating he could apply for any opening he desired. Numerous attempts at obtaining both assistant and head football coaching jobs have been blocked by JCPS Superintendent, Sheldon Berman. Perhaps his non-renewal as Superintendent of JCPS will now serve as a notice to him.

I kept quiet when it came to exposing Berman for the charade he would put on for the media, because my friend still had to work for him. It was amazing how he could say Stinson was eligible for any coaching job within JCPS, because every time Stinson applied for a position, something would happen to block it.

At first, nobody wanted to admit that Berman was involved, but over time it was apparent who was blocking Jason's return to coaching, and the obstruction was at the very top of the JCPS ladder (hierarchy). It seems the only coach in JCPS that had to have a contract signed off from the top was Jason Stinson, and the person who had to approve his contract was Sheldon Berman.

There were multiple schools that inquired about Jason after his acquittal, but no offer stood out more than his alma mater, Fairdale High School. This one stood out because so many people wanted to see this hire take place. Jason had grown up in Fairdale, and his parents still live in and are active in the community. However, when Jason applied for the job it made some waves. Jason simply bowed out, and once again walked away to do what was best for the kids at FHS and to avoid any further drama.

Jason finally was allowed to serve as an assistant coach for PRP's freshman basketball team. It was amazing, because practically every local news station made it a story and felt they had to report on it. Perhaps it was made a big deal because it meant he would now apply for other coaching positions, including football.

Jason now has been hired as an assistant football coach at Iroquois High School, located near historic Churchill Downs. Iroquois has not had many successful seasons in football, and it made some wonder why he would take an assistant's job, especially at a school that regularly finishes last in their district. Jason explained it to me again, as if I had forgotten. He was not concerned about a win-loss record on the field, but he *was* concerned with a player's win-loss record in the game of life.

———

The book was originally scheduled for release on September 17, 2010, on the 1-year anniversary of the verdict. At that time we were attempting to self-publish but were running short on money. In early 2011, Acclaim Press took over publishing responsibilities, which has allowed us to get this story out to the public. I believe this book will serve as closure for many, as it did for me. Yet when I look back on all of this, some things still get under my skin. Many of the actions of the procecutors were highly criticized. The performance that Stengel and Sgt. Butler put on for the Grand Jury is something that should be made public. Unfortunately, Grand Jury proceedings are private, so this charade has never been released to the community.

On September 16, 2010, the day before the book was originally to be released, it was announced that a settlement had been reached in the lawsuit against the PRPHS coaching staff. No one but a handful of people knew the book wasn't going to be released on time, so many were expecting it to be available the next day. It was rumored that a review copy of the book and its original release date helped push along settlement talks. Whether that is true or not will probably never be known, but it sure is a nice feeling to think I may have contributed by pointing out obvious facts that most chose to ignore. If that was the situation, you're welcome, anything I can do to help.

The wrongful death lawsuit was settled for a fraction of the $19.5 million that Max Gilpin's parents and their attorneys were originally seeking.

JCPS' insurance carrier made the decision to settle for $1.75 million, and the coaches had no say in the matter. JCPS admitted no wrong doing, and they felt to settle was a business decision. It is actually this lawsuit that demanded an afterword be written, because I left a few things unsaid. The last thing I wanted to do was make the situation any worse, so on many occasions I kept my opinions regarding the lawsuit to myself, and now I don't have to do that anymore....

First of all, I don't care what myths or speculations were circulating after the settlement about how the whole legal process was pursued to help raise heatstroke awareness or obtain answers, because it wasn't. From the time Max collapsed, during his stay in the hospital, at the funeral home and church services, and in many private conversations afterwards, it seems Michele and Jeff may have been influenced by others more interested in financial gain than finding the truth and answers to why it happened.

I regularly think about the approximately $312,000 each parent received from the settlement, and I wonder if it was worth it. I am sure they would trade that money 10 times over to have Max back, and for over a year I held a great amount of sympathy for Max Gilpin's parents. I, along with many others, have said on numerous occasions it is hard to imagine what they went through losing a child. I still feel great sympathy for them today, but enough is enough. It now seems Jason Stinson was dragged through the mud and back for a few hundred thousand dollars.

At one point the plantiffs said they were looking for answers, and this lawsuit would help bring about these answers. After the criminal trial and civil deposition of Jason Stinson, they were still seeking answers. When the appeal was filed and there was no further activity on the case, they were still looking for answers. No new information came in, and apparently enough questions were finally answered that a settlement was reached, but I do have a question. Did you get your answers? I don't think so, because the answers you were probably looking for could not and would not ever be found. It seems that they were not willing to explore the possibility that something or someone other than Jason Stinson could have been responsible for what had happened to Max. When it was all said and done, Jason had absolutely no responsibility for the death of Max Gilpin.

Sports Illustrated published some disturbing allegations against Jeff Gilpin. I was aware of these claims, but I was not willing to cover them. There was a fine line on what I was willing to print, and many of these very personal things I decided to leave alone, especially if it didn't have anything to do with the criminal case. When Thomas Lake from *Sports Illustrated* came to town, and started asking the tough questions, Max's parents clammed up. According to Lake, Michele canceled follow-up interviews, and Jeff's only interview proved too awkward to warrant more. However, it was nice for a journalist to press them for the truth. So many times they have been allowed to say whatever they wanted, and no one ever called them on it.

Jeff Gilpin granted several television interviews after the settlement. As detailed in chapter six, he has changed his story, yet local reporters never seem to want to challenge him on it. I thought it was the job of a reporter to get to the truth, but instead Jeff Gilpin was allowed to contradict himself with no dispute.

Since the final edits were completed on this book, several people have moved on to different positions. Tim Amshoff has moved to Moore High School, Steve Deacon has moved to Westport Middle School, Julian Tackett has been promoted to Commissioner of KHSAA, and Jason Stinson has been promoted into an administrative-type position at PRPHS. Who knows? Maybe next year we can call him a head coach again. This situation will not be entirely corrected until he is returned to the position he was holding before this all began.

Please remember to refer to www.factorsunknown.com for additional information and content including a link to the aforementioned *Sports Illustrated* story written by Thomas Lake.

About the Author

Rodney Daugherty was born, raised and has spent most of his life in the Louisville, KY area. With years of experience as either a player, coach and even co-owner of a semi-professional football team Rodney could be described as an avid football enthusiast. Rodney led the fundraising efforts to support Coach Jason Stinson, and he was inspired to write his first book after witnessing the criminal case waged against his friend.

Rodney has a B.S. in Information Technology and he is the General Manager of the Louisville, KY based tech firm Digital Solutions of KY, Inc. He currently resides in Louisville with his wife Ann. He has one daughter, Kendall and one step-son Christopher. Oh, and two cats Lucy and Trixie.

Rodney Daugherty and Jason Stinson first met one another in 1987 at Fairdale High School in Louisville, KY. They were reunited in early 2005 as their paths crossed in the PRPHS weight room. Little did they know that a few years later they would stand in the eye of the storm as football and legal history swirled around them.